History of American

Paul S. Boyer, General Editor

Abraham Flexner

The Politics of Philanthropy

Abraham Flexner and Medical Education

STEVEN C. WHEATLEY

The University of Wisconsin Press

The University of Wisconsin Press
114 North Murray Street
Madison, Wisconsin 53715

The University of Wisconsin Press, Ltd.
1 Gower Street
London WC1E 6HA, England

Photo credits: p. ii, courtesy of the Rockefeller Archive Center and Frederick Bradley; pp. 108, 109 top, 110, 111, courtesy of the Rockefeller Archive Center; p. 109 bottom, the MIT Museum

Cover illustration: (Left to right) Edwin A. Alderman, Frederick J. Gates, Charles W. Eliot, Harry Pratt Judsen, Wallace Buttrick, Wickliffe Rose, Hollis B. Frissell, John D. Rockefeller, Jr., E. C. Sage, Albert Shaw, Abraham Flexner, George E. Vincent, Anson Phelps Stokes, J. Starr Murphy, Jerome D. Greene. Hotel Samoset, Rockland, Maine, July 8-10, 1915. Courtesy of the Rockefeller Archive Center.

Library of Congress Cataloging-in-Publication Data
Wheatley, Steven Charles, 1952–   .
The politics of philanthropy.
(History of American thought and culture)
Bibliography: pp. 231–243.
Includes index.
1. Medical education—United States—Endowments—
History.   2. Medicine—Research—United States—
Endowments—History.   3. Flexner, Abraham, 1866–1959.
Medical education in the United States and Canada.
I. Title.   II. Series.
R745.W44   1989   610'.7'1173   88-40199
ISBN 0-299-11750-2
ISBN 0-299-11754-5 (pbk.)

For Linda-Marie

Contents

Preface

This is an essay in political history—but it concerns politics of a special kind. The politics it attempts to describe and analyze are those of the management of organized knowledge. In particular, it is concerned with the politics involved in the philanthropic reform and support of medical education from 1890 to 1950. This is not a work in the history of medicine, however, but one in the history of philanthropy. It was under private philanthropic stewardship that many areas of social action were rationalized and that the mechanisms of national management which formed the core of the organizational society of the twentieth century were produced. During this period, private philanthropy was crucial to dramatic changes in medical education which helped produce the system still in use today. A disjointed collection of institutionally weak medical schools, universities, and hospitals developed into a functionally related national system. My central focus is on Abraham Flexner, by far the most important in the sequence of philanthropic managers of medical education. Flexner's model of national philanthropic management greatly expanded the range of philanthropic power and created a new standard of national policy-making.

Flexner's achievement is important precisely because of what it tells us about the relation between politics and organizational life. Americans today take for granted a political economy of institutions which is a puzzlement to the rest of the world. Other societies make a fairly clear division between the role of the nation-state and that of private initiative. Institutions of social management tend to be parts of official, national bureaucracies. Private organizations may locally supplement state action, but the "commanding heights" of social management are state institutions. In the United States a bewildering variety of institutions and organizations—governmental, private, voluntary, national, local—are knit together by networks of personnel and financed by grants in arrangements which vary across fields and locales. More important, social policy is both developed within and determined by the limits of this organizational hodgepodge.

The unwieldy nature of this process of social management is not necessarily an argument against it. American higher education and university research may have become the objects of global admiration precisely because of the institutional variety which characterizes those enterprises. But this peculiar organizational culture does call for a historical explanation, and an essential point of that explanation is to acknowledge that this seeming hodgepodge is a system, one whose contours have been politically determined as surely as if it were an *etatized* structure. It is the aim of this work to help explain how political values and understandings conditioned the development of that structure by examining one of the most powerful instances of its operation.

The early efforts at philanthropic social management were all of a piece with the now historiographically familiar "search for order," Robert Wiebe's suggestive description of the changes which took place in the United States in the early twentieth century.[1] The philanthropists who invented the general-purpose foundation at the turn of the century were bent on rationalizing social organization just as they had made their fortunes rationalizing economic organization. In patronizing learning and organizing expertise the foundations filled a role in the United States played by the state in Europe.[2] But the impulses of Rockefeller and Carnegie were crucially shaped by those upon whom they depended for advice. As the philanthropists' once-personal benevolence became a formal organization, the level of decision making shifted.

It was the bureaucrats and not the plutocrats who did the decisive managing. Rising professionals and professionalizers like Flexner were able to use the power of the foundations to advance their own agendas. To be sure, these philanthropic managers were obliged to drape their programs in mantles acceptable to the philanthropists, but the rubrics of Progressive reform were more than broad enough to accommodate their designs. While the philanthropists continued to hold a veto power over policies, the managers had the crucial power of initiative. Flexner made the most of that advantage by forging a rhetoric which legitimated his management within and beyond the foundations.[3]

The organizational revolution which helped produce the institutional landscape of modern America has been much discussed, but we need to deepen our analysis of it, particularly of its political dimension.[4] For many scholars, this bureaucratizing process was antipolitical in both content and effect. The substitution of professional expertise for partisan discretion, the development of executive procedures to take the place of collective deliberation, the promulgation of universalistic standards as opposed to personal favoritism were indeed all stated goals of reformers in general. Moreover, scholars have recently suggested that it was just these changes which helped lower the amount of popular political activity from its nineteenth-century zenith to today's lamentable level.[5]

There can be no question that the new advocates of organization and management, including the philanthropic reformers, were out of sympathy with the political regime of their youth: the "state of courts and parties" where the reach of government was severely constricted and the mediator of the public realm was the political party.[6] But to analyze this process through simple dichotomies like organization vs. partisanship, or bureaucracy vs. politics, is to make a double error. First, the reform organizers were not bereft of political ideas; they had a reasonably sophisticated political vocabulary which guided and enabled their action. Second, to rely on such straightforward opposites as analytical devices is to confuse the regime of nineteenth-century politics with the political culture in which it was rooted and which survived it. That political culture has been remarkably consistent in its bias toward representativeness and its distrust of power. There are "centrifugal" tendencies to American democracy which resist centralization and tend toward pluralism. While these tendencies were too inchoate to prevent the growth of bureaucratic power, they militated against the formation of coherent national policies even after the rise of national bureaucratic organizations. The relation of modern institutional life to that political culture is something which needs to be historically understood.

The rise and fall of Abraham Flexner's managerial system constituted a revealing chapter in the American organizational revolution and its relationship to American democratic values. To him, the organizational implications of scientific philanthropy and scientific medicine were congruent: new universal standards were applicable to situations which had previously been locally, personally, and intuitively managed. It is in this sense that philanthropic reform bureaucratized medical education. Whereas the entrepreneurial egalitarianism of Jacksonian democracy had permitted the growth of commercial and quasi-commercial medical schools, Flexner trumpeted new standards. Through the adroit placement of foundation funds, he was able to transform diverse local medical schools into organizationally similar institutional bases for a national network of academic physicians. Where consensual arrangements among local medical elites had formerly sufficed to connect hospitals and medical schools, Flexner insisted on contractual arrangements. Hierarchy and definite lines of authority were introduced into collegial faculties. Flexner's aim was to remove the medical profession from control over the means of its own reproduction and put in its place a distinct learned discipline of clinical science.

One point needs to be made explicit: Flexner did not develop modern medical education in intellectual terms. The scientific discoveries, pedagogic reforms, and practical techniques which formed the core of modern medical education had gathered a critical momentum long before he began to campaign for them. In his careful and well-documented history of American medical education, Kenneth Ludmerer goes to great lengths to emphasize a point with which Flexner would have heartily agreed: that the reform of medical education was based on ideas and practices which had been developed and instituted in academic medicine long before the "Flexner report" proclaimed them to the nation. Nor, of course, was he the sole administrative reformer. University presidents, professional leaders, and local philanthropists had already begun to institutionalize the intellectual innovations and educational ramifications of scientific medicine while he was still a Louisville schoolteacher. But what Flexner did do was to crystallize these local reforms into a national policy. As Ludmerer notes, despite their negligible contributions to the intellectual development of modern medical education, philanthropists and reformers from outside academic medicine were influential in helping to determine the "final [institutional] form" assumed by American medical education, a corporate form which has perdured despite subsequent intellectual changes in the content of medical education.[7] It was Flexner's political and organizational achievement within the Rockefeller philanthropic boards which helped structure not only medical education but also the "grants economy" which now organizes the diverse range of American institutions we negatively and inadequately refer to as "nonprofit."

Flexner's rhetoric was an alloy of the Mugwump dream of a society both deferential and democratic with the idiom of Progressive reform. In addition to being a politically effective formula, it was a blueprint for transinstitutional management. The intertwined evils of corruption and inefficiency were serviceable for castigating opponents, and the ideal of science formed the initial basis for institution building. Flexner was frankly dedicated to nurturing an elite, and, though he eschewed the term, he found the bureaucratic organization of knowledge in the German university system a compelling example of how to form such an elite.

By 1920, Flexner's efforts at reform, institution building, and networking had seemingly come to complete fruition. Because he envisioned an ultimately self-regulating academic elite, Flexner felt justified in exercising an often contentious and heavy-handed management of the nation's leading medical schools. But in so doing he had seriously overestimated his power, and the means of resistance to it.

The order brought about by the bureaucratization of medical education produced another set of problems which proved more intractable than had the commercial localism of the nineteenth century. Crosscutting professional and institutional loyalties resulted in a new political fragmentation which Flexner's managerial model could not accommodate. Moreover, the short half-life of viable political rhetoric worked against him. Flexner's institutionally routed elitism had become unacceptable to a new generation of managers in both the foundations and medical education who premised their careers on the earlier reforms. This new managerial cohort responded to the accumulated pressure on Flexner's program and, employing a language drawn from popular politics, forced him out of Rockefeller philanthropy. The centrifugal tendencies of democracy had asserted themselves except on a bureaucratic plane.

The passing of what we might call the Flexnerian moment in American history—the brief heyday of unvarnished enthusiasm for social management—marked the beginning of a new stalemate in policy-making for medical education. The philanthropic managers who succeeded Flexner were either unwilling or unable to engage in his sort of strategic leadership. The final chapter is meant to suggest the diffusion of power which occurred within the Rockefeller Foundation, a diffusion which reflected the balkanization of the national policy process. With ever-increasing numbers of actors in the politics of educational organization, there was less leadership. The institutional coherence which Flexner had envisioned proved chimerical.

Previous work in this area has not satisfactorily addressed the problem of the politics of private bureaucratic management. Much of the literature from the history of medicine is concerned with chronicling the emergence of scientific medicine against a background of quackery and mediocrity. This approach treats the philanthropic role in the transformation of medical education as a fairly straightforward implementation of the best scientific knowledge available and minimizes the question of the politics of reform.[8] Conversely, recent studies from a Marxian perspective have emphasized the political dimension of the process to the exclusion of any other. These scholars see philanthropic reform as the means by which the capitalist class established definitive control over the American health care system. In these renderings, scientific medicine is seen as "scientism": an ideological Potemkin village concealing the oppressions of capitalism.[9] This is the historiographical school which sees foundation philanthropy as the means by which the capitalist class transformed its economic power into cultural and political hegemony.[10]

Between those two poles another group of scholars has begun to stress the role that organizations and institutions play in the "ecology of knowledge."[11] This concept does not deny the internal logic and integrity of scientific growth, but recognizes that the social forms in which knowledge is cultivated can be important determinants of which disciplinary hybrids flourish and which wither. Work taking this approach has drawn attention both to previously underestimated scientific advances in nineteenth-century American medicine and to the contemporary cultural validity of practices now scientifically discredited.[12] It examines the "politics of ideas" which redefined professions and the institutions crucial to successful careers without suggesting that the political implications of the scientific ideas render them ipso facto bogus.[13] Similarly, I believe that any analysis of the philanthropic foundations which does not take into account the real disputes within the foundations and the real limitations on their power has explained away all the important questions.[14]

These points underline the importance of a figure like Flexner, someone who had definite ideas about the proper ecology and organization of knowledge and who was a political success in promoting them in the Carnegie and Rockefeller philanthropies. My emphasis on Flexner is not meant to imply that he alone was responsible for the strengths or ills of the organization of medical education as it eventually developed. Indeed, the fact that medical education today is a distortion of his hopes underlines this point. His system of management and reform was but one of many important elements in the development of modern medical education. Scientific advance, individual and collective professional ambition, technological development, economic growth, and social change were all factors. The significance of Flexner's rise and fall was in his acceptance of the political challenge of managing those various forces. The problematic combination of bureaucracy and democracy which plagued him in that effort remains today a pressing question.

Acknowledgments

Almost any work brings with it to publication a history crowded with benefactors, but this is especially true of a book which began as a dissertation. I would like to acknowledge gratefully the assistance of many of those who have been true philanthropists to me.

The expert, cheerful, and even indulgent assistance of archivists both makes possible and enriches historical research. The bulk of my research was carried out at the Rockefeller Archive Center, Pocantico Hills, New York, where the skill of the staff is equal to the vastness of its holdings. I would like to thank in particular Dr. Joseph Ernst, Director emeritus, J. Warren Hass, and Tom Rosenbaum for their help and apt suggestions. Dr. Ernst and Curtis Clow provided essential guidance to the collections of the Rockefeller Family Archives in Rockefeller Center, New York. Nancy McCall was most helpful during my visit to the Alan Mason Chesney Medical Archives at the Johns Hopkins Medical Institutions. Florence Anderson of the Carnegie Corporation of New York provided me not only with documentary materials, but also with an incisive oral history of that organization. Albert Tannler helped me navigate the archipelago of holdings in the Department of Special Collections. Carleton Chapman, former president of the Commonwealth Fund, provided me with an invaluable opportunity to plow through the Fund's files.

I also want to thank the staffs of the Nathan Pusey Library, Harvard University; the Countway Library of Medicine, Boston; the Department of Special Collections, Sterling Library, Yale University; the Yale University History of Medicine Library; the History of Medicine Division of the National Library of Medicine; the Manuscript Collection of the

American Philosophic Society; the Harvey Mudd Library of Princeton University; the Department of Special Collections, and the President's office, Columbia University; and that of the Manuscript Division of the Library of Congress.

Friends and colleagues provided encouragement, criticism, and advice at many stages in the research, writing, and rewriting of this book. I would like to thank in particular Ted Calhoun, Jack Michel, Ken Cmiel, David Farber, Kathleen McCarthy, Ellen Condliffe Lagemann, and Robert Mc-Caughey. Their counsel brought many improvements; the errors which remain are of course my own. Barbara and Lee Kreader deserve special mention not only for several careful and helpful readings, but also for timely transfusions of morale. I also want to thank my parents, Charles and Elisabeth Wheatley, for their support of me in this process, especially since its length occasionally, and justifiably, puzzled them.

Margaret Browning not only typed large portions of one stage of this manuscript but, more important, in dreary days, believed in better ones and for that I thank her. Susan Tarcov gave the manuscript a thoughtful and careful editing which saved me from many embarrassments. K. Bridget Gibbons went beyond the call of duty in helping to produce a revised manuscript under difficult circumstances. The good advice and easy humor of Barbara Hanrahan of the University of Wisconsin Press was crucial in turning manuscript into book.

This work began as part of the larger project on the history of philanthropy and public policy at the University of Chicago directed by Stanley N. Katz and Barry D. Karl. The financial support of that project by the Ford Foundation, the Rockefeller Foundation, the Alfred P. Sloan Foundation, and the Lily Endowment helped me undertake the travel to archive collections which was essential for my research and to provide the wherewithal to persist in the final years of graduate study. I want to thank those foundations for their help. Happily, my relationship with both Stan Katz and Barry Karl continues. Stan is a reliable source of intellectual insight and organizational energy, one I have resorted to often. That we now work together on many of the problems of the organization and support of knowledge which are the subject of this book is to me a very satisfying irony. My intellectual and moral debt to Barry Karl is considerable. The influence of his ideas on this work will be clear to all who know him; I hope to be faithful to his personal example of scholarly and humane sincerity.

My wife, Linda-Marie Delloff, contributed to this work in more ways than she knows. Dedicating this book to her is but small thanks for that and her many other gifts to me.

The Politics of Philanthropy

Introduction

The oldest medical school in the United States was founded with the expectation of public patronage. When John Morgan inaugurated medical instruction at the College of Philadelphia (later the University of Pennsylvania) in 1765, he confidently predicted that "when two such important institutions, as a medical college and a well regulated hospital, contribute mutually to the advantage of each other, all ranks and conditions of people would chearfully unite in support of a common interest, so beneficial to useful literature, and so advantageous to the province in general." Morgan's expectation was premature: it was not until the twentieth century that public support, first private and then governmental, became widespread and important to medical education.[1]

When Morgan's address was reprinted in 1937, it was published with an introduction by Abraham Flexner. Those two names bracket the decline and rise of public support for medical education in America. More than any other single person, it was Flexner who came to symbolize the fulfillment of Morgan's hopes for a generously supported and, more important, well-ordered system of medical education. In order to understand Flexner's achievement it is necessary to sketch its background. That background reflects the corrosive effects of democracy on a profession whose status in Britain was supported by the state.

Morgan and the early medical elite had hoped to bring to American medical education some of the system and hierarchy which they had come to know in their European medical training. That attempt soon ran afoul of the rambunctious egalitarianism of young America. In the absence of any authoritative social or political regulation, medical schools in

America became numerous but institutionally weak, with a seamy under-
side of commercialism. Mid-nineteenth-century efforts by the medical
profession to influence educational policy were unavailing.[2] However, a
little more than a century after Morgan began his school, educational
leaders such as Charles W. Eliot and Daniel C. Gilman, aided by increasing private philanthropy and a nascent scientific elite, were able to establish new institutional models for reform. These models drew on transatlantic scientific and educational ideals. These local reforms were the
basis from which Abraham Flexner subsequently developed a program for
the national management of the organization of knowledge in medical
education.

Before 1765, American physicians were trained by apprenticeship sup-
plemented by occasional European study.[3] In that year, after returning
from a three-year sojourn at the medical centers of London, Edinburgh,
and the Continent, John Morgan felt the time was ripe for building
American institutions of medical education. "I was further induced to
it [offering a full course of lectures] from a consideration that private
schemes of propagating knowledge are unstable in their nature, and that
the cultivation of useful learning can only be effectually promoted under
those who are patrons of science, and under the authority and direction of
men incorporated for the improvement of literature."[4]

The opening of the Philadelphia medical school was but one part of an
effort by an erstwhile elite of physicians like Morgan to introduce some
hierarchy into colonial medical practice. In eighteenth-century England,
health practitioners were divided into three classes: surgeons, physicians,
and apothecaries. The division of practice implied by these categories was
not as firm as the social distinction of their corporate organization. The
Royal Colleges of Physicians and Surgeons were made up of members
from upper social strata who had not only formal medical training but
also university training in the wider intellectual values of society. Morgan
recognized that on the very frontier of the empire it would be impossible
to maintain the division of labor implied by the English categories, but he
hoped to produce a medical leadership conversant with higher culture
which would be a worthy object of emulation by its inferiors. Founding
medical colleges was the first step in this process. The next was to link the
schools with medical societies which would have some legal relation to the
regulation of practice. The Revolution suspended but did not terminate

this movement. After the American victory at Yorktown, schools were founded in Boston, New York, and Baltimore. Medical societies, often closely overlapping with the college faculties, followed.[5]

But the new United States did not have the social or institutional infrastructure to support a system of medical education on a European model. Whereas in Britain the relation of the Royal Colleges to a definite social order helped preserve a professional hierarchy, attempts to create such institutions continually failed in America. Americans were leery of national organizations, especially any with an elitist flavor. The failure in 1844 of the National Institute for the Promotion of Science was only the most prominent wreckage of such attempts to formalize a national elite. Local institutions were too weak to serve as the basis for an exclusive professionalism. American colleges remained predominantly centers of denominational piety, and what scientific and professional schools that existed were held warily at arm's length. The support of education and particularly of science was haphazard in nineteenth-century America. It was only when would-be recipients could produce a likely combination of opportunity and ideology that any gifts were forthcoming.[6]

Medical education, however, was excluded from even this sporadic traffic because it was conducted largely as a business. The organizers of the Philadelphia school founded by Morgan had adopted the practice of the University of Edinburgh of having the fees for each lecture be the property of the professor in question. In Scotland, where the university was an established institution, the system worked well, but in America it ran wild. Given the makeshift quality of most American medical schools, dependence on fees became both institutional and personal. In order to maintain enrollments, entrance requirements were continually lowered. In an educational application of Gresham's law, the devalued M.D., in Britain a specialist's degree, quickly drove the Bachelor of Medicine (M.B.) degree out of America.[7]

American political culture reinforced this disintegration. In a country where John C. Calhoun could marshal arguments and a considerable following for the belief that it would be unconstitutional for the federal government to accept James Smithson's bequest for "the diffusion of knowledge," it was impossible to rely on the federal government to regulate or support medical education.[8]

The rise of Jacksonian democracy attenuated the already weak regulation of medical education and practice by the state governments. Since the political culture was biased against the exclusive grant of privileges to any organization—bridge company or medical school—there was no impediment to any group of physicians' incorporating themselves as a school with the attendant benefits in fees and prestige. Local communities saw the foundation of medical schools as an advantage in the fearsome competition to become important cities in the rapidly filling interior. Any personal, political, or a professional dispute within a medical faculty often resulted in a schism which produced two rival schools. Daniel Drake, one of the most prominent physicians of the early national period, remarked from bitter experience that "the establishment of medical schools is a prolific source of discord in the profession."[9] With the commercialization of medical education, medical schools and medical societies had opposite interests; the former wanted to increase the number of students while the latter strove to decrease the number of practitioners.[10]

The absence of public support and the feebleness of government regulation of medical education did not imply a scientific dark age in American medicine. Many American physicians were members of the community of world science, made significant contributions to the growth of medical knowledge and technology, and were alive to the implications of the most recent discoveries for medical practice.[11] But those scientific advances were channeled and mediated by an institutional context which through most of the nineteenth century recognized social and political claims as at least equal to those of science. Two institutions are pertinent examples: hospitals and formal professional organizations.

The nineteenth-century hospital was seen as primarily a charitable, not a medical, institution. The patients—or, perhaps more accurately, the inmates—were almost entirely the urban poor. Hospital governing boards were composed of the local elite traditionally concerned with the social control and moral uplift of the submerged classes. To be sure, these boards recognized that physicians played a vital role in the institution, but this recognition was circumscribed by the boards' conceptions of the hospital's mission. Medical and charitable values could and did clash on questions of admissions (ascertaining that the patient was deserving) and therapeutics (the administration of alcohol to patients). More significantly for medical education, the determination of the lay boards to guard their institutional independence meant that the appointment of medical college faculty members to hospital staffs, as well as the availability of the wards for clinical teaching, was subject to uncertainty.[12]

Similarly, the existence of sectarian medicine was an impediment to strong professional organization. Intellectually and in daily practice, "regular" and homeopathic approaches to medical care were by no means mutually exclusive, and both were grounded in the science of the age. But in politics these differences became systematized into rivalries. Aspiring professional leaders employed contemporary political rhetoric to resist licensing requirements which they felt might discriminate against their putative constituents. As George W. Winterburn, editor of the *American Homeopath*, asserted: "Every man has the right to employ any other man to do any thing for him. . . . We would not submit to legislative enactment compelling us to patronize John, the butcher, and Dick, the baker . . . and we see no reason why they should be compelled to have a doctor endorsed by government."[13]

Rather than choose among the competing claims of the various sects or devise different "portals of entry" to medical practice, many states abandoned licensing altogether. "The ultra-radical version of the axiom that all men are born free and equal" lamented Oliver Wendell Holmes, Sr., to the Harvard Medical School class of 1844, "has invaded the regions of science."[14] In the face of this, aspiring leaders of the medical profession attempted to organize. With stricter licensure a political impossibility, reformers concentrated on medical education as the only available fulcrum on which to raise professional solidarity. Medical colleges were exhorted to stop "the ignoble rivalship to see which could have the greatest number of students." As Daniel Drake put it:

> A state which establishes and conducts a medical institution on these principles, will have little need of what are styled laws to regulate the practice of physic. If the fountain of supply be pure, the stream will seldom be tainted, and its waters will require but little clarification. It will regulate and depurate itself.[15]

The American Medical Association itself grew out of an 1846 meeting called to help establish national standards for medical education, and that subject was its chief focus of activity for the first seventy-five years of its existence. But after several decades of agitation its leaders readily admitted that their reform efforts had yielded little fruit. Partly this was a result of the organizational weakness of the association in the Jacksonian climate.

As historian James Burrow has pointed out, until the reorganization of the AMA at the end of the nineteenth century, it was chiefly a collection of aspiring urban practitioners from the eastern seaboard and the Midwest.[16] Opponents seized on this point to decry the "aristocratic feature" of changes advocated by the association. "It is oppression towards the poor, for the sake of crippling the principled Medical Colleges," objected one defender of the prevailing nonsystem.[17] More positively, William Ellery Channing maintained that "the characteristic of our age, then, is not the improvement of science, rapid as this is, so much as its diffusion to all men."[18] But after the Civil War, as America grew in wealth, power, and self-confidence, the aspiring medical elite again sought to assert its legitimacy.

In 1877 Philadelphia was still warmed by the afterglow of the World's Fair celebrating the American Revolutionary Centennial when, in succession to John Morgan, William Pepper delivered the inaugural address of the Medical Department of the University of Pennsylvania. Pepper took as his theme the mingled pride and self-examination inspired by the exhibition. He saw the occasion as a "searching" test which the still relatively new nation had passed. "Has it not stamped, with marks of strongest approbation, the achievements of our country in almost every branch of human industry? Has it not registered the fact that in the brief space of a century we have taken such vast strides in material development, that in many things we approach the older nations, and that in many we equal or even excel them?" But despite the "world-wide applause" for American achievements in "everything that requires skill and business enterprise and mechanical ingenuity, and that contributes directly to material prosperity," Pepper noted that "our defects are equally glaring." Chief among these was America's "degraded system of medical education."[19]

Pepper noted that the debilitating commercialization of American medical education was the result of the absence of "an intelligent and powerful government [which] exercises supervision over the interest of education." Had such a government "extended its protection to our system of medical education at an early stage . . . the medical profession of America would never have fallen to the low estate it has reached." Pepper realized, however, that "the exercise of such control would not only have been impossible, it would have been hostile to the spirit of our people and the principles of our national government."[20] But acknowledging the role of undeniable political principles in producing the unhappy situation did not make it any more acceptable. Indeed, as Pepper noted, the problems of medical education in the country were a rebuke to American pride, and not just by comparison with Europe:

> Even in countries which, like Mexico and the republics of South America, we are disposed to regard as only semi-civilized, and where the instability of government and the frequent convulsions of social order would seem to render any fixed and comprehensive educational policy impossible—when we see that in each and all of these a thorough plan of medical education is held essential for the welfare of the community, for the development of medical science, and for the interests of the medical profession itself, it is surely time to consider carefully if we are not sadly at fault in this; and if, while elsewhere the requirements of medical education have been made to keep pace with the growth of medical knowledge, with us they have not been controlled by other and far less proper influence.[21]

Pepper's contemplated solution belied his nationalist rhetoric, however. His proposal—that the individual states rely on the expertise of acknowledged medical luminaries in devising new and more stringent licensing requirements—was, given the political realities, wishful thinking.[22] Reform which depended on governmental authority was stymied. Instead, the reconstruction of American medical education came from the development in private institutions of a national elite capable of determining and enforcing coherent policies for the creation and administration of a national system of organized knowledge. Educational leaders bent on creating an American university were one early component of that network.

Charles W. Eliot, who became president of Harvard in 1869, was one of the most important of these leaders. Eliot reformed the undergraduate curriculum by introducing the elective system, nurtured the growth of Harvard's graduate school (although he had some misgivings about it), and helped promote the transformation of the law school. But nowhere were his reforms more thoroughgoing than in regard to the Harvard Medical School. In later life, Eliot pointed to his effect on the medical school as his proudest achievement, and it was said of him that he found the school brick and left it marble.[23] More important than materiel however, were the organizational changes Eliot effected.

The Harvard Medical School had been founded in 1732, and prior to

Eliot's tenure its administrative connection with the parent university was tenuous. The school was conducted by the faculty, which was one branch of Boston's social elite. If the early teaching in the school was mostly didactic lectures and the graduating exercises were in the manner of a classical dissertation defense, there was at least the assurance of social breeding. When William James graduated from the school in 1869, he was worried that his dissertation on the common cold would not be approved. But after one perfunctory question, chief examiner Oliver Wendell Holmes, Sr., cheerily asked the nervous student, "Well, James, how is your father?"[24]

In his first annual report as president, Eliot declared that "the whole system of medical education in this country needs thorough reformation." The requirements of medical schools (as well as law and divinity schools) were so low that "the term 'learned profession' is getting to have a sarcastic flavor." Eliot conceded that such schools "may, indeed, be the best which the hastily organized, fast-growing American communities will support," but "the spectacle of so large a crop of poor doctors" made him shudder.[25] Eliot was resolved to improve the situation at least at Harvard.

One of his first steps in that direction was the creation in 1869 of a department of physiology under Henry P. Bowditch. Bowditch had studied in France and Germany and was determined to introduce experiments into teaching alongside didactic lectures. This department was to become a national exemplar in the very discipline which in turn introduced laboratory methods into medicine.[26] Within the school, Bowditch became the leader of a scientific cadre whose restlessness was a double-edged sword to Eliot. In battles with the old guard, they provided the president with useful allies, but as entrepreneurs making independent overtures to local wealth, their ambitious plans sometimes created problems for Eliot's always careful and frugal management.[27]

In 1871 Eliot exercised for the first time in living memory the right of a Harvard president to chair a meeting of the medical faculty. In that capacity he proposed a series of reform measures. The opposition to these reforms was led by Henry J. Bigelow. This conflict focused on the debatable nature of medicine: was it an "art" or a "science"? Bigelow held that medicine was an art: that at the core of the profession there was an indi-

visible and indeterminate content which was both deeper than and beyond mere book knowledge. This debate echoed repeatedly through the
controversies surrounding the reform of medical education, with the en-
trenched elites employing the rhetoric of "medicine as an art" in order to
resist the claims of rising groups which waved the banners of science.[28]
Bigelow developed the argument that medicine was an art to defend the
educational autonomy of the medical school and the social autonomy of
the profession. He felt that since medical discovery was "generally not
made by workers in chemical and physiological fields but by subsequent
and more purely medical workers," the schools should not "encourage
the medical student to while away his time in the labyrinths of Chemistry
and Physiology." Moreover, he felt that it was foolish to try to dictate the
development of students since "most eminent men are in a large degree
self made, and have pursued their subject from the attraction before
them, and not from a stimulus behind." To Bigelow, the source of that
attraction in post–Civil War America was clear: "In this vigorous country, where the pursuits of business exhibit so many striking examples of
early capacity, and where the aim of every young man is to find himself
in active life, it is plainly difficult to fetter the ambition of the student
with a view to insuring greater cónventional and average competency."
He continued: "Medical teaching should not be too much interfered with,
nor its machinery hampered by those who are not familiar with its working." Finally he asserted that "a university cannot judge accurately of
medical men." The very deficiencies of American education, Bigelow argued, particularly the lack of university hospitals, made it essential that
the medical school be autonomous so that it could make the best of a bad
situation.[29]

Bigelow demanded to know why change was so suddenly necessary
after years of peaceful functioning of the school; Eliot's calm reply was
that it was necessary because there was a new president.[30] Oliver Wendell
Holmes, Sr., was "amused" at the spectacle of "this cool, grave young
man proposing in the calmest way to turn everything topsy-turvy."[31]
But it was more than a personal confrontation; it was a reflection of a new
social basis for institutions like Harvard. The university's Overseers, one
element of the Harvard Corporation, had recently been reconstituted;
they were now elected by the alumni and not the Massachusetts General

Court. That change reflected the increasing institutional integrity of the university.[32] The Corporation supported Eliot, and Bigelow was left sputtering at the lack of professional autonomy:

> Does the Corporation hold opinions on medical education? Who are the Corporation? Does Mr. _____ know anything about medical education? Or Rev. Dr. _____? Or Judge _____? Why, Mr. _____ carries a horse-chestnut in his pocket to keep off rheumatism! Is the new medical education to be best directed by a man who carries horse-chestnuts in his pocket to cure rheumatism?[33]

Eliot's triumph did not immediately open floodgates of private philanthropy, but it did help put in place the crucial precondition. As he later put it: "So long as medical schools are conducted as private ventures for the benefit of a few physicians and surgeons who have united to form a corporation of faculty, the community ought not to endow them."[34] Eliot used the reforms to plead for new endowments. Although the Panic of 1873 set back fund-raising, by 1900 the Harvard Medical School had an endowment of nearly $1.1 million.[35]

Educational leadership and philanthropy also were combined in the creation of the second new model in medical school organization: the Johns Hopkins University School of Medicine. The creation of the new university was itself an example of the transition in philanthropy which took place in the nineteenth century. Johns Hopkins was a Baltimore Quaker merchant who made a fortune in railroading. Much of his early giving had been the sort of traditional charity that concentrated on that new and troublesome class: the urban poor. As Baltimore grew, his beneficence became more completely identified with institutions. He was reinforced in this direction by one of the first modern American philanthropists, George Peabody. An ex-Baltimorean, Peabody had left the United States and made a fortune in London banking. Imbibing English notions of noblesse oblige, he had begun endowing institutions in England and America. One was the Peabody Institute in Baltimore, and on a triumphal return to open the institute in 1866 he urged Hopkins to think along similar lines. Hopkins took up the suggestion, and in his will he made legacies for a hospital and a university. Significantly, Hopkins instructed the hospital trustees: "you will bear constantly in mind that it is my wish and purpose that the institution should ultimately form a part of that university for which I have made ample provision in my will."

The origins of this provision are obscure—Hopkins may have intended nothing more than the most efficient use of resources—but its effect was clear. It not only made certain that the new university would have a medical school, but it created a model of institutional integration which was crucial to subsequent reforms.[36]

It was D. C. Gilman who transformed Hopkins' general philanthropic intentions into a new educational paradigm. Hopkins died in 1873, soon after making his pledge; and in searching for a president for the new institution, the Hopkins trustees consulted other college presidents. Eliot was the first to suggest Gilman, and his nomination was heartily endorsed by James Angell of Michigan, Noah Porter of Yale, and Andrew D. White of Cornell. The unanimity of their sentiment reflected the growing sense of national community among the leaders of American higher education.[37]

In 1873 Gilman was serving as president of the University of California. Dismayed at the choice of Noah Porter, a defender of the old regime in education (his endorsement of Gilman notwithstanding), as the president of Yale, Gilman had moved westward in the previous year in search of an opportunity to construct a model of nonsectarian, rigorous, and engaged higher education. One of his notable achievements during his brief three-year tenure in Berkeley was in bringing about the unification of a private medical school with the state university. Gilman was active in his supervision of medical education and articulated many of the themes (high standards, coeducation, clinical training, scientific background) which would later characterize the Baltimore school. In California, Gilman experienced firsthand the problems that democracy posed for his educational vision. Charges of corruption by publicist Henry George, resentment of Gilman's forthright nondenominationalism, and populist charges that the university was not meeting the needs of farmers and workingmen produced legislative investigations. While Gilman was exonerated of any wrongdoing, it was clear that California was less than the educational promised land, and he accepted the call to Baltimore in 1874.[38]

On assuming the Hopkins presidency, Gilman searched the Western world for uprootable scholars. Although some of his finds were foreigners, the increasing transatlantic traffic of previous years made it possible to staff the first graduate university in the United States mostly with

Americans. The grand tour had always been a requisite finishing for aspiring young American men, but about mid-century it took on an increasingly academic cast: the wanderers came back armed not only with sketchbooks but with Ph.D.'s. These young men, fired by zeal for learning qua learning and the ideal of university culture, provided the personnel for Gilman's enterprise.[39]

The medical faculty was one of the last Gilman recruited, but the same principles held there. In beginning the school ex nihilo, Gilman had an opportunity to break the localism of American medical education. In selecting the medical faculty, Gilman fused two intertwined but potentially divergent traditions of medical education. His first appointment was that of William H. Welch to be professor of pathology. It was a crucial choice. More than any other individual, Welch captured and magnified the transforming influence of the German university on American medical education. Trained at Breslau, Welch had struggled upon return to the United States to find time and resources for his research and was obliged to pursue it only in the most modest of circumstances, until his appointment to Johns Hopkins. Like physiology, pathology held out to medicine the promise of useful laboratory results and scientific rigor. Welch's students subsequently helped develop pathology as a learned discipline in the American university. Moreover, these "Welch rabbits," when placed throughout the country, formed a network of discontent, dedicated to promoting their discipline as a paradigm for the reform of the whole medical education.[40]

Another important figure selected by Gilman was William Osler. Osler, a Canadian, was broad in his outlook and had served as a pathologist, but he was more closely associated with the British tradition of clinical medicine which stressed the professional role of physicians. This tradition was also bent on reform; one of Osler's legacies at Baltimore was the introduction of the clinical clerkship, a requirement designed to assure the development of the student in actual hospital practice.[41] In time, however, it became clear that the differing outlooks of Welch and Osler reflected conflicting values and even personalities. The nineteenth-century clinician's natural orientation was toward society. The brisk decisiveness, broad range of interest, and personal flair of an Osler might be pinched by the confines of laboratory disciplines of patience, precision, and isolation.[42] But when the Hopkins medical school was beginning, there was sufficient room to reform American medical education from both standpoints, and for more than thirty years these two traditions dovetailed productively.

The organization of the school in which these remarkable individuals served enhanced their impact. Gilman sought to maintain university conditions in the school insofar as possible. One of the early rulings of the board of trustees was that "medical education in the United States now suffers from the fact that the chairs are almost always filled by practitioners. . . . It is thought best here to initiate our Medical School by appointing several teachers who shall not engage in practice." Also, the Johns Hopkins Hospital did not follow the then-common practice of rotating heads of clinical services: there was continuous control by one chief. Gilman took an active interest in all aspects of medical education; he not only chaired the medical faculty but also became the first administrative head of the hospital where he oversaw with equal sedulousness the purchase of linens and the determination of lines of authority. It was this introduction of an internal hierarchy which helped make Johns Hopkins unique in American medical education.[43]

While these innovations were of enduring importance, the new medical school electrified the reform movement by its requirement of an undergraduate degree for admission. This too came about through philanthropic prompting. Despite all Gilman's efforts the university's medical school was still held back by its relative poverty; Johns Hopkins' provisions had not been as "ample" as he anticipated, particularly when the stock of the Baltimore-Ohio railroad, which made up most of the university's assets, plummeted in value. The hospital opened in 1889, but resources for the school were not at hand. At least $500,000 was necessary.[44]

Into this breach stepped a syndicate of wealthy women who promised to raise a portion of that figure if women would be admitted to school on the same basis as men. Led by M. Carey Thomas, later the president of Bryn Mawr College, the women managed to overcome Gilman's distaste for the prospect of coeducation. One of their number, Mary Garrett, who contributed the bulk of the total sum necessary, wanted to ensure not only the admission of women but their admission to a school with the highest standards. Involved negotiations eventually produced the requirement of a college degree for admission.[45]

By 1890, philanthropy was coming to be seen as a solution to the institutional underdevelopment of "a nation born in a day." Martin B. Anderson, the president of the University of Rochester, provided a theological interpretation:

> God has graciously adjusted our financial strength to the moral burdens which he has called us to bear. Unless our benevolence in giving shall more than equal our capacity for accumulation, the forces of ignorance, evil and superstition, will take possession of our fair land; and in spite of our boasted freedom of thought and action, we shall become a by-word and a hissing and a shaking of the head among the nations.[46]

The growing importance of private philanthropy to higher education in general and medical education in particular was becoming clear. Early pleas for philanthropic support were apologetic about soliciting funds from outside the profession, but this outward reach was soon turned into a positive virtue. Its advocates portrayed medical education not just as a mechanism for the professional development of individuals but as a medium of social management. The editors of the *Journal of the American Medical Association* stressed that "the giving of money for the proper endowment of medical colleges will not . . . be a charity to a few medical teachers, but a means of protecting the public."[47] It was regretted "that the many wealthy and generous men in our country who have made endowments to schools and colleges have almost uniformly overlooked medical institutions . . . medical colleges have been allowed to shift as best they could."[48]

The accumulation of medical school endowments was slow and painful. In 1881 only seven medical schools had productive endowments, and giving trailed behind that to theological education.[49] Even as late as 1908 the president of the American Association of Medical Colleges noted that "the greatest single difficulty in the way of progress in medical education is undoubtedly poverty. Beside it all other difficulties appear trivial."[50] Indeed, one Chicago leader of the profession was so impatient with the slow growth of private benefactions that he urged the federal endowment of schools.[51]

Such voices were in a minority, however. The growth of private philanthropy was seen as a vindication of American democracy. University presidents were quick to defend its value and its political legitimacy. In soliciting funds for Harvard Medical School, Eliot maintained not only that giving would accelerate the pace of medical education reform but also that "in this country endowment is the best means of giving the privilege of high education to the children of the poor."[52] Eliot saw no conflict between the growing wealth of private institutions such as universities and American democracy, and throughout the nineteenth century he stressed how complementary they were. Indeed, the very categories of public and private were not strictly appropriate, he maintained:

> The fact that the property of these public trusts is administered by persons who are not immediately chosen or appointed by the public, obscures to some minds the essential principle that the property is really held and used for the public benefit; but the mode of administration does not alter the uses, or make the property any less property held for the public.[53]

The luxuriant growth of these institutions was made possible by private endowments, "a phenomenon without precedent or parallel, and . . . a legitimate effect of democratic institutions."[54] When in 1874 the Massachusetts government considered restricting the exemption from taxation of college endowments, Eliot was rousing in their defense. He criticized as "ungrateful and absurd" the idea that "anybody in this country [was] obstructed, as to his rights, duties, or enjoyments, by any endowment or foundation provided by the living or the dead."[55] Such organizations were essential, Eliot maintained:

> The public services of these institutions can hardly need be enlarged upon. All the professions called learned or scientific are fed by these institutions; the whole school system depends upon them; they foster piety, art, literature and poetry; they gather in and preserve the intellectual capital of the race . . . they maintain the standards of honor, public duty and public spirit, and diffuse the refinement, culture and spirituality without which added wealth would only be grossness and corruption.[56]

Eliot acknowledged that the exempted corporations were answerable to the state for their stewardship and that periodic review of their functioning was a good thing. "[They] must admit the ultimate right of the State to inquire into the administration of their affairs." But he stressed that allowing the growth of endowments was the most appropriate and efficient means of maintaining private institutions. He criticized as "sophistical and fallacious" the suggestion that the system of government grants would be better. "The exemption method leaves the trustees of the institutions untrammelled in their action, and untempted to unworthy arts or mean compliances. The [government] grant method . . . puts them in the position of importunate suitors for the public bounty, or worse, converts them into ingenious and unscrupulous assailants of the public treasury."[57]

This new institutional formula—the American university supported by private philanthropy—seemed to promise at least a partial solution to the Jacksonian decay of the institutions of American medical education. Elite institutions seemed to be much better engines of "reform" than either professional organizations or state action. Morgan's prediction in 1765 that all classes of people would "chearfully" support medical education had been succeeded in 1900 by the realization that all classes were not needed—the wealthy alone could serve the purpose.

The organization of knowledge could thus be insulated from the corrosion of the wider political culture. However, Eliot's expectation that private benevolence would guarantee the institutional autonomy of the university would shortly prove to be overly sanguine. Just as the retreat from state action had altered the balance of the reform movement, so the development of a new consciousness among the wealthiest men in America would upset the balance he sketched between donors and the institutions. But while Eliot urged philanthropists to support local institutional leaders, what was developed was a mechanism for national leadership through the medium of those institutions.

1 Experiments in Philanthropic Reform

The growth of large fortunes like those of Andrew Carnegie and John D. Rockefeller changed the scale and form of the philanthropy which educational leaders like Charles W. Eliot had praised as a solution to the deficiencies of American culture. With the new sources of wealth, philanthropy was transformed from a system of individual patronage to a matrix for the resolution of issues of public policy. Associated with this transformation were two terms which jointly revealed the religious origin and secular direction of charity: the "gospel of wealth" and "scientific philanthropy." The devotion of private wealth to public uses—the gospel of wealth—was intended to help lend political legitimacy to the presence of large wealth in a democracy. The efficient organization of that benevolence—scientific philanthropy—was intended to distinguish it from the impulsive charity of the past. The "scientific" flavor of the new endeavor in both method and object reflected the search for new values to replace an increasingly battered religious orthodoxy.[1]

Medical education was a logical field for the new philanthropy: it promised general and permanent improvement rather than individual, fleeting palliation. But it was only after cautious experimentation that the philanthropy of the great magnates was committed to that object. The field was quite "thick," in institutional terms, and the best means of leverage were not immediately apparent. Puzzles abounded: Were medical teaching and research inextricable? How could the philanthropic motives of the donors be squared with the commercial aspect of medical education? Most important, could the philanthropists intervene in this area and not become entangled with the various political projects and political controversies latent in this area?

It was the advisers to the philanthropists, Frederick T. Gates in the case of Rockefeller and Henry S. Pritchett in Carnegie's case, to whom the task fell of devising policies which could preserve the organizational integrity and political legitimacy of the new philanthropic mechanism. The results of their policies laid the basis for the more extensive philanthropic program Abraham Flexner would later implement. They sought to mediate between their patrons' hesitations, their own understandings of the proper organization of knowledge, and the opportunities which were presented to them. Gates became enthralled with the potential of medical research, but was uncertain about the existing state of university medicine. His experiences with medical education, in particular with the efforts of William Rainey Harper to acquire a medical school for the University of Chicago, soured him on the field. The independence of the Rockefeller Institute for Medical Research, created in 1902, was a reflection of this ambivalence. Pritchett was more adventurous. He called the medical profession and the universities to public account and then sought to enforce that call with an educational survey, the so-called Flexner Report, which would organize the agenda for further reform. It was that effort which initiated Abraham Flexner's career as an influence on American medical education.

The uneasy position of great wealth in a democracy was a persistent problem for the development of modern philanthropy. Carnegie in particular, although he relished the approval and company of the Gilded Age elite (his circle included businessmen, conservative Republicans, university presidents, and other guardians of the genteel tradition), retained enough of his radical Scottish Chartist heritage to want to befriend the little man and to distrust mighty institutions. Most of the time this tension was manageable. His most famous—and in some ways most typical—program, the donation of libraries, caught these contradictions. The library could be a means of individual mobility; giving only the building prevented pauperization of the recipient community, and the charity could be diffused through many communities.[2] "Pauperization" was the specter haunting the philanthropists: the distinction between "worthy" and "undeserving" objects of benevolence. The word conveyed the fear that charity, if not correctly applied, could reduce those in temporary need of assistance to a position of permanent dependence on external generosity.

At an ideological level, Carnegie tried to fuse a hope for the perfectability of man with the gloomy metaphysics of Herbert Spencer. However, the phrase "gospel of wealth" was not Carnegie's but that of the English editor who reprinted Carnegie's two essays "Wealth" (published in June 1889) and "The Best Fields for Philanthropy" (December 1890) after their original American publication. Carnegie himself was not conventionally religious; he drew a "clear line . . . between theology and religion, the one changing and the other surviving, the one of man and the other in man."[3] Carnegie's father had left Scotch Calvinism to experiment with Swedenborgianism. As a child, Andrew attended a Swedenborgian church, but never found it ultimately satisfying. His substitute for theological explanations became the works of Spencer and Darwin. "These works were relevations to me," he wrote, "here was the truth which reconciled all things as far as the finite can grasp them, the alembic which harmonized hitherto conflicting ideas and brought order out of chaos."[4] But the synthesis which Carnegie produced was as much a product of his own personality as anything else. A "sublime optimist," Carnegie attempted to apply principles freely drawn from Spencer and Darwin in a way which justified his position and held out hope for the future. Like many American interpretations of European thought, Carnegie's rendering of these philosophies filtered out much of their world-weariness and substituted an uplifting hope.[5]

The professed task of Carnegie's essays—that of strengthening the "ties of brotherhood that they may still bind together the rich and poor in harmonious relationship"—was less than a ringing call for the free working of natural selection in society. To be sure, Carnegie was a convinced capitalist, but according to him that system required not vindication but only assertion. "One who studied this subject will soon be brought face to face with the conclusion that upon the sacredness of property civilization itself depends—the right of the laborer to his hundred dollars in the savings bank, and equally the legal right of the millionaire to his millions." The insertion of "legal" on the prosperous side of the equation alluded to Carnegie's larger point: that it was the "duty of the man of wealth . . . to consider all surplus revenues which come to him simply as a trust fund, which he is called upon to administer, and strictly bound as a matter of duty to administer in the manner which, in his judgment, is best calculated to produce the most beneficial results for the community."[6]

Determining those uses was of course the crucial question, "for one of the serious obstacles to the improvement of our race is indiscriminate charity." In a telling paraphrase of Oliver Wendell Holmes, Sr.'s, remark concerning the American pharmacopoeia, Carnegie asserted that "it were better for mankind that the millions of the rich were thrown into the sea than so spent as to encourage the slothful, the drunken, the unworthy." Rather "the best means of benefiting the community is to place within its reach the ladders upon which the new aspiring can rise."[7]

In his second essay, Carnegie considered "some of the best uses to which a millionaire can devote the surplus of which he should regard himself as only the trustee." Carnegie was convinced that "the founding or extension of hospitals, medical colleges, laboratories, and other institutions connected with the alleviation of human suffering, and especially with the prevention rather than the cure of human ills," was "one of the wisest possible uses of wealth." Carnegie saw "no danger of pauperizing a community in giving for such purposes, because such institutions relieve temporary ailments or shelter only those who are hopeless invalids." The steel magnate stressed in particular the importance of laboratories for medical colleges.[8]

Despite this endorsement, Carnegie the philanthropist was not as interested in medical education as Carnegie the publicist. Much more of his surplus went to libraries, parks, and public swimming baths. Carnegie was so put off by the commercialism in medicine that it was not until he came into sustained contact with Henry S. Pritchett after 1906 that he displayed any significant interest in medical education.

John D. Rockefeller was much less voluble than Andrew Carnegie, but his philanthropy was much more cautious and deliberate. The founding of the University of Chicago was a crucial passage in the development of his giving pattern. What began as an effort to assure denominational piety became a development of national importance in the institutionalization of knowledge. It marked the transition of his giving from episodic patronage to strategic planning. Perhaps the most important aspect of the episode was the acquaintance he made with Frederick Taylor Gates.[9]

Gates was to become a vital figure in Rockefeller's philanthropy and was the man responsible for interesting him in medical research and education. Gates's career exemplified the transformation of nineteenth-century America. Born on an upstate New York farm, he grew up with the country on the western prairie and died in the suburbs of an industrial metropolis. Ideologically he went from conventional protestant belief to religious skepticism combined with a faith in science; in his work he went from local congregations to international business and philanthropic organizations. These changes were not sudden lurches, however, but a logical progression; when his path crossed Rockefeller's he was at a critical turning point.[10]

By 1880 Gates was dissatisfied with local pastoral work, and he joined one of the growing denominational bureaucracies which were in many ways prototypes of the later philanthropic foundations. The American Baptist Education Society had been formed by Northern Baptists in 1888 to regularize support of the denomination's educational academies and colleges. Upon studying the situation, Gates was dismayed to discover that the Baptists were not supporting their schools as generously as either the Methodists or the Presbyterians. This, Gates felt, was a reflection not on Baptists' spirit but on their organization; their schools were poorly located, widely scattered, and too numerous. The society was designed to be a central clearinghouse for potential givers which would bring order to the field.[11] Gates also hoped that such a system would solve what he perceived to be evangelistic malingering: the dispensers of funds could become the moral guardians of the schools. As Gates wrote to a fellow divine:

> What you say regarding the religious life of our institutions, ashamed of Christ and ashamed of this denomination, is, I fear, too true. It is curious that this sensitiveness to being too religious or Baptist is in pretty strict ratio to the amount of endowment they have. More endowment, more independence of the churches, more carelessness regarding the Gospel. I sometimes seriously question if it would not be much better to try to get a fund of several millions in the treasury of the Education Society as an Educational Endowment fund. Instead of distributing the principal as now to needy schools let the interest only be distributed. . . . Our institutions would then own their parentage and honor the Gospel or else find their income suddenly withdrawn and transferred to some other institution not puffed up.[12]

The intent of the American Baptist Education Society also appealed to Rockefeller. With the growth of his fortune, the oil magnate found responding to individual suppliants increasingly burdensome. As he wrote in 1889 to a friend, "I am more and more disposed to give only through organized educational agencies."[13] Thus, when Gates put forth the idea that the society sponsor the creation of a new college that would be the acme for the denomination's rationally organized educational structure, Rockefeller was inclined to participate if his contributions were matched by others. After a tug-of-war within the denomination over the location of the proposed school was settled in favor of Chicago, William Rainey Harper, Yale professor of Semitic Languages, was selected to head the new enterprise.[14]

Harper, it was hoped, would solve the problem of maintaining religious faith in the face of secularizing intellectual trends. As Gates wrote of Harper to a fellow Baptist, "He is really a mediator between Higher Criticism and Orthodoxy and as such I think is destined if he continues to maintain his discretion to work an important service to Christianity."[15] Gates had been assured that at Yale Harper annually secured a number of conversions.[16] Harper, however, hesitated before accepting the charge. His position at Yale was influential, and he had great ambitions. Like Gilman, Harper was a product of the Sheffield Scientific School and hoped to revitalize education on as broad a front as possible. Chicago interested him only to the extent that it would become a major institution. It was only when Rockefeller pledged $2 million for a divinity school for the university and, more important, implied more substantial aid to come that Harper accepted the opportunity.[17]

The relationship between Harper and his patron remained anxious. The scope of the emerging university rapidly outgrew denominational bounds, and appeals were made to wealthy Chicagoans of all creeds. A major national, even international, institution was created, but the ultimate reliance was always on Rockefeller's purse. Without denying Harper's achievement, Rockefeller was troubled by Harper's ambitious planning and often overly optimistic financing. As Gates later put it, "the struggle for economy and financial order" was "a great struggle to reconcile and maintain harmony between two antipodal natures. . . . I warned Dr. Harper. I warned him many times. I warned him at work, in deed and in every possible way. At times I thought I have made an impression . . . but when he would return to Chicago he would inevitably fall from grace or drift helplessly in a current which he had not the force to resist."[18]

Gates was in a good position to observe the struggle because he had left the Education Society in 1891 and entered into Rockefeller's personal employ. Rockefeller had been impressed with Gates's management of the Chicago founding, and told the former pastor that "the pressure of appeals for philanthropic causes on his time and strength had become too great to be borne; that he was so constituted as to be unable to give away money with satisfaction without inquiry as to the worthiness of the cause," and that he wanted Gates to be his full-time benevolence officer.[19] Gates's duties included investigating a number of Rockefeller's philanthropic and business interests, but one of his chief tasks was to try to rein in Harper. As Harper's plans grew apace the urgency in the New York office to curb potentially crippling deficits also increased. This conflict came to a head over the question of a medical school for the new university.

What was to become the long and troubled relationship between the University of Chicago and Rush Medical College began out of mutual need. Rush was the oldest medical school in Illinois, having been founded in 1837 when Chicago was not much more than a growing village. Many of the leaders of the local profession graced its faculty which staffed the Presbyterian Hospital and had access to the burgeoning Cook County Hospital. One of the better schools of its type, Rush maintained relatively high admission and graduation standards but still managed to remain one of the largest producers of M.D.'s in the nation. In 1890 Rush had a loose affiliation with Lake Forest University, but in the national institutional reshuffling that was taking place Lake Forest was scaling back its ambitions and becoming a college and so some of the leading personalities of Rush began to look for a more capacious academic harbor for their school. Even before the university opened, Rush faculty member E. Fletcher Ingals inquired of Harper about the possibility of merging their two institutions.[20]

Some tried to advise Harper to spurn the advance, warning of "the great wrong that would be thereby done to the University as an institution of higher culture by the consummation of such an arrangement." "I beg in the name of higher medical education, that you pause and think before committing what seems to me, the fatal mistake of making the proposed combination in order to get your Medical Department on its feet at once," wrote one correspondent.[21] The eagerness of Rush and other schools for union with the university reflected how little they had to offer. But Harper was easily seduced. A medical school, as well as other professional schools, was essential to his educational vision. The sort of university he was constructing would combine the ideals of research, teaching, and utility, and no institution more clearly held out that possibility than a medical school. Harper was concerned about criticism of Rush, but after Ingals assured him that adoption of the highest standards was a proximate goal, the two began planning for union.[22]

It should have become immediately apparent how unstable the contemplated alliance was. Ingals constantly had to urge Harper to keep discussions confidential "for as soon as it shall become known whatever is done or not done, it will start two or three hundred people to do everything they can to circumvent our desires."[23] The younger faculty apparently did not feel that they would get benefits from the proposed affiliation. Ingals urged Harper to get Rockefeller's ear on the subject and nail the union down while he still controlled his uneasy faculty. Gates cautioned Harper to take no action until the president saw the philanthropist himself. When the New York office refused to endorse any plans for medical education, Ingals agreed to be patient and not "burn our bridges."[24]

It has been suggested that Rockefeller was unwilling to support the affiliation with Rush because he was a believer in homeopathy.[25] That is at best a partial truth, one that Ingals and others eagerly seized upon as an explanation of their rejection.[26] Rockefeller did patronize homeopathic physicians, but the disinclination of the New York office to endorse a union with Rush reflected more specific fears. Their main concern was the institutional and fiscal integrity of the university and ultimately its claims on their office. When Harper proposed affiliation with another local institution as an attempt to create a technical school, he was also rebuffed. Gates's words on that occasion were indicative of the suspicion with which Rockefeller's office viewed any suitors of its institutional child, the university:

> I have had so much experience with persons who are disposed to take every advantae of rich corporations that I have great fear that before you get through with it you will find [the technical school] a thorn in your side. Perhaps our own experience has made me unduly cautious about putting a possible club in the hands of evilly disposed persons. If you could be here in this office and see the exhibitions of human meanness, and even dishonor, among otherwise respectable men when they come to negotiate with Mr. Rockefeller's wealth, you would appreciate better than you can how this perhaps unnatural caution has arisen.[27]

Moreover, there was ample reason to distrust Rush apart from its alleged sectarian perspective. Trusting in Harper's goodwill, Ingals was frank in his comments about his colleagues. Dr. A was "well educated but a poor presence and a poor teacher." Dr. B was "a disgrace to the college and is obscene & profane in class room"; Dr. C "appears sadly lacking mentally, is certainly no ornament"; Dr. E "does not enjoy the confidence of those who have come most in contact with him. His loyalty & integrity are doubted."[28] Overall faculty performance was poor, and the college administration was lax. Ingals lamented that one colleague "thinks the college ought to keep men simply because they have been there a long time. His sense of justice is much stronger than his inclination to get the very best man for the work."[29] Rush's troubles were the result not only of a failure of will, however, but also of its ramshackle organization. When Harper suggested that a particularly useless member be dropped from the faculty, Ingals protested that the individual's personal connections allowed the college use of the dispensary and he could not therefore be let go. While Rush was not an outright proprietary operation, it had some suspicious features. Ingals baldly admitted that one of the ways of compensating the faculty was "giving them a rank where their prestige will increase their practice," and that the higher the rank the less they were obliged to teach. The school had no endowment and was dependent on fees not only for expenses but also for retirement of its considerable debt. Since most of the debt was owed to the senior faculty who had purchased its bonds, the faculty had an interest in maintaining a large class.[30]

Even so, Harper continued to feel that Rush would form a valued part of the university and hoped he could convince the New Yorkers of the virtue of that position. His hopes were no doubt excited when he received a letter from Gates in 1897. "I am just now reading," Rockefeller's almoner wrote, "the recent book on the practice of medicine by the head of the Johns Hopkins Medical School, and have scarcely read anything more interesting."[31] In his enthusiasm over the volume Gates not only misstated William Osler's position but must have forgotten Harper's low combustion point; for the president immediately tried again to push for approval of union with Rush. It was a dangerous miscalculation on the educator's part, one which reverberated beyond his own institution.

By his own testimony Gates's summer idyll with William Osler's *Principles of Medicine* was the origin of the Rockefeller philanthropic ventures in medical research and education. This was not a random encounter; Gates had sought the volume out. His father had studied to be a physician before becoming a minister, and Gates had long been interested in medicine. During his Minneapolis pastorship he had often discussed medical theories with physicians in his congregation. While the ministrations of these parishioners had not given Gates great confidence in contemporary medicine, he had obviously not given up on it. In New York he asked a former parishioner studying medicine at Columbia to recommend the best possible text. His question could not have been one of mere curiosity; Gates was already preoccupied with finding outlets for Rockefeller's rapidly growing hoard. The student recommended Osler's book, and Gates took the volume on vacation to the Catskills.[32]

At first glance Osler's book must have seemed an unlikely candidate to change Gates's low opinion of medical practice. The book was replete with frank confessions of medical ignorance of particular disease agents and unflinchingly noted the often fatal consequences of therapeutic impotence. But what Gates accurately read was the possibility which was implicit in Osler's terse but illuminated prose. Osler's recitation of the history of discoveries relevant to the particular diseases showed that definite progress was being made. His book was, in effect, a long outline whose many blank spaces had the prospect of being filled in soon by the progress of medical research.[33]

While still on vacation, Gates composed a memorandum for Rockefeller proposing the creation of an institute for medical research. Such an institute would constitute the most basic and symbolic expression of the ideal of scientific philanthropy: the quest for disease cures was much more important than mere mitigation of suffering. Gates was not so naive as to believe that a cascade of discoveries would be loosed by one blast from Rockefeller's financial arsenal; but if Rockefeller's initiative only inspired others it would be money well spent.[34]

Before Rockefeller had any reaction to the institute idea, Harper seized on Gates's enthusiasm to press again the issue of affiliation with Rush. Patience would have served him better; the university was the logical site for the contemplated institute, but his impetuosity was only adding to the image the New York office had of him as overly impulsive. Representatives of the medical college and the university agreed on the conditions of affiliation. The present Rush trustees would resign and be replaced by men who were also trustees of the university, admission requirements would be raised, and the debts would be paid off. All appointments would be subject to university authority. The first two years of instruction would take place at the university's South Side campus, and clinical teaching would continue at Rush's West Side plant. Even when these conditions were met, the trustees of the university made it explicit that they were not pledging an eventual full union with Rush.[35]

Gates was infuriated: "I see nothing whatever to be gained in the affiliation with Rush Medical College, possibly something to be lost," he pointedly noted.[36] When Harper raised the issue of sectarian medicine and suggested that it could be settled, Gates put that issue in perspective:

> I have no doubt that Mr. Rockefeller would favor an institution that was neither allopath or homeopath but simply scientific in its investigation of medical science. That is the ideal. For that the University would wait and reserve the great weight of its influence, authority, and prestige instead of bestowing the same gratuitously on Rush Medical College. Such an institution would have to be endowed and would be run on a far higher principle than the principle of Rush College or any other of the ordinary institutions.[37]

Nevertheless, the trustees voted, with Gates in the minority, to go ahead with the affiliation. Gates termed the move "a very serious blunder" and treated it as a personal and moral affront. He saw Harper's act as "an absolute breach of faith," and he felt it keenly.[38] Gates wrote to a fellow trustee that the affiliation had destroyed "one of the dreams of my own mind": "of a medical college in this country conducted by the University of Chicago, magnificently endowed, devoted primarily to investigation, making practice itself an incident of investigation and taking as its students only the choicest spirits, quite irrespective of the question of funds."[39] This incident could not but have increased Gates's Lear-like conviction that the distribution of philanthropy produced ungrateful children. If any university was to become a home for the future institute it would have a heavy legacy of mistrust to overcome.

With Chicago unsuitable as a possible site for the institute, the question lay dormant for three years. Rockefeller junior and Gates continued to encourage the idea and began to take steps to implement it. In 1900 they seemed to consider the possibilities of affiliation with either Harvard or Columbia. In the early summer of 1900 Rockefeller junior asked retiring Columbia president Seth Low what he thought of the possibility of setting up in the United States an institute similar to the Pasteur Institute. From his summer post in Maine, Low wrote to such leading academic physicians as T. Mitchell Prudden and William H. Welch, asking whether it would be "a matter of great advantage to medical science, and through it to humanity," if such a step were taken, and what would be the best organizational arrangements for such a project. He assured his correspondents that "this is not an idle inquiry, although I cannot say, on the other hand, that it will certainly lead to anything."[40]

The replies were of course glowing: "I do not know of any other means by which with so much certainty individual suffering and misery could be relieved and prevented and research be fostered along lines involving the highest general welfare," Prudden wrote.[41] Prudden and Welch, Low felt, "would be universally considered, I think, two of the best authorities in the country." He agreed that such a new venture should be affiliated with a university; an academic relation would provide both prestige and support in the allied sciences. As Low, clearly not disinterested, noted to Rockefeller junior, "the best men value very highly the university connection."[42]

Rockefeller senior finally approved the idea of forming an institute. The physicians selected as the first directors of the Rockefeller Institute for Medical Research were among the most eminent in the nation: William H. Welch, T. Mitchell Prudden, L. Emmet Holt, and Theobald Smith. At their second preliminary meeting they resolved: "It was the general consensus of opinion that for the first year it would be better to make use of existing laboratories in this country and Europe rather than to start a new laboratory." Welch sent out signals to find out who among his network would have projects available for funding. Thus was begun one of the first interuniversity research grant programs.[43]

Gates, however, remained uncertain of the virtue of a university connection for the proposed new institute. While both university presidents and the academic medical elite wanted the institute either rooted in or at least supportive of university medicine, Gates held out for an independent foundation. The definitive formation of the institute took ten years; between 1900 and 1910 the university forces tried to entice Gates to support academic medicine, but he was wary of their entreaties. For the first few years of the institute's existence the maneuvering was particularly feverish, but Gates would not be moved and repeatedly rejected proposals which would have meant a sustained Rockefeller participation in the structure of medical education.

There was no shortage of schools interested in acquiring the new benefaction. Not easily discouraged, Harper tried again, prompted by his anatomy professor, Lewellys F. Barker. Barker had come to the University of Chicago in 1900 from Johns Hopkins where he had been a protégé of anatomy professor Franklin P. Mall. Mall was in many ways the distillation of the new trends in medical education. He would not engage in formal teaching of his students, only make himself available to assist their own inquiries. Mall expressed disgust at the commercial values of American society which prevented a reverence for scholarship and learning. Having correctly read Gates's similar ideas, Barker took up that theme in order to attract Rockefeller patronage.[44]

"Could not the Rockefeller Institute for Medical Research though temporarily lost to us be recaptured?" an eager Barker inquired of Harper. "That Mr. Rockefeller would be susceptible *still* to appeals for the Institute from the University is obvious . . . why should we not have a school where in both preclinical and clinical branches the side of *research* is emphasized." Barker urged Harper to think of the "ultimate aims" of development of the medical faculty.[45]

Barker outlined those aims in an address to the western alumni of Johns Hopkins in 1902 entitled "Medicine and the Universities." The address was a frank "plea for the better organization and endowment of medical departments of the universities."[46] Barker proposed that clinical men should be full-time researchers and teachers, just as instructors of laboratory subjects increasingly were:

> I should like to see what the result would be if men with these capacities who were bred to university careers, were placed in charge of hospitals especially constructed and endowed for university purposes, and were sufficiently paid to permit them to give up private practice entirely and to devote their whole time and strength to teaching and investigating in such hospitals.[47]

Barker's address was the earliest comprehensive statement of what eventually became known as the "full-time plan," the scheme which was the keystone of Abraham Flexner's administration of Rockefeller medical philanthropy. Although Barker would eventually oppose the plan, he was at this point honestly expressing what he felt were the ultimate goals of medical education reform. The clear purpose of his presentation, however, was to display his sturdy moral weave, and by implication that of the university, to Gates. Barker made a point of personally presenting Gates with a copy of it when it was "just off the press." The idea was clearly in line with Gates's predispositions, but patience was not Harper's long suit.[48]

While Barker attempted to lure Gates with evidence of Chicago's moral awakening, Harper tried again to secure New York's blessing of the organizational relationship with Rush. In 1902 Harper proposed a formal union of the university and medical school corporations in place of the existing affiliation. To sweeten the proposition it was planned that Rush raise $1 million to wipe out its debt and put in on a proper basis to facilitate the merger. The New York office provisionally consented to the arrangement rather than be "in the position of standing between Rush and a million dollars."[49]

In 1903, after Rush actually raised the money, it turned out that there was no agreement on its expenditure. Much of the money was raised for purposes extrinsic to the merger and only $300,000 was available for university purposes.[50] Still, Harper could not bear to let even that amount of money and the opportunity for union pass by. He proposed to go ahead with the merger hoping rather blithely that "we may confidently look for further contributions for the purpose of medical teaching and research from the people of Chicago in the near future." In attempting to maneuver the Rockefeller office he mentioned the fear "that if a union is not effected at this time, the interests of medical education will be put back ten years." Joining with Rush was a "risk [which] had to be taken."[51] Chicagoans even boldly suggested to the Rockefeller office that the aims and ideals of Rush were "substantially" those which Barker had outlined.[52]

In this strategy, Harper was being too clever by half, for he was caught between two imperatives. On the one hand, he was obliged to avoid taking on new possible debts. To do that he worked out an arrangement with Rush that faculty salaries would be tied to the school's receipts. On the other hand, that strategem moved the enterprise away from the ideal which Barker had exalted, as Rockefeller junior and Gates were quick to point out. If Rush were to meet the higher standards of medical education and be on a parity with the other departments of the university, much more than $1 million, let alone the $300,000 already raised, would be necessary. Since Rush had repeatedly proven a failure at such efforts, such funds would have to come from the founder. On that score Rockefeller junior and Gates were modulated and precise:

> On the question of assisting the university either at present or in the future, to discharge the financial obligations necessarily involved in organic union with Rush, and on the further question of carrying out the plans for medical education which is the main purpose of the union, we find the founder not prepared to make any committals, or, indeed, to offer any encouragement. . . .
>
> Since the affiliation with Rush, Mr. Rockefeller has embodied his own ideals for medical education in the Institute for Medical Research, an institution devoted exclusively to research, not united organically with any medical college or school, hospitable alike to all.[53]

Again, the question of homeopathy and sectarian medicine was raised not so much as a scientific commentary but as a comment on the self-seeking of the Rush faculty.

The university trustees gamely attempted to respond to these assertions by stressing the synergy of research and teaching and by insisting that "the preparation of medical practitioners of the best type, is quite as much the function of a University as is the promotion of research."[54] But from the New York point of view, ideals were relevant only when the university deficits had been lessened, and even Rush might still be less than adequate. Harper had failed to lure the Rockefeller support he so desperately wanted. In 1905, before a cancer operation from which he never recovered, Harper poignantly wrote to Rockefeller senior that "it would have been a source of great satisfaction to me if I could . . . have added Technology, Medicine and Music, thus rounding out the institution. But if it is ordered that someone else is to do this in place of myself, I am ready to accept the decision . . . let me say goodbye."[55]

In 1902 Columbia president Nicholas Murray Butler was another suppliant for Rockefeller medical bounty. In his eagerness to appeal to the philanthropist Butler vouchsafed that he, too, shared the ideals Barker had presented in his address on full-time (although Butler, like Barker, was to oppose them a decade later).[56] In dealing with the Rockefeller office, Butler displayed carelessness, ignorance, and unfounded pride as well as the impulsiveness which marked Harper but without the latter's winning humility. Butler boldly solicited $3 million. The president made confident allusions to other gifts and expected administrative changes, expectations which were without any visible support. He made extravagant claims for his school ("the medical school which, in the whole United

States, has the most considerable reputation and the widest influence"),
which someone of even limited acquaintance with medical education
would be skeptical of. When the Rockefeller office pointed out discrepan-
cies in Butler's calculations, the president pleaded understandable confusion over the different practices of the many schools of his educational
empire, typographical errors and, as a last resort, unexplainable lapses.
Such management did not merit a gift, let alone a relation with Gates's
"dream Institute."[57]

Harvard came the closest to winning the new benefaction. As the institute was being organized, Harvard was engaged in a campaign to raise
funds for a new medical campus. Relocation of the medical school to a site
closer to the teaching hospitals and an expansion of laboratory facilities
had long been on the school's agenda. These steps had not been taken
earlier because of the fiscal conservatism of the corporation and President
Eliot. The school's modernizing faction, led by Bowditch, chafed under
this restraint and attempted to pressure Eliot to move faster. Although
Eliot's reforms had attracted some (chiefly local) support, the growth in
giving had not kept pace with the capital needs mandated by new scientific
developments. Harvard sought to solve this dilemma by tapping national
wealth. An overture was made to Andrew Carnegie, but it was rebuffed.
The steel baron was not interested in aiding medicine or large universities. J. P. Morgan agreed to fund three of the contemplated five buildings as a memorial to his father. The occasion may have been modern but
the form of the intention was ancient: a limestone edifice memorializing
the dead.[58]

When Rockefeller junior heard of Morgan's gift, he expressed interest
in the growing school. Accordingly, Gates recruited Starr J. Murphy,
a Wall Street lawyer and a suburban neighbor, to make a survey of
the Harvard opportunity. In contrast to Morgan, the Rockefeller office
was interested in endowing research work and not in erecting monu-
ments. What most appealed to Murphy when he made his survey was the
organization and educational ideal of the Harvard school. The university
management's practiced frugality was a happy contrast to Harper's prof-
ligacy. The school's access to clinical facilities was admirable. In order to
ascertain the attitude of the school's leaders toward the aims of medical
education, Murphy asked some leading questions: "is not the proper
work of the school to make doctors rather than bacteriologists or scientific

investigators? If the work of the school is limited to that of teaching, are such elaborate facilities as those proposed required?"[59] The replies were all he could have hoped for. Faculty member F. B. Mallory asserted that "the proper training of the students demands a strong teaching staff who are developed from those students who show originality of mind. The original work produced by the staff of a department and by the students making researches under their direction adds just so much towards the advancement of medical knowledge."[60]

Murphy's September 1901 recommendation that Rockefeller senior donate $500,000 to the new Harvard campus was accepted. In his report to the Rockefeller office, Murphy made it clear that the work of the Harvard Medical School would complement and not conflict with that contemplated for the Rockefeller Institute. There is some evidence that a more direct relation was considered. Gates later maintained that Harvard was thought of as a possible site for the institute. In early 1902, Harvard professor Theobald Smith, one of the institute's directors, was asked to become the director of its heart, the bacteriology department. Smith, however, demurred.[61]

When Smith declined, an offer was made to Simon Flexner. Flexner had not been in the original group of directors, but had joined them at their second meeting at Welch's suggestion. Flexner was part of a remarkable Louisville, Kentucky, family which was using the changes in professional career paths to make an enduring mark on American institutions. Simon had graduated from the University of Louisville medical school and had gone into practice with his older brother in connection with a third brother's drugstore. When Gilman created postgraduate fellowships in the basic medical sciences, Flexner became one of the first "Welch rabbits," protégés of William H. Welch who virtually created the academic discipline of pathology. But the network was formed before there were places to fill, and there was a period of anxiety as to how to fit the new ideals into the existing opportunities. From Louisville, Simon's brother Abraham urged him "not . . . to mutilate your career" by taking an inferior position,[62] and accordingly Simon waited until he secured a research position at the University of Pennsylvania, the post in which he received the Rockefeller offer.

While contemplating the directorship Flexner again raised the question of the institute's university connection.

The work of the Institute cannot fail to be affected by the scientific atmosphere that surrounds and pervades it. A question, therefore, that may well be discussed is whether the best interests of the Institute will be favored by complete independence or by some kind of attachment to an institution of learning where study in collateral branches of science is carried on. In other words, would the work and success of the Institute be furthered by affiliation, entailing, however, no sacrifice of identity with an established university.[63]

Gates, however, was determined to keep the new enterprise independent.

Simon Flexner accepted the directorship on that basis and began to build the institute's operations. The institute was to be an exemplar of the strictest scientific ideals. Still, the new board was kept on a short leash. In May 1902, the directors urged that a $5 million endowment would be appropriate for the contemplated venture. But Rockefeller was cautious— he would begin with a $1 million gift, advising his son that "we cannot say anything about five millions now." Moreover, he would hold all real estate in trust for the institute rather than turn it over to the directors themselves. Confident as it was in their scientific ability, Rockefeller's office did not trust their business acumen and was not willing to risk the new venture on it.[64]

Gates's anxiety over the management of institutionalized research was a function of changes in his own views. His new faith in science did not carry with it any organizational model. With many of his generation, Gates saw in the ideal of science the ultimate solution to contemporary problems and a substitute for his withering orthodox Christian faith. Gates continually meditated on his "consecration" to organizing the Rockefeller fortune for productive uses, and would periodically set out the priorities of possible giving.[65] Despite the pulpit phraseology, received religion was being displaced in Gates's worldview. Medicine was always near the top of his list of philanthropic possibilities; religion, in contrast, suffered a diminution of importance. In 1905 he listed the promotion of Christian ethics and Christian civilization as a proper philanthropic goal. But in 1908 he would specify only "morality and religion."[66] When philanthropic work in China was considered he maintained that modern medicine was the most effective expression of Christ's gospel.[67] Gates found in medical science a persuasive morality which he no longer found in religious orthodoxy. In the 1920s, toward the end of his life when others might be tempted to consider anew eternal propositions, Gates was single-minded; by then he considered medicine alone an appropriate expenditure of philanthropic funds.[68]

Along with medical sciences the other elements of Gates's new trinity of social order were the corporation and system. The adviser saw the corporation as the harbinger of a material utopia. He put the case in biblical terms: the "corporation unites in itself the natural rights of men and certain supernatural rights or privileges brought about by government, which may be likened to the sons of God. So the corporation is very like the great human giant of scripture in its hybrid origin, the union of the daughters of men and the sons of God." Gates stretched this metaphor to an almost blasphemous point. "Sons of God, they are capable of bringing in almost the New Jerusalem, so far as the New Jerusalem can be brought by material means, out of Heaven, and founding it here on earth. They can transform any country into a paradise."[69] Gates's devotion to the corporate mechanism, however, did not imply a desire to organize society on the basis of the free market. Like many of his generation, Gates hoped that the age of laissez-faire would yield to a more cooperative period. He was devoted to the ideal of "system," a concept he defined thus:

> A scheme to be justly called a system would have to answer, I suppose, to four main characteristics. First, to form a system the members must be comprehensively and efficiently distributed and not partially and inadequately. Second, to form a system the members must be related to each other harmoniously and helpfully and not hurtfully. Third, to form a system the members should be each within its assigned compass, complete or supplemental to others and not fragmentary. Fourth, to form a system the scheme, as a whole and in all its parts, must be essentially stable and permanent and not temporary or fluctuating.[70]

As Gates looked about him, very few of the aspects of American civilization met those criteria. Education, religion, government were all fragmented. He was no more sanguine about laissez-faire economics: "the competitive system is a contradiction in terms. . . . The competitive system is a sort of human cannibalism, by which people eat each other up, take bites out of each other's flesh. Is that system, or is it heap?" The professions were no help to that situation. "Three-fourths of the ministers, nine-tenths of the lawyers, three-fourths of the doctors . . . are producing nothing on earth of the slightest real benefit to society, but are simply eating each other up, snarling, cursing, knifing, cheating, deceiving and swindling, anywhere, everywhere and everybody."[71]

Yet how to systematize science remained a problem. Perhaps because he had such a strong sense of the failings of medical education and its potential, Gates was continually hesitant about involvement in it. The issue of supporting university medical education was raised again in 1907 when William Osler of Hopkins appealed to Rockefeller on behalf of his alma mater, McGill. Gates forwarded the appeal to the institute board for comments, noting that he gave particular weight to the request because it came from Osler. After a "full discussion" the board demurred passing on the application without "a somewhat extended statement of its views regarding the general needs of medicine in this country." Welch was directed to draw up such a statement.[72]

In his statement Welch began by noting that "the agencies and conditions which determine the advancement of medical knowledge are so manifold and complex that it is not possible . . . for any single institution or foundation, however broad its scope, to embrace them all." "The directors of the Rockefeller Institute have hitherto considered their functions circumscribed by the conception of an independent institute promoting medical research in its own laboratories," and they did not deny that usefulness. Welch clearly saw Gates's question as a possible invitation for the institute board to begin a large-scale grants program and treated the question as such. "It is believed that the membership of the Board of Directors is such as to enable them to make such a survey intelligently and to justify them in assuming additional responsibilities in this field, if entrusted to them."[73]

Welch's view was unequivocal: "The relation of medical education to medical research is of fundamental importance." "Investigation is the fruit of a tree which has its roots in the educational system, and if the roots are neglected and unhealthy there will be no fruit." There were, of course, invocations of the model of Germany with its "liberal government support of its system of laboratories and hospitals connected with its universities." Since "the future of the Institute is closely connected with the improvement in the conditions of medical education in this country," the institute, as Welch delicately put it, "should not be indifferent to the conditions of education in our better medical schools and should not rest upon the assumption that the educational side can be safely left to take care of itself."[74]

Welch urged that only a select group of schools be aided. The criteria for the selection of such a school were familiar: university basis, adequate and productive laboratories, a demonstrated interest in research. Explicitly leaving state universities out of consideration, Welch listed Harvard, Columbia, Johns Hopkins, Western Reserve, the University of Chicago and, "in part," McGill as fulfilling these criteria. Those institutions, he proposed, should be aided not only by gifts for specific investigations but also by "permanent gifts of money." "It is believed that occasional grants for specific purposes could not be made to serve the same useful purpose as permanent endowment, for it is only upon assurance for the future that the proper organization and work of laboratories can be securely effected."[75]

Welch concluded with an expression of readiness to assume the task:

> The Directors of the Institute realize that they would be assuming functions of great responsibility and requiring much thought, investigation and wisdom in their execution by attempting to carry out such a broadened policy as that indicated or by giving advice along the lines suggested, but they would be willing to assume such functions in the interest of medical science and they could endeavor to exercise the same care and thought which they have hitherto given to the interests of the Institute.[76]

Gates seems to have taken this plea under advisement. The Rockefeller office did not make a grant to McGill, and other appeals were turned down, including one from Hopkins in 1907. Within the Rockefeller offices at the Standard Oil Building, Murphy seems to have been eager to enter the field; Gates, however, remained cautious. He wanted to see the institute firmly established, something not accomplished until it was re-chartered in 1910.[77]

Although Gates constrained the development of a direct institutional connection between the Rockefeller Institute and the nation's medical schools, the institute did become an incubator for a group which aspired to lead in reforming medicine and medical education. The ultimate goal of this group was the development of clinical science as a learned discipline. This aspiring elite thus placed itself at the conjunction of several strands in the reform of medical education.

Ever since the failure in the early national period of John Morgan's model of professional leadership, the position of America's medical elite had been problematic. So long as the AMA remained a self-selecting organization composed mainly of the urban leaders of medicine, its political power and effectiveness were limited. At the turn of the nineteenth century, the association was reorganized to become an inclusive representative of the entire profession. Although this strengthened the association politically, the elite became increasingly dissatisfied and sought new organizational foci. The American Physiological Society, founded in 1887, was one of the first such attempts. It was followed by the formation of the American College of Physicians, the American College of Surgeons, the American Association of Physicians, and such regional organizations as the Inter-Urban Clinical Club.[78]

These groups reflected the increased importance of the university to medical reform. Between 1892 and 1902 four journals were founded restricting publication to original research: the *Journal of Experimental Medicine*, the *American Journal of Physiology*, the *American Journal of Medical Research*, and the *American Journal of Anatomy*. These developments encouraged those who hoped to develop medicine on the model of other university disciplines. Leaders of this movement such as Welch stressed that the "historical and proper home of the medical school is the university, of which it should be an integral part coordinate with the other faculties."[79] Such changes would mean a new structure of ambitions. As Welch wrote to his associate Mall in reference to two of the latter's students: "What a splendid position for Harrison! Also for Flint! How do you manage to place your pupils so advantageously? Anatomy is really becoming a career."[80] The opening of the Rockefeller Institute accelerated this trend by underscoring the importance of research. The institute took over publication of the *Journal of Experimental Medicine*, and its fellowship program helped recruit new cadres for the university elite.

At a certain point the organizational agenda of a learned discipline was incompatible with that of a profession. The institutional home of a learned discipline was clearly the university and related institutions, whereas a profession existed across the span of society. Professions tend to be internally cohesive and semidemocratic in their corporate organization, while learned disciplines are dependent on hierarchies of influence and prestige. Since professions strive to control and regulate the "portals of entry" to their memberships, control of the medical schools by an elite answerable only to itself would be dangerous from a professional point of view.[81]

This potential conflict was manageable in the laboratory branches of medical science. All segments of the reform movement agreed that the laboratory subjects should be taught by instructors who would give their entire time to the university and not engage in practice. But clinical medicine, the actual practice of medicine on patients, was a different case. That clinicians should apply the gains of laboratory research to their practice seemed clear, but it was not nearly as universally agreed that clinical medicine could be organized and pursued as a learned discipline.[82]

The growth of the Rockefeller Institute provided an opportunity for those who aspired to turn the practice of clinical medicine into the learned discipline of clinical science. The organization of the institute's hospital provided a new model for the institutional location of such a discipline. The hospital had originally been intended merely as an adjunct to the work done in the basic science laboratories of the institute. But Rufus Cole, who was called from Johns Hopkins to administer the hospital, had other ideas. Cole recognized that if clinical medicine was to become a learned discipline it had to have regularized control of its material, both laboratories and patients. Cole therefore insisted that the hospital be not merely an arena where the findings of the institute's laboratories could be applied but a laboratory itself, coequal with the basic science laboratories.[83]

Another voice from the Rockefeller Institute promoting the notion of a learned discipline of clinical science was that of Samuel J. Meltzer.[84] In 1903 he helped found the Society for Experimental Biology and Medicine, later known as "the Meltzer Verein." He was also a leader in the formation of the American Society for the Advancement of Clinical Investigation. In his 1909 presidential address to that group he urged that "clinical medicine must reclaim some of the brawny young men who were enticed by the sciences of medicine." In a frank plea for the extension of the process of specialization to clinical medicine, Meltzer rejected the view that "the relation of clinical medicine to the sciences of medicine is that of technology to science in general" as "logically erroneous and practically harmful." He saw no valid objections to clinical medicine's assuming the mantle of science. Some would contend that clinical medicine was not subject to experimental proof, but Meltzer answered that all tenets of pure science were not experimentally verifiable and that, in any case, animal and even some human experimentation could be carried out.

Moreover, "each disease is an experiment which Nature makes on the organism."[85]

Meltzer pointed out that the clinical scientist was more than a successful practitioner. "The investigator in clinical science must devote the best part of his time and intellectual energies to the cultivation and elevation of this field just as the physiologist does in his domain—or at least he ought to do." Practice and science were incompatible to Meltzer. Whereas practice "avails itself of acquired knowledge for the purpose of attaining a certain useful end," science aimed only at "truthful knowledge" and could not afford to be "side-tracked by any extraneous motives," such as practical utility, which "obscures its vision." He felt that both practice and science would benefit if "clinical research should be raised to a department of clinical science and be theoretically and practically separated to a considerable degree from mere practical interests."[86]

While the clinical science zealots were growing in numbers, the profession at large was also pressing forward with its agenda. One important step was the rejuvenation of the AMA. Previously crippled by its elitist and unrepresentative cast, the association reorganized itself in 1901 to become more inclusive of all regular physicians and to do away with intermediate organizations between it and its members.[87] One facet of the association's rejuvenation was the creation of the Council on Medical Education which gave a new national framework to the reform movement. At the second annual conference Dr. J. A. Witherspoon exhorted his colleagues: "Now, gentlemen, the Council on Medical Education for the American Medical Association recognizes no state. We are Americans. . . . It matters not what may be your feeling now, I want to say to you, you are your brother's keeper, and it is your duty to help every section of this country to rise up and elevate and meet the requirements of the day, and that is what this organized body should do."[88]

The council began in 1906 a program of classifying the nation's medical schools according to criteria of endowment, hospital affiliation, professed admission standards, and the results of its graduates on state examinations. The council's standards were aimed high enough to exclude the most flagrantly commercial schools but, given the polity of the reformed association, they were low enough to ensure that the majority of the schools were given at least tentative approval. The other leading professional organization dealing with medical education, the Association of

American Medical Colleges, was similarly limited by the need to placate its membership. Frustrated reformers were considering setting up a more rigorous organization when the Carnegie Foundation for the Advancement of Teaching (CFAT) was formed.[89]

The CFAT was a typical product of Andrew Carnegie's very individualized approach to philanthropy. Carnegie had long kept a private pension list to which he periodically added those he felt were particularly deserving. He also proposed to set up a pension fund for ex-presidents of the United States, but public outcry made him shelve the offer. College professors were, however, politically suitable objects for his bounty, and upon learning how many former teachers ended their lives in straitened circumstances, the steel baron planned an endowment which would pension all superannuated college and university teachers in the nation. To direct this effort he selected in 1905 Henry Smith Pritchett, the retiring president of MIT.[90]

Henry Smith Pritchett represented the second generation of his family to have made a career in science and education by exploiting the frontier materialism of American society rather than by resisting it. Pritchett's father had supervised a college in rural Missouri which could not have aspired to that dignity if not for the rude state of the area. Henry was part of the first wave of American Ph.D.'s, receiving his degree in astronomy from the University of Munich. After some teaching, Pritchett found a place in the federal service in one of those few areas in the nineteenth century where science was deemed essential to the national interest: President McKinley appointed him director of the United States Coast and Geodetic Survey in 1897. Having been credited with removing the agency from the clutches of partisan jobbery, Pritchett moved to Boston in 1900 to take the presidency of the Massachusetts Institute of Technology.[91]

Pritchett's MIT service anticipated the direction and focus of his philanthropic career. The new president hoped that the strengthening of engineering education would help put the engineering profession in a better position to assume the economic, social, and political leadership that industrial society required. His model of professional education combined a thorough background in liberal arts and an enlightened view of professional responsibility. Toward that end, Pritchett agreed with Charles Eliot's proposal that Harvard and MIT should merge.[92] This move prefigured his attitude toward the reform of medical education: he leaned toward reform through consolidation rather than the sort of institutional purification Gates favored. Pritchett saw consolidation as the lesson of the age even on a geopolitical scale. Here again, Germany was a model:

> In the place of some forty jealous and independent kingdoms and principalities stood a German nation. No event in the history of Europe has been of greater significance or more far-reaching in its results than this substitution of a nation and a national policy in the place of isolated states with discordant and oftentimes hostile political programmes. But the political significance of United Germany has been only one of the results achieved. Not less remarkable and not less significant is the industrial progress of Germany since it became a nation.[93]

When the proposed unification of the Cambridge institutions failed Pritchett's authority at MIT ebbed, and he accepted Andrew Carnegie's invitation to head his new educational foundation. Pritchett had been cultivating Carnegie for some time, and their relationship was a peculiar hybrid. They shared a desire to construct a new moral culture based on institutions of broad, sympathetic education, but had different inclinations as to means. Throughout his active life Carnegie maintained his bias toward the smaller institutions, whereas Pritchett favored the growth of large institutions through the absorption of smaller ones. Lifting another metaphor from contemporary events, Pritchett said that just as railroads were consolidating, colleges must also. But Pritchett never let these differences become explicit and skillfully adapted Carnegie's general impulses to his own agenda.[94]

The CFAT president's first step in that direction was to align Carnegie's desire to pension superannuated college teachers with economic realities. Even Carnegie's fortune could not begin to accommodate all who could make a claim on it under the general criterion of "college teacher." Once the philanthropist accepted that there would have to be some conclusive regulations, Pritchett had an opportunity to use the foundation as a "technology of influence." Standards, including the famous "Carnegie unit," were set which would determine the admission of institutions to the list of those whose faculty would be eligible for pensions.[95]

Pritchett perceived the Jacksonian openness of American education as a national embarrassment. "The pioneer stage of national development is so near to us in time that many of its habits still rule in social and political matters. This is particularly true in education. We can scarcely claim as yet to have a system, at least in higher education."[96] Pritchett was eager to make sure the public understood that the CFAT was "not a charity but an educational agency." He belittled the fear that "a great gift like this in the hands of a limited number of men might prove a centralized power which would hinder rather than aid the progress of education." [97] A centralized power was, indeed, something to be wished:

> It is, in my judgment, a wholesome influence in education to have a few such centralizing influences. Our tendencies in the past have been almost wholly along competitive lines. . . . Heretofore the tendencies have nearly all been centripetal and the outcome is seen in the multitude of weak, badly organized, and in some cases unnecessary institutions. The establishment of an agency which is concerned with the larger outlook and the wider field can scarcely fail to make for educational coherence and in the end for educational unity. [98]

But even at this moment, perhaps its zenith in American political culture, the idea of centralization was regarded with suspicion as a threat to local autonomy and self-development. "All great social and economic efforts—such, for example, as the attempt to educate the youth of a nation in formal schools—develop themselves between the tendency to loose standards on the one side and to over-organization on the other," Pritchett noted. [99] He feared that the "danger of the narrowness and rigidity which come from formal administration" could in "each species of instruction . . . run away with the deeper underlying purpose which gave it birth." However, he conceded, "organization is indispensable" if America was to have continuity and efficiency. [100]

Pritchett proposed to navigate between the shoals of frontier dilapidation and stultifying regimentation by means of consensus. In place of rigid organization he favored elite guidance. The composition of the CFAT board—representative college presidents—was a reflection of this idea. He did not see this notion of enlightened elite leadership as incompatible with democracy. As he commented at the opening of the University of Cincinnati Hospital,

> Democracy is on trial in this experiment, as it is on trial in all such institutions of the people, but it is on trial in a new way. . . . If here in Cincinnati you can develop an ideal of politics under which the politician shall be considered worthy to stand with the teacher and scientist, you will have contributed to democracy something greater than even the building of a University and a Hospital. [101]

However, before the professions could become forces of social equilibration Pritchett recognized that they required reform. "Like the other branches of education," he noted, "the training of men for the learned professions has not yet outgrown the pioneer stage." Professional schools had "no common standards and no relation to the general system of education."[102] Pritchett was not seeking merely a more rigorous technical training; he wanted to imbue in professionals a consciousness of their social role. That role entailed a rejection of privatism:

> Aside from all question of intellectual basis or content, the distinction between a business and a profession does not lie in any difference of honor in the pursuit of one or of another, but in the obligations which one assumes. . . . He who enters a profession . . . undertakes certain obligations to the calling itself and to the public. He is under obligation to consider the interest of the public as well as his own, and this is one reason why these great callings have differentiated into professions. . . . That debt [of the professional] devolves upon him who enters one of these great professions the obligation to fit himself for it, the obligation to conserve the honor and advance the cause of his profession, and above all to remember in his practice his duty to the state as well as to himself. It is only through the observance of these ideals that a profession can remain a profession.[103]

To guide the reform of professional education, Pritchett inaugurated in 1908 a series of educational surveys. The most famous and effective of these was the foundation's Bulletin No. 4, *Medical Education in the United States and Canada,* by Abraham Flexner, published in 1910. In selecting Abraham Flexner to make the survey, Pritchett knew he was choosing someone with important connections to the emerging leadership in academic medicine and someone eager to join the forces of philanthropic reform. What Pritchett did not anticipate was that Flexner would transform the reform process from one of elite consensus to one of bureaucratic management.

The Civil War had just ended when Abraham Flexner was born on the hinge between North and South at Louisville, Ky. Flexner's father was a Moravian Jewish immigrant who built up a substantial business as an itinerant wholesaler but was wiped out by the Panic of 1873. Despite penury, his sons were able to build substantial careers. Simon and Bernard made their marks in the quintessential professions: medicine and law, respectively. Abraham was a professionalizer: he redefined professional circumstances from the outside. He was an example of the type of strategic elite which the increasing interrelatedness of society required. With an agile command of resonant symbols and ideals, he became a manager of the organization of knowledge.[104]

4 6

Abraham was one of the first graduates of the new Johns Hopkins University, where he took advantage of Gilman's flexibility to finish the undergraduate requirements in two years. Interestingly, at the beginning of the educational age of specialism and science he majored in classics. After graduation, he returned to Louisville to teach and help support the struggling family. Abraham soon became impatient with his work at the local high school and embarked independently on a program of preparing the sons of aspiring local families for admission to the eastern colleges, graduation from which was becoming increasingly important to the middle class. While his school was all male, he did consent to tutor privately Anne Crawford, the daughter of a Louisville banker, whom he eventually married.[105]

Once his brothers had been set on secure career paths Flexner undertook to broaden his own credentials by going to Harvard to study psychology with Hugo Munsterberg. At Cambridge Flexner found experimental work frustrating and Munsterberg tedious, although he was quite taken with Josiah Royce.[106] What he saw most keenly was that career opportunities were already becoming tied to credentials. As we wrote to his brother Simon in 1906:

> I am not *trained* & that stares me in the face constantly . . . I am sure that in philosophy or psychology I can never be on an equal footing with men of my age who have been trained systematically. . . . It is . . . a warning to me not to make a one-subject specialist of myself, no matter how fascinating the chase may become.[107]

Disappointed with Harvard, Flexner went to Europe where he wrote a short book, *The American College,* critical of contemporary higher education in general and Harvard in particular, and which approvingly quoted CFAT president Pritchett.[108] When Flexner returned to the United States he sought employment with the CFAT. At their second meeting Pritchett suggested that Flexner undertake a survey of medical schools in the United States and Canada. Flexner, who had followed his brother Simon's career with such care that he frequently offered pungent advice, unconvincingly demurred that he was not a medical expert. Pritchett replied that that was fine; he wanted the problem studied from an educational point of view, not a medical one.[109]

The report was an exercise of Pritchett's reform-by-consensus approach. He was careful to secure the cooperation of the Council on Medical Education of the AMA. He and Flexner met with N. D. Colwell and Arthur Dean Bevan of the council, and it was agreed that while Flexner could rely on their advice and connections his inquiry would be independent. This was useful to both parties. The council would gain an ally in its efforts to raise standards, one that could be more unsparing in its criticism since it was not responsible to those it was investigating. Similarly, most medical school officials welcomed Flexner to their campuses. Perhaps hopeful of Carnegie gifts, many made a point of their school's deficiencies.[110] Flexner focused his inquiry so that he could ascertain "in the course of a few hours" the relevant information about each school under scrutiny. His questions were in five areas: entrance requirements, the size and training of the faculty, the nature of and extent of endowment, adequacy of laboratories and laboratory teaching personnel, and the availability of clinical resources and nature of clinical appointments.[111]

The report was typical of the agenda-setting surveys of the Progressive Era. It combined the assurance of authoritative expertise with the muckraker's whiff of intriguing scandal. The published report had two parts. The first was an exposition of the proper basis of medical education as Flexner understood it, and the second was a description of each medical school in the United States and Canada according to the crucial criteria Flexner had isolated. Implicit in the descriptions was a plan for the future organization of medical education. As Pritchett put it in his introduction,

> The attitude of the Foundation is that all colleges and universities, whether supported by taxation or by private endowment, are in truth public service corporations, and that the public is entitled to know the facts concerning their administration and development, whether those facts pertain to the financial or to the educational side.[112]

Similarly, Flexner cast himself in the role of exposing a "powerful and profitable vested interest [that] tenaciously resists criticism."[113]

Flexner's report was most immediately effective in energizing those schools which were both already reforming and had a strong central administration which could respond to his recommendations. Washington University in St. Louis was the most dramatic case.[114] The establishment of the university as a modern institution was due largely to the efforts of one man, cordage magnate Robert S. Brookings. Brookings had re-endowed the moribund school and in 1909 continued to dominate its management. Brookings was typical of the philanthropists who helped modernize American medical education. He had left his native Maryland to seek his fortune elsewhere and had developed a loyalty to the place where he made his money. An autodidact with an abiding respect for learning, Brookings had a somewhat naive expectation of its transforming power over social institutions and an impatience with the often abstruse deliberations of the learned. One of the early faculty members of the re-formed university had been Henry Smith Pritchett who had held the chair in astronomy.[115] Indeed, Pritchett stressed to Flexner the importance of calling on Brookings if the report on Washington University was to have any effect.[116]

Flexner's initial report excoriated Washington University, finding it lacking in all the familiar ways: failure to live up to even its own lax ad-mission standards, inadequate facilities and endowment, a poor relation between laboratory and clinical teaching, and no formal relation with the hospital where clinical teaching took place. He found it "a little better than the worst . . . but absolutely inadequate in every essential re-spect."[117] There was, Flexner stressed, "no 'team work,' no training in method, no governing purpose."[118] The clinical branches of the school were "in wretched condition"; the dispensary did "more to demoralize than to train." Flexner recommended "heroic measures" to "make the medical department of a piece with the rest of the university."[119]

Brookings was astonished when he received a copy of Flexner's prelimi-nary report which Pritchett forwarded. He went immediately to New York for a conference where he asked Flexner to return to St. Louis to give him a tour of the school. That tour convinced Brookings of the ac-curacy of Flexner's assessment of the school's problems and of the neces-sary solutions. On the afternoon following the second inspection the trustees determined on a policy of reconstruction which would require the resignation of the entire medical faculty, its replacement by more aca-demic physicians, and the reconstruction of the school on an endowed basis.[120]

This reorganization set a pattern Flexner later followed in New Haven, New York, and Rochester. Through Brookings' leadership of the St. Louis philanthropic elite, Flexner was able to secure hospital connections for the university. Flexner's agenda brought together both the traditional charitable concern for the poor with the new emphasis on stimulating the possibilities of organized knowledge.

The point of the reconstruction was to achieve both changes in personnel and a realignment of authority. In place of the general faculty meeting, the authoritative body was to be the Executive Faculty composed of the newly recruited chairmen of the newly endowed and organized departments. There was to be no intermediate authority between this body and Brookings himself; the dean was merely the first among equals elected by his fellow department chairmen, and while the chancellor was ex officio a member of the Executive Faculty he had only one vote.[121]

Thus in one afternoon Brookings achieved at Washington University a reform of the medical school similar to that which had taken Eliot years at Harvard. The relative ease of his achievement owed much to the different histories and complexions of these two institutions, but it is important to note the changing relation of local and national authority. Whereas Eliot was a local leader sensitive to national and international standards, Flexner was part of a national organization which felt a responsibility to promulgate authoritative, universally applicable institutional models. Brookings was a local leader who felt responsive to that national leadership. Whatever the specific content of the reforms, the form also mandated a strengthening of those local hierarchies and leadership which supported the national agenda.

Flexner's survey had a similar effect at other schools. The report had been only recently published when the secretary of Yale University sent Flexner a copy of votes passed by the Yale Corporation "mainly in line with your views." The corporation had concurred with the "opinion of impartial experts, such as Dr. Flexner in his report to the Carnegie Foundation, that there is an unusual opportunity for developing in New Haven a small University Medical School of the highest standards," and it had voted to begin a $2 million fund-raising drive toward that end.[122]

Other administrators welcomed Flexner's comments on their schools, even if they were not altogether favorable. Although he was "fully conscious of the limitations of the School, especially in its equipment," the president of Howard University was "deeply gratified" by the report's "favorable representation."[123] The president of the University of Cincinnati was "glad to get the report at this time, as it supports me in all that I am trying to do," but felt that a slightly different phrasing would help him attract more contributions.[124]

Other officials were not as positive. "The report disappointed me," the

president of Northwestern University, A. W. Harris, wrote to Pritchett;
"I have looked to it for help in making improvements; in its present
form, I fear that it would only arouse antagonism." He stated accurately,
"The general tone impressed me as that of one inclined to make the worst
of things."[125] There can be no question that Flexner's survey was a
snapshot technique which deliberately did not reveal the overall trend of
improvement in American medical education. This was noted by the *New
York Times,* which commented that while the report was "very searching,
very candid, and in some respects very severe . . . the tone . . . is in
some, not numerous but marked, passages slightly tinged with the spirit
of the advocate, slightly contentious and unnecessarily irritating."[126]

One of the most substantial objections came from F. W. Hamilton, the
president of Tufts College. Hamilton complained to Pritchett that the report was "neither fair nor accurate and is misleading even where its statements are not technically incorrect." But his criticisms went beyond
details to the assertion that "the investigation which Mr. Flexner has
undertaken is utterly worthless because of its vicious method of approach." He felt that Flexner had "adopted certain arbitrary standards as
to methods and he has reported as to whether or not the schools conform
to those methods which may be interesting to him but is worthless for
anybody else."[127]

In reply, Pritchett tried to be irenic without yielding on principle. "Let
me suggest mildly," he wrote, "that until you have brought forth for
a season the peaceful fruits of righteousness in this matter, you can
well afford to be sweet-tempered over our criticism." He responded to
Hamilton's specific complaints by defending the accuracy of Flexner's
characterizations of the Tufts facilities and by pointing out that better
things were possible. "We have in this country become habituated to
the use of these makeshifts so completely that men conducting medical
schools are not infrequently under the impression that the arrangement is
satisfactory and inevitable,"[128] but administrators must face up to new demands. He concluded by invoking the New Testament injunction: "The
time of ignorance God overlooked, but now he commands all men everywhere to repent."[129]

But Hamilton was "unconverted" to the new regime. He did not want
his school to be "whitewashed," but he felt that "the investigation which
you have conducted is not of real value." In frustration he leveled the

ultimate insult, impugning the expertise of the expert: "Mr. Flexner is not a medical man . . . I wish you would have a medical man make an actual investigation."[130]

To that attack Flexner directly responded. "As a matter of fact the question is not a medical question, but an educational question. It is a question of relations. . . . The problem is to define the goal and to ascertain the bearings of a number of factors upon each other with reference thereto. . . . When one sees what medical education has come to in this country in consequence of being left entirely in the hands of medical men, one realizes perhaps that that very fact makes it important that the whole subject should be viewed and criticized from a standpoint that is educational rather than professional."[131]

Criticism was only Flexner's initial goal, however. He was interested in planning a new structure of medical education. He asserted that "when public interest, professional ideals, and sound educational procedure concur in the recommendation of the same policy, the time is surely ripe for decisive action." The plan which the report put forward was indeed decisive. It rested on the conclusion that "the necessity of a reconstruction that will at once reduce the number and improve the output of medical schools may now be taken as demonstrated." This recommendation was graphically portrayed by the juxtaposition of two maps: one with the location of all existing medical schools and one with "the suggested number, location and distribution of medical schools." The 155 medical schools in the United States and Canada would be reduced to 31, the unfortunate 124 "wiped off the map."[132] In his introduction to the report, Pritchett called for "an educational patriotism on the part of the institutions of learning and a medical patriotism on the part of the physician" which would lead to the elimination of "unnecessary and inadequate medical schools."[133]

In making this recommendation, Flexner was only accelerating a trend which was already under way, as he himself noted in the report. The growth in licensing requirements, the increasing cost of medical education, and the reports of the AMA's Council on Medical Education had already begun a reduction in the number of medical schools and the graduates thereof. What was more important to the subsequent development of philanthropic policies toward medical education was how that reduction was to be achieved.[134]

The report contained two strategies for achieving a smaller number of medical schools, strategies which turned on the problem of who would control medical training. Pritchett hoped to achieve the reduction by combining the best of the existing schools. During Flexner's inspection tour, the CFAT president had instructed Flexner to seek out a common ground on which the leaders of the various schools in any particular locale could form a union.[135] Pritchett continually stressed the importance of command of sufficient clinical material (patients) to the training of physicians. His primary goal was securing adequate facilities for professional training, and he thought it could best be achieved by combining the clinical departments of the better schools with the basic science departments of the several local universities. What would be produced were clinical schools on the lines of the English hospital-centered schools.[136]

But while Pritchett's goal was reform of the profession, Flexner was more concerned with the production of conditions which would make possible the growth of learned disciplines in medicine. The supremacy of the university form was therefore critical. As for clinical education, he felt that "the profession itself has in large measure still to be educated; the clinical faculty often stands between the university administrator and a sound conception of clinical training." Flexner predicted that the reduction in the number of medical schools would make it possible to make hospitals "exclusively and continuously the laboratory of the clinical departments of medical schools," and to have "faculties composed in the first place of scientific teachers of clinical medicine."[137]

Simply aggregating existing schools would not achieve his desired end. Flexner stressed that "unless combination is to destroy organization, titles must be shaved when schools unite. There must be one professor of medicine, one professor of surgery, etc., to whom others are properly subordinated." He wanted to avoid the sort of annexation under which "faculties have become unmanageably large, viewed either as teaching, research, or administrative bodies."[138]

Clinical professors, Flexner maintained, must be not representatives of the local profession but "simultaneously teachers and investigators." He stressed that they should be "professors in the ordinary acceptation of the term: they hold chairs in an institution resting on a collegiate basis—a graduate institution." This was not a role a busy physician could fill. "The practitioner usually lacks impartial and eager scientific spirit; he can at best give set hours to teaching, and these are not infrequently interrupted by a patient's superior claim; of course he has little or no time and rarely any zest for research."[139]

In the report and throughout his career, Flexner rejected the idea of an explicitly bifurcated structure of medical education: one set of schools for training researchers and another for training practitioners. This was politically astute since the universalistic quality of his program made it more salable in a society which had always rejected a formal elite.[140] More important, his prescription of uniformity was the basis of a new dynamic for medical education. Once a number of individual medical schools could be reconstructed on the basis of Flexner's university model, the "demoralizing" commercial competition of the past would be replaced by the general scientific competition "to which all well equipped, well conducted, and rightly inspired university departments throughout the civilized world are parties."[141] A new elite, organized as a learned discipline, would arise out of that competition.

The experiments of Gates and Pritchett established philanthropy as a directed influence on the reform of medical education. New institutions were built and expertise was mobilized to help set a public agenda. The Rockefeller Institute for Medical Research provided not only a signal announcement of the increased importance of medical research but also an institutional base for a new group of reforming zealots. Pritchett's development of the Carnegie Foundation for the Advancement of Teaching had been quite deft. He had accurately apprehended that developments within the universities and within the organized medical profession were converging to the point where a dramatic public report could have a significant effect in speeding those developments.

Two things were clear. One, philanthropy had established itself as a national influence. Two, the strengthening of institutions was both the means and the end of that influence. What was not clear was what relationship organized philanthropy would sustain to other institutions. Different elites saw in philanthropy the potential for their own enhancement and were pulling it toward greater involvement in medical education. University presidents wanted institutional support, the AMA saw the endowment of medical schools as a useful standard which would exclude the less reputable institutions, and the emerging research elite saw the potential in philanthropy to realize goals of constructing a learned discipline of clinical medicine. But complete philanthropic support for any one of these groups would mean conflict with the others. Could philanthropy develop a formula which could accommodate that conflict and yet still give the foundations maximum effectiveness?

Gates was wary of working with these competing elites, and Pritchett was reluctant to work against them. Because of his experience with Harper, Gates was unwilling to extend Rockefeller's philanthropy too far beyond his immediate corporate control. Pritchett was careful to secure some representative legitimacy for his organization and his program—if only through a convergence of existing leadership.

Flexner, however, had another vision: the philanthropic management of reform *through* institutions, in this case the universities. So long as the reform of medical education was seen as an educational problem, then the untrustworthy profession need not be involved in its solution. Flexner's goal was plain: he favored the further reform of medical education on the model of the learned discipline. Moreover, he had already elaborated a political view which supported that goal.

Flexner confronted the tension between democracy and philanthropic planning without trepidation or hesitation. Indeed, he saw it as an opportunity. In 1911, he analyzed how those processes could be brought into congruence. The problem, he felt, was clear:

> The fact is that we have discovered that democracy needs—more so than any other social form—to be both intensively and extensively educated albeit extensive and intensive organization is not itself native to the genius of democratic society. Here we once more rub up against a fundamental contrast. Organization comes relatively easy to monarchical, aristocratic, or other kinds of paternal government.[142]

But not to a democracy.

Flexner understood and appreciated that organization did not serve the same functions in a democracy as it did in an aristocracy. Flexner described Prussian education as "the steel framework which tends to keep society and the distribution of social functions pretty much as they are now." The purpose of the American system of education, he felt, should be "to promote and to take advantage of social plasticity" by looking to the "reassignment of the individual on his own merits."[143]

However, American education could not become an efficient meritocracy if it waited for government leadership.

Democratic government . . . tends necessarily to be inadequate to represent the total interest of its own society. . . . The sphere within which a government can act which must first obtain the consent and the support of the public tends always to be restricted to a minimum. Democracy lacks therefore, driving force; it is deficient in initiative, in the ability to conceive and to execute comprehensive designs. The veto is very easily applied even by a minority. . . . Democratic governments are therefore apt to lag a long way behind really intelligent opinion.[144]

So to Flexner the task was obvious; "[an] organized educational system being necessary if democracy is to handle its undertaking, a way must be found to overcome, in the first place, its disinclination to comprehensive systematization; in the second, the defects to which such systems are liable."[145]

Flexner felt that the solution was to expand the arena of democratic policymaking. "Democracy marks itself off from aristocracy, not only in governing itself through agents of its own choosing; it goes far outside official lines in self-governance." He stressed that "the successful, responsive, progressive democracy is that in which official and non-official agencies are found in close sympathy and interaction." With the exercise of "conscience, intelligence and good will," these agencies could produce a "harmonious relationship" among the then-dissonant components of the American educational system.[146]

Flexner rhetorically presented this process as one of cooperation. "We have in America no way of achieving rational ends except by voluntary submission to rational ideals."[147] But in fact Flexner realized that firm leadership would be required in any substantial reform. If the reform of clinical education which his report contemplated was to be carried out, there would surely be opposition. But Flexner, at least, was untroubled by the political problems involved. As he put it in his famous report, foreshadowing an attitude he would hold throughout his career:

Reorganization along rational lines involves the strengthening, not the weakening, of democratic principle, because it tends to provide the conditions upon which well-being and effectual liberty depend.[148]

2   The Transformation of Philanthropic Reform

"And so opens a new chapter!" an elated Abraham Flexner wrote to his brother Simon in late 1912.[1] The permanent position Abraham had just accepted with the Rockefeller-endowed General Education Board marked not only a new departure for him but an important shift both in the management of philanthropic foundations and in the foundations' role in the reform of medical education. Before the implications of the changes were fully worked out, Flexner would greatly expand the capacity of organized philanthropy for national policymaking in medical education. Ultimately, he would direct more than $78 million of Rockefeller's fortune to medical schools throughout the United States.[2] In so doing he left an ambiguous legacy to future foundation administrators. Some have considered his career a titanic achievement never to be equaled but always to be emulated. Others felt he took organized philanthropy to an exhilarating but politically dangerous precipice from which it would be best to withdraw. What is certain is that Flexner kept philanthropy in the vanguard of the American organizational revolution by helping to shift its focus from the development and support of institutions to the management of transinstitutional networks.

In 1912 the "scientific philanthropy" practiced by millionaires and their advisers was still frankly experimental. The general-purpose foundation was only just emerging. The failure of the Rockefeller Foundation between 1910 and 1913 to win a congressional charter showed just how novel and distrusted the new organizations and their founders were. It was not apparent what role would be acceptable for the foundations to play in social change. How to translate the general principles of the "gospel of wealth" into coherent and politically salable programs remained a problem.

In the field of medical education, two approaches had been tried between 1890 and 1910. The policy favored by Frederick T. Gates, John D. Rockefeller's philanthropic adviser, was the patronage of research. In contrast, the goal of Henry S. Pritchett, president of the Carnegie Foundation for the Advancement of Teaching, was the improvement of professional education. Gates conceived of medical research as a quest which was moral in both conduct and goal. The former Baptist pastor saw this effort as a stark contrast to the dismal self-seeking of the commercialized medical colleges. The independence of the Rockefeller Institute for Medical Research from any university and its lack of institutional connection with medical education reflected Gates's uncertainty about the reliability of professional education as a means of social change. Pritchett, without gainsaying the deficiencies of contemporary professional education, saw the professions as potential sources of industrial society's self-equilibration. To help reform the professions he started a program of educational surveys. Flexner's *Medical Education in the United States and Canada* was the first and most famous of these surveys.

These two programs reflected perceptions of the political limitations of philanthropic reform. Gates hesitated to involve Rockefeller philanthropy with independent organizations lest it be charged with attempting to control them. After the experience of dealing with William Rainey Harper (who managed Rockefeller philanthropy more than it managed him) and social gospel preacher Washington Gladden (who questioned whether Rockefeller's "tainted money" could be devoted to good work), Gates was comfortable with only a relatively narrow coterie connected with the Rockefeller office. Pritchett was much broader in his sympathies and acquaintances, but he was also cautiously aware of potential conflicts in philanthropic operations. His approach was to broker a consensus among all elites relevant to any given reform. He was careful, for example, to secure the cooperation of organized professional and educational bodies in the execution of the Carnegie Foundation's surveys.

Flexner was bolder than either of these men. The success of his report on medical education in establishing him as an "expert" only whetted his appetite for the educational leadership he felt the foundations must supply. As he wrote to his brother in 1912:

no far reaching medical changes can be put through except with the aid & backing of a central money supply—a sort of General Education Board devoted to medicine. That agency would have to do what in Germany the government does, —develop a policy & offer inducement enough to force its acceptance. Mr. Pritchett hopes the Carnegie Corporation may undertake this task: some one must.[3]

While that statement overestimated Pritchett's aggressiveness, it accurately anticipated Flexner's career in philanthropy. When opportunities to work in medical education in the Carnegie organization dimmed, Flexner joined the staff of the GEB. From that position he sought to test the limits of the power of foundations to develop a national policy. The centerpiece of his effort was the "full-time plan."

Simply put, the full-time plan was the policy that the clinical departments of university medical schools should be controlled and partially staffed by faculty who received no income other than their university salaries. Previously, clinical professors had customarily been paid at most nominal salaries and derived their living from a private practice which benefited from their university prestige. Clinical appointments under this system tended to reflect local professional eminence, often of a distinctly social sort, rather than a national frame of reference. The ultimate aim of the plan was to supplant these local cliques with a new national network of clinical science. This network was to take the form of a learned discipline rather than that of a profession.

As others have pointed out, Flexner did not originate the full-time plan.[4] Most of the notions he propounded had been bruited about for ten or twenty years. Flexner cheerfully admitted this lack of originality on every possible occasion, prominently but selectively ascribing the components of his program to others.[5] This ritual self-effacement was a vital part of his technique. For Flexner was promoting more than just a technical reform. His achievement was that he developed the full-time plan into an ideological and organizational solution to the problem of the political limits on the philanthropic role in American medical education. Flexner skillfully crafted the plan into an adamantine tool: its several facets reflected different images to different publics but, even so, it had a durable point. By alternately emphasizing the themes of the positive promise of science and the corrupting force of clinical commercialism, Flexner appealed not only to Gates but to the Progressive temper as well. He turned the tables; local clinical elites which opposed him found that it was *their* political legitimacy which was weak. The emphasis on corruption made it possible to discuss frankly the distribution of power in medical schools and to intervene to change that distribution.

Since the plan—for both its adoption and its operation—required that a school have a unitary administrative hierarchy, the transformation of the structures of medical school politics became one of Flexner's chief concerns. He constantly spoke of the importance of proper "organization" to the growth of "ideals" in science and education. In sociological terms which he would never have used, Flexner sought the routinization of scientific charisma. But the bureaucratizing force of Flexner's policies was not limited to the medical schools which adopted his plan: he was also changing the balance of forces in the evolving structure of philanthropy. In promoting the full-time plan he continually expanded his influence, first within the Rockefeller boards and eventually with philanthropists and philanthropies across the nation. That a confessed generalist in a rapidly specializing world should achieve such a position was a tribute to Flexner's visionary power and political adroitness.

A 1911 lunch shared by Flexner and Gates was the beginning of Flexner's career in Rockefeller philanthropy. In his autobiography and elsewhere, Flexner recounted the crucial conversation as typical of the terse incisiveness with which like-minded men could conduct philanthropic business. "What would you do," challenged Gates, "if you had a million dollars with which to make a start in the work of reorganizing medical education?" Flexner's unhesitating reply to what he must have known was not merely a speculative hypothesis was: "I should give to Dr. Welch." William H. Welch, the dean of the Johns Hopkins Medical School, merited such support, Flexner went on to suggest, because he and others had already made Johns Hopkins the source of personnel and inspiration for reform of schools elsewhere. On this basis, Gates asked Flexner (subject to his temporary release by Pritchett by whom Flexner was still officially employed) to go to Baltimore and make a report on the medical school's needs.[6]

The offhand adventuresomeness with which Flexner endowed this exchange conceals the congruent needs which came together that midday. At forty-two, Flexner was still seeking a secure career in foundation philanthropy, his position with the CFAT being only temporary. Gates was shopping for both program and personnel. Ever mindful of the necessity of disbursing Rockefeller's accumulating wealth, Gates knew he needed new avenues of expenditure since the Rockefeller Sanitary Commission was winding down, the Rockefeller Institute was fully endowed, and the agricultural and other work of the General Education Board (a foundation established in 1889) was not capital-intensive enough to be easily expanded. At this time, Gates and his associates were in the midst of an effort—ultimately unsuccessful—to secure a congressional charter for the Rockefeller Foundation and were fundamentally unsure what shape or scale that agency would have. But Gates was not looking aimlessly; he had some specifics very definitely in mind. He had already discussed with Welch the possibilities for reform of the clinical departments at Johns Hopkins, and, in fact, he had been thinking about a version of the full-time plan.

Even Gates, though, had no fixed notion of what the precise nature of the reform should be. Welch continued his entreaties for general support, and by January 1911, two months before his lunch with Flexner, Gates was willing to take action. "It seems to me that the thing for us to do is to figure out now the ideal thing, whatever it may come to and however appalling the financial total."[7] The "ultimate ideal" Gates had in mind was the restriction of professorial practice to "the merest nominal charge for consultation or other service."[8]

Between 1900 and 1910, Welch had continually sought Rockefeller support for Johns Hopkins, but Gates had been reluctant to aid the school in any major way. Welch had reasons to be receptive to a new proposal. In 1911, the future of Hopkins was as problematical as either Abraham Flexner's career or the course of the Rockefeller philanthropies. The original combination of factors which had propelled the school to prominence—novelty, personnel, and ideals—had begun to lose its force. As changes in medical education proceeded and other schools reorganized, Johns Hopkins was no longer unique. Moreover, as the school became established, there was the inevitable diffusion and dissipation of the original energy and institutional power. For example, enrollment was creeping toward levels incompatible with ideal designs. The uneasy feeling that Hopkins was not as robust as it had been was shared by faculty and students alike.[9] In addition to that disquiet, there simmered a conflict between the clinical and preclinical faculty. This conflict was evident in tiffs between William Osler and Franklin P. Mall over Mall's inductive method of teaching anatomy (which included very little conventional teaching). For Osler, science leavened teaching: for Mall the requisite task was to minimize teaching so as to maximize science. Their frames of reference were also different. Osler was devoted to the profession at large and to the students as nascent professionals; Mall looked to the discipline. While Osler was perhaps the most prominent of the Hopkins faculty, within that group Mall had a close ally in Halsted and dominated Welch with "moral supremacy." Osler recognized that his departure to Oxford in 1904 tipped the balance and said to Mall, "Now I go, and you have your way."[10] It was to this group that Flexner brought Gates's charge.

Those who engineered the adoption of Flexner's plan at Johns Hopkins had to combine the secrecy of conspirators with the patient endurance of besiegers. Flexner took Gates's offer of $1 million to Baltimore to "get the judgment of the faculty as to the uses to which the income of this sum could be put." On the evening of his arrival, Welch hosted a dinner at the Maryland Club for Flexner, Mall, and Halsted. Mall's suggestion that "every penny" of the proposed fund be used to put clinical chairs on a full-time basis could not have been unexpected or unwelcome to the like-minded group. Flexner spent three more weeks in Baltimore producing the report which secured him both permanent Rockefeller employment and lasting hostility.[11]

The report was a triumph of the Flexnerian philanthropic style of a studied straightforwardness which ignored distracting ambiguities and possibly troubling implications.[12] The outward form of the document was that of an option paper which after a précis of the relevant facts presented three alternative uses for the sum: the financing of full-time; the construction and financing of additional laboratories; and the financing of the expansion of the school's enrollment to four hundred undergraduates. The latter two were not serious considerations from the standpoint of scientific philanthropy, representing as they did a choice of quantity and mere improvement as against a fundamental advance. Full-time was Flexner's recommendation "because it achieves what is presumed to be the main purpose of the proposed sum—it sets up a school that will be in essential respects a model to stimulate endeavor throughout the country."[13] Flexner obliterated any possible ambiguities by casting his argument for full-time in the self-reinforcing Progressive idiom: the plan was the result of a historical teleology which had been previously thwarted only by the greed of perverse individuals. "The successive stages of modern medical development prepare one for this view [i.e., that full-time was necessary] . . . it is true because the very nature of scientific medicine forces it." Scientific medicine was incompatible with commercialism. Flexner found the relative decline of Johns Hopkins to be "traceable to one cause, namely, the displacement of science and education by business." Even though the school's clinical departments were "probably more productive than any other in the country," "one must in all fairness admit that, considering the conditions provided by the institution and the ideals which have been set up, the clinicians have with very few exceptions proved too easy victims for the encroachments of profitable practice." Flexner minced no words: in the department of medicine "neither the professor nor the clinical professor can be called productive, the publications of both being small in volume and largely popular in character." Gynecologist Kelly "has for some years published nothing of original scientific value," another gynecologist was "wholly unproductive" and his "best years, scientifically speaking, are apparently already over." The private wards of the hospital were being conducted as "high-priced sanataria" where patients were seen "not because they are scientifically interesting, but because they are pecuniarily worth while." If a "huge fee" was in prospect, "routine teaching and hospital work go by the board." [14]

Such commercialism had long offended the members of the Hopkins preclinical faculty. As Mall had written after returning from study in Germany: "one sees it all over in America—the philosophy is altogether wrong. . . . Education does not necessarily put one in the best society. The result is that man's only object is money." [15]

Gates felt vehemently that the asymmetry of knowledge between physician and patient meant that medicine should be outside of the market realm. [16] To Flexner, commercialism was no mere tawdry distraction but a dynamic malignancy from which the clinicians must be "protected." He saw no sphere of coexistence for full and part-time men within the hospital: if "the extremely prosperous physician or surgeon should have a place in the Johns Hopkins Medical School . . . he will inevitably exploit his prestige for his own pecuniary benefit . . . [a] spectacle [which] is not a wholesome one for students to witness." Following that logic to its conclusion, Flexner raised almost casually the touchiest point of his scheme: clinicians should be absolutely prohibited from any private practice; if they were to see other than charity patients the fee charged would be imposed, collected, and used by the university.[17]

Once the clinicians were insulated from the siren call of lucre, their ambitions would be channeled by institutionalized science. Competition was one of Flexner's crucial notions, however. He recalled in his autobiography his early enthusiasm for Social Darwinism; for himself and his brothers, "Darwin, Herbert Spencer and Huxley . . . replaced the Bible and the prayer book."[18] The structure of medical education which he envisioned was the inverse of the commercialized nightmare he had exposed in his report: in the one competition for tuition devalued science, in the other competition for public and philanthropic support exalted it.

Flexner was proposing nothing less than a transformation of the occupational basis of academic medicine. The full-time plan would create the new learned discipline: the science of clinical medicine. Flexner praised the "ideal situation" in the preclinical departments: "while the heads of these departments have retained their posts, despite repeated efforts to attract them elsewhere, the junior staff has been in constant flow: a steady succession of teachers and investigators has been trained, drafted by other institutions as soon as they were ready for independent responsibility." The departments were thus able to maintain "an equilibrium between teaching and investigation" by posing to their younger members the "stimulating alternative" of "be called [to other teaching posts] or be dropped." In the clinical departments, however, local private practice had rooted junior men in Baltimore and thus "blocked the line." Only through the creation of one of "the most powerful incentives to scientific devotion—the prospect of a career" could there be "the complete development of a distinctive race or school." Distributed across the nation like the pupils of Welch, Mall, Howell, and pharmacologist Abel, these new academic clinicians "would lead in the rehabilitation and modernization of American medical science and education." In order to create this new discipline, Flexner had to dislodge the old profession of practicing clinicians.[19]

Careerism was one of the enthusiasms of the age, and Flexner was keenly aware of its motivating power.[20] Although he took pains in his autobiography to present his life course as a series of happy coincidences whose haphazard nature somewhat amused even him, he was always conscious of the necessity of a career and alert to the variety of particular career strategies becoming available. The Flexner family functioned as a mutual aid and criticism society in promoting each other's careers. In the 1890s Abraham repeatedly urged Simon not to go into "any popular work": "under no circumstances would we permit [financial matters] to be a controlling factor" in any job choice but only "satisfactory scientific equipment and possibilities."[21] In this, Abraham Flexner was consistent across time and gender: he encouraged his wife's successful playwriting career and his daughters' careers in law and scholarship.[22] The emerging values of careerism—cumulative development, institutional routedness, and competitive evaluation—were exactly those that Flexner and others wanted to build into the medical education system.

Like "science" or "research," "career" was one of the several allusive images which gave Flexner's program tremendous rhetorical force. Such images could attract adherents to the organizational expedient of the full-time plan to whom those terms might have widely differing implications. The focus on career embodied a Horatio Alger stress on personal virtues and competition that was a convenient halfway house for a generation unused to the collectivism which institutionalization might connote. For Gates, full-time was a strategy that guaranteed moral fidelity. In this it resonanted deeply with the Protestant hermeneutic. As Flexner later noted to one colleague who questioned the stress on full-time: "full-time is not itself the thing but it is the outward sign of the spiritual rejuvenation which we week."[23]

Flexner's Hopkins report captured—more explicitly and pointedly than his early report for the Carnegie Foundation—the elements of the program he was to promote within the Rockefeller boards: the mutually reinforcing forces of education and science, the need to scourge commercialism, and the concern for secure career paths. However, Flexner presented and clearly understood these themes in organizational terms. For Flexner, science was an assumed value; what was important to him was not the particular content of scientific thought or its promise of applicable discovery but its organizational mandates. Education required the logic, openness, and evaluation which science provided. The combination of private practice and education was distortive, manipulative, and fraudulent.

Even so, Welch was uneasy over the relentless logic with which Flexner focused on the commercial aspect of clinical reform. One draft of the report shows his marginalia questioning the assertions that the staff's pursuit of profit had displaced a class of moderate-income patients for whom Johns Hopkins' will had made provision.[24] But Gates had no qualms; he found the report excellent and with eager bravado wanted to proceed directly with a conditional gift. Flexner wisely advised that it should appear that the proposal came from the university.[25] So a furtive but elaborate game of musical clinical chairs began with the General Education Board supplying the music and Welch in charge of the timing. Even though Flexner and Welch quickly won the approval of the interlocking boards of the university and the Johns Hopkins Hospital, Welch also wanted to secure at least the appearance of faculty support for the scheme, so he bided his time. While the interval allowed the opposition to marshal their arguments, it also gave them time to submit to the inevitable and adjust to the new regime.

"I have many times wished for your presence and council [sic] these past days," Howard Kelly wrote to Osler in Oxford. "We have had some stirring times." Kelly had shared the view that Hopkins needed some important reforms, but the dealings with Gates and Flexner had been entirely on Welch's initiative. Flexner did not visit Kelly while drawing up his report; indeed, the gynecologist was unsure whether it was Simon or Abraham who was the author of the "most frankly critical" but as yet uncirculated report, the conclusions of which Kelly had been assured were "such as we all agree to." "The difficulty comes in working out the situation in a practical way without doing unnecessary injustice to individuals."[26]

But the merely practical was slippery ground on which to meet such a carefully articulated program as Flexner's and, aware of this fact, Kelly's correspondence with Osler took on a tone of resigned defensiveness. He conceded that the "heavy burden" of his private sanatorium had tended to "seriously interfere with my services to the Hospital" and that he wanted to correct the situation, but he denied that greed had been his motivation. He did, however, divine personal interests in the motives of others: Halsted would triple his salary without having to give up a practice since he had none; obstetrician J. Whitridge Williams would gain control of the combined obstetrics and gynecology departments; and the laboratory men as a whole would be able to ask for higher salaries to match what the full-time clinicians would be paid.[27]

What disturbed Kelly most was the disruption of collegiality. "I have often felt . . . as if the old spirit of our Institution were departing. There is less hearty regard for the work of others in the various Departments, more of an undercurrent of criticism, occasional little outbreaks of hostility. . . ." This feeling was intensified when someone pilfered copies of Flexner's report from Welch's desk and distributed them widely. Kelly was outraged that the report was so "excessively personal, taking up different heads of department and their associates and in many instances severely condemning their work and methods."[28] By the end of May 1911, he had become quite livid:

> I further object to Dr. Welch's stirring up such an investigation in a democratic body like our Faculty, and presenting such a report without consulting us first. . . . Dr. Welch's dogma that individuals do not count in adjusting important business problems smacks very much of the Guggenheims as I have met them in the smelters of Mexico, and calls up a picture of the train of the suicides which followed Rockefeller's early days as he was building up the Standard Oil monopoly. If we could see all the little white stones which mark the graves for which the Rockefeller and Carnegie interests have been responsible, I wonder if the mountainsides would not look as if a snowstorm had struck them. [Hopkins psychiatrist Adolf] Meyer whispered in my ear recently that he was appalled that Standard Oil was acquiring such a large interest.[29]

Still, Kelly would not allow his emotions of personal slight, even when cast as populist principles, to stand in the way of what he saw as inevitable. His very ethic of collegiality compelled acquiescence: "If they do make the changes, I will try to give it all the hearty moral backing that lies in my power, that the trial may be a fair one. For after all, injustice seems to be a part of all readjustments in human affairs."[30]

Barker took up the issue directly with Flexner. Since moving to Baltimore and inheriting Osler's practice, Barker had found that his 1902 ardor for full-time had cooled. Some of his old arguments, he wrote to Flexner, were "impracticable and erroneous," and he hoped a "judicious compromise" could be made between his radical suggestions now being backed by the GEB and the status quo. Barker maintained that he had been opposed to commercialism only "in the bad sense" and did not want to abolish "that opportunity for increase of material reward by improvement of the quality and quantity of effort [which] is one of the most powerful stimuli to work of all sorts." To Flexner's ears this was the voice of avarice adorned with professional piety. Indeed, Barker reiterated the importance of money in eight of the thirteen points he enumerated against the plan. His arguments, however, did have a focus and consistency beyond mere greed. He was arguing that the viability of the medical education system was assured only by its integral relation to society; that both the cognitive and practical aspects of medicine required close communion with the swirl of social circumstance. Professional ethics mitigated the socially ordained market orientation from which the physician could not safely isolate himself. To Barker the full-time plan reduced a holistic relationship to one involving a single type of client and interest.[31]

In a subsequent address, Barker continued what Flexner labeled "his Jesuitical efforts to find a good reason for resisting what in his heart he approves."[32] Barker said:

> It would be a mistake to start with any cut and finished garment that we should ask the medical schools immediately to don. . . . The ideal clinic can scarcely be attained by proclamation. . . . Nor would, in my opinion, the limitation of every professor in a university to the material rewards of an insufficiently salaried position prove a panacea or a magic "open sesame" to the medical millennium. . . . Men who now occupy the clinical chairs and who have of necessity ordered their lives for the double function of professorship, on the one hand, of consultative or operative work on the other, have become so involved in obligations that they could not suddenly change to a salaried basis without great hardship to themselves and their families, and loud complaints from the public. . . . Above all, all honest, earnest, hard-working men should be protected from the zeal and over-statements of headlong advocates who insinuate the "absence of ideals" among clinical men, or talk of "graft," "rascality," "commercialism" and the "exploitation of the clinical chairs for private profit."[33]

From across the Atlantic, Osler let fly with a similar blast against what he termed the "climax of doctrinary madness."[34] He excused Flexner's report as due to the "perhaps pardonable ignorance" of a layman, but hoped that it would not cause the trustees to "risk termination of that close affiliation with the profession and the public which has made their clinical school the most potent distributor of scientific medicine in the United States." Even though Osler yielded to none in his regard for the laboratory, he saw clinical medicine as a question of "the translation of Science into Art." He maintained that there were "wider problems of social reform so closely associated with disease" that it would be "subversive to the highest ideal of a *clinical* school . . . to hand over young men who are to be our best practitioners to a group of teachers who are *ex officio* out of touch with the conditions under which these young men will live." He feared that the full-time plan would begin "the evolution throughout the country of a set of clinical prigs, the boundary of whose horizon would be the laboratory, and whose only human interest was research, forgetful of the wider claims of a clinical professor as a trainer of the young, a leader in the multiform activities of the profession, an interpreter of science to his generation, and a counsellor in public and in private of the people, in whose interests after all the school exists."[35]

As the discussions among the Hopkins faculty stretched through 1912 and into 1913, Flexner became increasingly impatient. He was leery of any compromise among the faculty and worried that "Mr. Gates may have to save them from themselves."[36] The collegiality which the irenic Welch hoped to salvage was an ephemeral consideration to Flexner. He wrote to one faculty member that "all you folks are much too tender [on the] clinical men who are going to be deposed. . . . Can not we drop them out of consideration absolutely and entirely, until the scheme is worked out?"[37] To Mall he expressed more exasperation: "Why doesn't Dr. Welch either shoot or give up the gun?"[38] In spite of the protests and the prodding, Welch maintained command of the situation "like a big father spanking all his children" and more or less successfully kept the dispute within the family.[39]

While the Hopkins faculty simmered, Flexner solidified his relationship with the Rockefeller philanthropies. Since his initial visit to Baltimore, Flexner had been doing studies for both the Carnegie Foundation and Rockefeller junior's Bureau of Social Hygiene.[40] Pritchett continued hoping to develop a medical program for either the CFAT or the newly incorporated Carnegie Corporation of New York and had secured board approval to retain Flexner on his staff—a possibility to which Flexner looked forward.[41] Still, Andrew Carnegie remained indifferent to the alleged promise of medical education, and Pritchett was Flexner's only ally in the Carnegie group. Aware of this fact, he encouraged Flexner to accept the General Education Board's offer of an appointment as assistant secretary under secretary Wallace Buttrick when it was offered in October 1912.[42] "I shall have opportunity under most friendly conditions," Flexner wrote to his brother of his new position; "it will be up to me to show what can be done with it and to win approval for any policy I can hammer out."[43]

At the GEB offices at 61 Broadway, Flexner moved to hammer out the full-time plan as a general pattern for medical education and to temper it with the heat of controversy. In trying to conclude the Hopkins full-time arrangements, Welch placed considerable importance on retaining Barker in the medical chair and offered him an additional $5,000 above the proposed $10,000 full-time salary. To Flexner, such largesse threatened the intent of the scheme, but fortunately from his point of view, Barker rejected the offer and prepared to resign and accept a part-time adjunct appointment.[44] The incident, however, underlined again a serious dilemma in the mechanism of grant making: how could the GEB be assured that its vision would be carried out after the grant was made? One idea proposed by the GEB office and eliminated at Welch's suggestion was to have a representative of the GEB appointed to the Hopkins' committee which would administer the full-time system.[45] The expedient ultimately agreed to addressed the problem legalistically. A contract was drawn between the school and the board under the terms of which the school would forfeit back to the foundation the principal of the gift if it deviated from the full-time plan as laid down by Flexner.[46]

While Welch was carefully shepherding the plan through its final paces in Baltimore, a challenge to the scheme arose from another source. A petition from the Harvard Medical School asking for an endowment to be used for the salaries of clinical assistants arrived at the GEB offices.[47] Such a proposal was too much in line with Flexner's version of full-time to be dismissed out of hand, and yet was sufficiently different from the Flexner outline to be unacceptable. The Hopkins plan was intended to be the cornerstone of a new medical education system. To approve the Harvard petition would be to sanction an alternative arrangement of a plan which was an all-or-nothing proposition. The subsequent negotiations with Harvard gave evidence of Flexner's skill and tenacity as a policymaker. With careful timing and artful dissembling, Flexner turned the negotiations from a threat to an advantage. By rejecting the Harvard version of full-time he established his version as the immutable policy not just of the GEB but of all the Rockefeller philanthropic boards. He had not only "hammered out" a new policy but also honed the very concept of policy into a managerial tool.

The Harvard proposal was expressed in the reform idiom. The litany recited was familiar: the unhappy contrast of American and European medicine; the baleful proprietary heritage of medical education; recent advances such as specialist instruction of laboratory subjects. "It would seem that the time has come to take the next step in medical education in America, if we are to gain our proper place in medicine, and that step involves the better organization of the clinical departments." The present deficiencies of clinical department organizations were seen as localism, distraction of practice, incomplete control of wards, and inadequate budgets.[48]

This diagnosis was Flexner's exactly, but the therapy suggested in the proposal was the milder perscription of placing only the assistants in the clinical departments on a "whole time" basis, not department heads as Flexner wanted. The Harvard authors contended that the recent appointments of outsiders Henry Christian, Harvey Cushing, and David Edsall had already put several Harvard clinical departments on a basis comparable to the best German clinics. In a lengthy appendix, the petition discussed possible limitations on the work of clinical professors. A general practice was ruled out, but a consulting practice was held to be important because the professor would gain experience of certain diseases that were rarely seen in a hospital setting. On the question of who should receive the fees from paying hospital patients, there was flexibility: "It makes no essential difference . . . the final result [concentrating the professor's efforts] is the same" so long as there was some limitation.[49]

Implicit in the Harvard proposal's slight but distinct modifications of the Flexner program were divergent conceptions of the nature of medicine and of social organization. The problem was discussed by the Harvard authors (chiefly Henry Christian) as one of creating the proper combination of teaching and practice. These functions were seen as mutually dependent: the professor must have some practice because practice was what he taught. The notion was that his task was one of transmitting to his students personally accumulated experiences rather than the employment and advancement of abstract knowledge. Research might animate teaching, but the Harvard proposal contained no hint of a vision of research pointing toward a distinct clinical science.

This difference in outlook was rooted in the contrasting institutional structures of Harvard and Johns Hopkins. Whereas Johns Hopkins was still a relatively new and compact institution, Harvard was defined by diffuse arrangements dictated by indefinable yet undeniable tradition. In Baltimore, the dyadic relationship of the university and the hospital had been decreed before either existed, while Harvard's plural combinations with several hospitals rested on a variety of imprecise agreements and conventions. It is possible to characterize these differences as reflections of foreign models of medical education: Johns Hopkins as German and Harvard as French.[50] But such descriptions perhaps gloss over the contrasting power arrangements from which the two universities confronted the reform process. Johns Hopkins was a more unitary agency designed to achieve certain specific ideals, once those of Johns Hopkins himself, now those of Welch and Flexner. As with a unitary state with power concentrated in the capital, once Welch controlled the core of the medical faculty he could achieve his aims. At Harvard, in contrast, the pluralism of organizations permitted a pluralism of ideals and gave a veto power to any faction in a circumstance which required consensus. Aware of the reforms being pursued in Baltimore, the Harvard petition to the General Education Board urged that "the exact nature of these changes should vary with different medical schools because of local differences in development of existing conditions."[51]

Whatever the document's rhetorical deficiencies, the backers of the Harvard proposal had touched every procedural base. There had been a full discussion within the faculty, particularly with the department heads concerned. The Harvard Corporation and President A. Lawrence Lowell had approved the petition. Former president Charles W. Eliot, a trustee of the General Education Board, and Jerome Greene, Eliot's former assistant who was soon to be secretary of the Rockefeller Foundation, had both given advice. The chances of approval would have appeared reasonable by any previous standard.[52]

To the growing astonishment of the New Englanders, Flexner upset these hopes by conducting the ensuing negotiations on the basis of fixed notions. What was not immediately apparent was that he proceeded according to a hidden timetable: disposition of the Harvard request had to await the final acceptance of the full-time plan in Baltimore. So, under the cover of the simply procedural, the process of making absolute full-time an unassailable philanthropic policy proceeded. A month after receipt of the Harvard proposal, the General Education Board formed a committee, of which Flexner was one of three members, to consider clinical questions. Negotiations with Harvard were put off at the board's request while the committee commenced its work. In the summer of 1913, Flexner was deputized to begin discussions with Harvard. In the course of the ensuing exchanges, Henry Christian, head of the Harvard negotiating committee, became only gradually aware that the petition's plan would not do and that it was a question of full-time for professors *and* assistants, or no aid at all. On October 15 Flexner finally made that stipulation plain, and Harvard began to take steps toward a new proposal.[53]

The Harvard principals were accordingly surprised when the following week, on October 23, the GEB made public announcement of their rejection of Harvard's March proposal. This was one part of that day's triple developments. Also announced was the not-unexpected conclusion of a GEB study committee that the full-time plan represented the best policy for medical education. These reports prefaced the long-awaited announcement of the $1.5 million gift to Johns Hopkins which was to be used to set up the "William H. Welch Endowment for Clinical Research and Training."[54]

Flexner's rhetorical skill lay in combining the components of philanthropic and educational ideologies: his managerial skill lay in keeping them separate so as to serve rather than confuse each other. This October 23 solution helped him preserve Hopkins as a pristine example of the full-time plan. Questions of alternative arrangements for clinical heads could be postponed until the movement took on a momentum which even rejection by prestigious Harvard could not slow.

Further discussions saw definition and redjustment of lines of authority and policy within both Harvard and the Rockefeller boards. After their initial rebuff, the Harvard authorities made an attempt to frame a proposal for full-time departments at the affiliated Brigham hospital which would meet Flexner's criteria. Christian, the Brigham chief of medicine, was willing to accept the Baltimore fee constraints provided that Harvard and Brigham forge agreements which would assure that he would remain in authority over beds and clinics; that Harvard would be represented on the Brigham board; and that certain improvements in the hospital would be made and supported.[55] As Christian's concern evidenced, unity of purpose of the Harvard and Brigham corporations had always been somewhat problematical. That disunity was the means by which Harvey Cushing, the Brigham chief surgeon, rejected this scheme.

Cushing felt that the Hopkins transaction was a desperate expedient. "It is my impression that the reasons for the adoption in Baltimore of the proposal from the General Education Board were based upon the feeling, chiefly on the part of the heads of the pre-clinical departments, that the school was getting into a rut, from which it should be extracted no matter how seriously the method adopted might temporarily wrench their machine." Such extremes were unnecessary at Harvard, he opined, since with his and Christian's appointment Harvard had begun such a reform on its own initiative. He concluded that "the injection at this time of a new element into the situation might seriously complicate it." The adoption of the "still more radical experiment" proposed by Flexner was not justified, and Cushing was skeptical that the Brigham trustees would support it. He indicated, however, that he would resign if his tenure was the only thing blocking adoption of a plan favored by all other parties.[56]

Cushing's reluctance to adopt the Flexner plan was not merely financial. Although he was one of the leaders in the development of the improved techniques and organization of the newly powerful medicine, Cushing placed paramount importance on the ideal of the independent physician. Even with more adequate salaries he feared that full-time teachers would be "enslaved" by the proposed system.[57] Harvard president Lowell saw Cushing's position as "reasonable," but continued to seek a possible accommodation.[58] Flexner urged the president to seek out all possibilities even as he himself was proposing privately to Cushing that Brigham set itself up independently of the Harvard Medical School on the model of a British hospital school.[59] Such a proposal puts Flexner's Germanophilism in perspective. Flexner had a strategist's loyalty to tactics; his goal was the production of a new learned discipline of clinical science. In pursuit of that goal he was willing to adopt inventive measures.

For more than a year, Cushing mulled over his alternatives: resignation, a full-time position, or subordination to a full-time head. Lowell, eager to retain the talents of the man he felt to be "the best brain surgeon in the world," tried to make the last option attractive, but Cushing kept his own counsel.[60] Walter Cannon, a physiologist and leader of Harvard's preclinical men, tried to coax Cushing out of his intransigence with an appeal to institutional loyalty. The full-time plan was spreading faster than anticipated, Cannon urged. Johns Hopkins was running well on it, and a full-time professorship would soon be instituted at Columbia. "Unless Harvard takes it up soon, therefore, this Medical School loses a place of leadership in an important improvement in medical education and re-

search. Loyalty to this Medical School makes me and others of your colleagues jealous of its good standing and desirous of keeping it at the front
of medical progress." Cannon said he had heard a "bewildering variety of
statements about your attitude." While some had suggested that Cushing
would be willing to take a special professorship under a new head, others
maintained that he would yield nothing and had so told the Brigham
trustees.[61]

It was, indeed, the hospital trustees who vetoed any such arrangement.
The board president wrote to Lowell that even though Cushing had expressed willingness to step down, "It was thought by some of us that
there would be certain well defined risks of friction in the Staff if we introduced a new Chief Surgeon."[62] Unlike Barker and Kelly in Baltimore,
Cushing could not be cajoled to move aside, and his independent relation
with the hospital trustees gave him an institutional redoubt.

As the Brigham situation was unraveling, the related issue of a proposed institute of hygiene further embittered relations between Harvard
and the Rockefeller office. In 1909, the final year of Eliot's presidency,
Milton J. Rosenau had been brought from the U.S. Public Health Service
to be professor of medicine and hygiene at the medical school. In 1913
Rosenau began jointly with MIT, the School for Health Officers, the first
such school in the nation. On his own initiative, Rosenau sent to Flexner
in early 1914 future plans and a plea for support from New York. Here
again was an opportunity which required careful philanthropic management if Flexner's evolving policy of medical education reform and the
network it contemplated were to be safeguarded.[63] Even though in January 1914 the GEB reinforced its commitment to the full-time plan by re-
solving to aid medical education only where the plan was involved, there
was still from Flexner's point of view a danger in the Harvard public
health proposal. The Rockefeller Foundation had recently created a new
subsidiary: the International Health Board. A substantial and respectable
project such as the Harvard school would have been an attractive initial
effort for the new board. Public health was a field in flux, and to help
chart its course and develop its institutionalization naturally attracted the
philanthropic imagination.[64]

Moreover, the Harvard proposal demanded sedulous consideration in
view of the rejection of the university's first full-time application and the
fading prospects of their Brigham proposal. Support for the proposed public

health school, however, would send the message not only to Harvard but throughout the medical education structure that absolute full-time organization was not the sine qua non of Rockefeller support. Although the General Education Board was a distinct entity, Flexner's position would have been weakened if another Rockefeller board supported an enterprise which contradicted his policies. In that case, the IHB might develop as an alternative to the GEB in support of American medical education.

Flexner dealt with this dilemma by employing the now trustworthy gambit of calling a conference which would appoint a committee to issue a definitive report. That sequence gave the appearance of broad participation, disinterested inquiry, and orderly procedure, but its very structure predetermined its outcome. The Rockefeller Foundation formally asked the General Education Board to make a survey of public health teaching. At an October 1914 conference called by the board, Rosenau and other Harvard delegates were joined by representatives from Hopkins and elsewhere. Welch and Wickliffe Rose were appointed to draft a report on the essential conditions of an ideal public health school. This report defined the situation in line with the principles of the Flexnerian policy: university status, research orientation, and full-time.[65]

The implications of such criteria were clear, and as a site selection committee of Rose, Jerome Greene, and Flexner visited New York, Philadelphia, Baltimore, and Boston, resentment arose at Harvard over what seemed to be a foregone outcome. When, during discussions, Flexner remarked that the hoary but legally imprecise relationship between the Massachusetts General Hospital and Harvard was an aspect of Boston life which troubled him, it was taken by some as proof that he was prejudiced against Harvard and all its works. Greene tried to assure Eliot of Flexner's fairness, but pointed out that "the authorities of the University seem to be more interested in getting the money than in adopting a rational policy for the Medical School."[66]

Eliot admitted that the full-time negotiations had been a "fiasco," but he felt that Harvard's position in medical education was nonetheless premier.[67] When it became apparent that the school was going to be placed at Hopkins, Eliot was angry. "This is the first time that a proposed act of a Rockefeller Board has seemed to me to be without justification or reasonable explanation." He characterized Johns Hopkins as "a small and weak university" compared with Harvard or Columbia and saw Baltimore as "a provincial community" which "conspicuously lacks [the] public spirit and beneficent community action" of either Boston or New York. Welch alone, he felt, was insufficient reason to found the institute on the Chesapeake.[68]

Flexner first attempted to assure Eliot that no decision had been reached and unconvincingly abjured any authority to make one; the Foundation would evaluate any of the committee's memoranda and reach its own conclusions. But the criteria were clear, he maintained, and had been approved even by the Harvard conferees as "thoroughly sound." Flexner asserted that since the problem was one of developing a cadre of public health teachers for future university chairs, internal conditions of the proposed school were more important than external factors, the "most important single factor" being the "character of the medical school organization: a thing which will surely endure."[69]

Thus the Johns Hopkins School of Hygiene was finally created and endowed by the Rockefeller Foundation in 1916. The distrust engendered by the decision did not, however, forestall yet a fourth round of discussion between the Harvard Medical School and the General Education Board. Harvard communicated its intention to make another proposal to the General Education Board for support of the clinical departments of its medical school. Despite the difficulties, all parties had too much to lose to let the matter drop precipitously. The indebted medical school needed a cash transfusion, and Eliot wanted to see completed the work he had begun in 1871. The venerable educational reformer had a moral lien on Flexner's cooperation, especially in view of his association with Rockefeller junior. Moreover, General Education Board secretary Wallace Buttrick had experienced considerable disquiet over Harvard's hurt feelings. Eliot conducted the negotiations for Harvard. President Lowell, who was disgusted with Rockefeller dealing, was more than happy to yield that role.

Greene was heartened by Eliot's intervention, and assured his former boss that both Flexner brothers shared that sentiment. "I am confident," he wrote, underestimating Flexner's inflexibility, "that whatever unfavorable prepossessions may have been formed, they are not incompatible with an entirely disinterested and sincere hope that the way may be open for the strengthening and enrichment of the Harvard Medical School."[70]

These 1916–17 discussions focused almost entirely on the organizational politics of the full-time reform. The Harvard committee, in addition to Eliot, consisted of men unquestionably of the new stripe of medical educators: Walter Cannon, David Edsall, and Reid Hunt. In their presentations to the General Education Board and among themselves these men were in entire agreement on the importance of the full-time reform. Their differences with the board concerned how the reform should be powered and empowered, that is, what institutional structures should advance the measure. This was the closest convergence of what eventually became two contrary attitudes toward full-time within medical education and, much later, within the Rockefeller boards. These differences over administrative arrangements evolved into differences over philosophy, in somewhat the reverse of the process by which the full-time plan originally emerged. In Edsall particularly Flexner found an opponent who matched his own determination and doggedness.

At the Harvard committee's request, William S. Thayer of Johns Hopkins was commissioned to do a survey of their school. Harvard, Thayer related, was not completely in tune with a medical education system which was national and even international in scope and hierarchical in form. In the past Harvard's clinical contributions had been "individual and occasional" rather than the "consecutive and co-ordinated work" which would come from units organized as continuous services under one professor. Even though recent changes had broadened the faculty, "clinically speaking, Harvard has been generally regarded as a local institution . . . representing the best which Boston could put forward rather than as a national institution representing the best in America." Thayer urged that Harvard create modern departments at the Massachusetts General Hospital. While Brigham had the closest geographical and administrative relation to the medical school, the MGH organization was similar enough to that demanded by the GEB to be allowed a fair trial. Moreover, the clinical and laboratory facilities of the MGH were unsurpassed.[71]

This thinking was reflected in the tentative proposal which the committee submitted to the GEB in December 1916.[72] It was understood by both sides that this submission was to be regarded as entirely unofficial; neither party wanted yet another formal rebuff to Harvard, so it was agreed that an official petition would be forthcoming only if acceptance was assured.[73] The committee's memorandum went far in meeting the problems of previous negotiations. Continuous service units were to be established under full-time professors and full-time assistants "as rapidly as suitable hospital affiliations and new income permit." This latter clause addressed the problem of what to do about people like Cushing: no present occupant would face displacement, and no present relations between the university and its hospitals would have to be upset. Since the initial goal was modest—the endowment of only Edsall's MGH department— Harvard was asking for only $90,000. The noble record and achievement of the "very favorable connections with several independent hospitals" which had been developed "through more than a century" were rehearsed, and it was asserted that this arrangement was adaptable to the full-time scheme. "Cooperative arrangements like those at present in use, however, rather than minute binding contracts would seem sufficient and most likely to run smoothly." The complexities of the governance of the medical school were also reiterated, with the assurance that "the result of this somewhat complicated arrangement is that the Dean and the Administrative Board are the real executive forces" of the school.[74] A similar note of special pleading was also evident in the discussion of appointments. Although Thayer advised against it, the memo delineated two distinct modes of appointments: worldwide searches for the best established talent, and promotion from within of promising men. "In a new and young institution it is obvious that only one of these methods is available. The Harvard Medical School uses both." This theme of diversity of historical development was one of the memorandum's strongest points.

> The Harvard Medical School believes that there is urgent need in the United States of a much greater number than now exist of men trained to medical research and well prepared to serve the American communities as directors of medical and surgical research, and as public health officers. The Rockefeller Institute for Medical Research is one useful source of supply, but a limited one. In addition, there should be four or five strong medical schools of high standard fully equipped for preparing young men in considerable numbers for the new service which the country needs. These four or five schools should be well distributed geographically, and need not be all of one type; indeed it would be better that they should vary in type in accordance with their different historical developments. The Harvard Medical School, in view of the contributions it has already made to medical education and medical research, of its excellent plant, its remarkable clinical facilities, and its high standards for admission and graduation would seem to be one suitable recipient of an appropriation from the General Education Board.[75]

The Harvard committee held that full-time was a valuable forward step which could be adapted to the contours of their present organization with some administrative readjustment. To the GEB, which maintained the Flexner view, the full-time plan was not merely a general tendency but the definitive embodiment of all relevant principles. Implicit in the Harvard proposal was the whiggish expectation that the reform would work itself out in the evolution of their academic organization.

To someone as ardent as Flexner, this incrementalism missed the point. The GEB was more disposed to see such an evolution as a pathology, gnawing at the vitals of a vulnerable organism. The policy Flexner had promoted was too tightly reasoned to admit of either organizational variety or alternative paths of historical development. Buttrick acknowledged receipt of the Harvard memo with the assurance that "Mr. Rockefeller, Mr. Gates and others, among whom I would like you to include myself, are anxious to cooperate with Harvard University in the promotion of its medical department." However, he noted that the policy of the board was to aid medical schools in putting work "on a strictly full-time basis" and added, "I do not think that the Board would now be ready to depart from that policy."[76] A perplexed Eliot responded that the memo contemplated no such deviation, but rather looked to the policy's fulfillment at Harvard.[77]

A GEB memo—bearing the marks of Flexner's draftsmanship—outlined the position more fully. The GEB plan looked to "the ultimate suppression" of part-time clinical departments and "the banishment of professional business from research and teaching clinics." The Harvard scheme did not give the envisioned full-time units "a commanding position as against the part-time units." "The full-time scheme was, in a word, meant to end one order of things and to install a new order of things. Dr. Eliot's proposition continues the old order and adds the new order." The only scheme acceptable to the board would be full-time units at Brigham (which was a known impossibility before the start of this round of negotiations) and their elevation above all other units. The Harvard proposal threatened the integrity of the board's policy; if accepted "the Board would be exposed to similar applications from many other schools, for the Harvard plan could be universally adopted without thorough reorganization."[78]

Taken aback by the GEB's rigidity, the Harvard committee sharpened its view of the best organization of reform. "It seems to me a misconception to fancy that we desire to suggest an essentially new scheme," Thayer wrote. The flaw in the GEB's logic was that "conditions existing in Baltimore and St. Louis . . . are essentially different from those which exist at Harvard," hence the effort "to adapt existing conditions to the plan suggested by the Board." Conditions were not uniformly good or bad; the size of Hopkins had facilitated an easy transformation to full-time, but the school remained too small to provide adequate instructional material, Thayer felt. Harvard's arrangements with several hospitals were therefore "an advantage not lightly to be thrown aside." Similarly, the logic of imposing upon clinical departments the history of preclinical developments was held to be "not quite apt," and "specious."[79] The demand for "suppression" struck Edsall as a "harsh proposal" which "conflicts in spirit if not in fact with the full-time platform as I have subscribed to it." Edsall discerned keenly that Flexner harbored a "direct desire to destroy the power and authority of any clinical teachers who practice their profession," and worried that "to demote them ipso facto . . . would have I believe a very reactionary effect upon the whole tribe of them." Frustrated by what he saw as increasing GEB obdurateness despite repeated protestations of openness and sympathetic understanding, Edsall suggested that Harvard "withdraw with dignity from any further negotiations."[80]

Before closing negotiations, Eliot privately protested to Buttrick what he felt was a deviation from "the policy . . . which I heard stated with great distinctness by Mr. Gates when I first joined the Board . . . namely, the policy of the Board not to interfere with the domestic management of an institution."[81] Buttrick's reply was indicative of the transformation Flexner had wrought: the older policy was relevant to the general support of institutions, not necessarily to "appropriations for specific kinds of work."[82]

After the final breakdown, F. G. Shattuck of the venerable Harvard medical family approached the Carnegie Corporation, perhaps at the suggestion of a GEB executive committee member.[83] Pritchett was willing to listen, but held out little hope since the corporation hoped to focus on southern medical schools. "How Mr. Eliot should have failed to get away with some of the Rockefeller money when he was himself a member of the Board is past my comprehension," the Carnegie official confessed.[84] Shattuck complimented his friend on not raising hopes he intended to dash, "a much more satisfactory way to be dealt with than that which the General Education Board has followed."[85] When Pritchett parenthetically questioned the competence of Harvard dean Bradford, the galling bitterness which the Rockefeller negotiations had engendered overcame Shattuck's Brahmin reserve:

> There are circumsized [*sic*] folk in NY, circumsized alike in pecker and intellect, who can see nothing good in the Harvard Medical School, Lowell, or Bradford— Every now and again the savor of their skunkhood comes my way. You are too wise to be beguiled by them.[86]

The Johns Hopkins and Harvard medical schools had been in the vanguard of American medical education ever since its emergence from the Jacksonian leveling. In gaining the adoption of the full-time plan by Hopkins, Flexner had secured a keystone for his contemplated learned discipline of clinical science. In withstanding the Harvard faculty's attempt to alter his plan he had gained something more: the definition of his program as the fixed policy of the Rockefeller boards. His rhetorical skill had projected the General Education Board into the midst of medical school organization: his skill at the management of institutional politics had made that transition to an active philanthropic role seem natural. Gates, once so reluctant to deal with university medical schools, was now eager to promote their reformation.

Flexner had found a means whereby philanthropic management could reach within and across institutions. Within the schools, the result of his activity was the reorganization of authority. In Baltimore, Welch and his allies dominated the reformed school. Partially as a response to the failure to win Rockefeller support, David Edsall became dean of the Harvard Medical School and subsequently energized that school. In the 1920s Edsall was to become one of Flexner's more effective antagonists. In 1916, however, Flexner seemed unassailable. He had established his power and his program; to preserve it, he now had to expand it.

3 Building a System of National Management

Once he was secure in his position at the General Education Board, Flexner moved swiftly to nationalize the reform of clinical teaching. The adoption of full-time by the Johns Hopkins Medical School was only the beginning of his plan to reorganize American medical education. The report he had submitted to Gates outlining the importance of clinical full-time envisioned Hopkins as the center of a national network of teachers and researchers. To ensure the growth of clinical science, Flexner wanted to have opportunities for those who would be trained by the reformed Hopkins, and he set out to reform other schools to accommodate this nascent academic elite. Like an antebellum sectionalist, he felt he had to expand the territory of full-time before his opponents breached new frontiers. The creation of a national network of reformed schools also meant the creation of a national system of policy management.

Circumstances favored Flexner's program. Medical education was still in organizational flux around the country and remained relatively malleable. Moreover, the Rockefeller boards were eager for a program as relatively acceptable politically as full-time. The growth of Flexner's system was accompanied by the growth of his own power within the philanthropic community. In the implementation of his plan, he gained the allegiance of local philanthropists while at the same time winning his independence from his earlier sponsors, Pritchett and Gates. Pritchett was unable to dissuade Flexner from absolute insistence on the full-time plan as a condition for assistance to medical schools. Flexner came into conflict with Gates when he sought to nationalize his plan in both scope and form by including publicly supported schools in his network. His victory in that struggle marked the zenith of his success as a national policymaker.

Interestingly, while Flexner had been establishing his program through the Harvard and Hopkins negotiations, public attacks on the foundations had increased for other reasons. The pervasive distrust of these charitable trusts was inflamed by an incident at Ludlow, Colorado in 1914. Ludlow was a company town of the Rockefeller-owned Colorado Fuel and Iron Company. During labor strife, a number of women and children were killed by police and private guards serving the company. The newly formed Rockefeller Foundation announced that it would investigate the incident as a part of its program of studying industrial conditions—a program headed by Canadian labor expert William Lyon Mackenzie King, the future prime minister. This program seemed to imply just the sort of propagandistic activity in support of brute industrial power which the critics of foundations had predicted. The U.S. Commission on Industrial Relations, set up by Congress to investigate economic conditions, announced that it would include the foundations in its inquiry. Public hearings were held at which the foundation officials were subpoenaed. Andrew Carnegie put on a charmingly garrulous performance and was treated lightly, but Rockefeller junior was mercilessly grilled by commission chairman Frank Walsh. It was a searing experience for the oil heir, and though he won some sympathy, public suspicion remained high. As a result of this incident the Rockefeller Foundation henceforth eschewed domestic philanthropy to a large extent and sought to develop its programs overseas.[1]

The way was thus cleared for Flexner to develop his program for the reform of medical education without any competition from another Rockefeller board. While some foundation activities excited public misgivings, Flexner's program had a certain appeal to the cast of mind which we think of as Progressive. The organized medical profession resented the full-time plan and the rift it represented between academic physicians and the local guild.[2] But the broader public had no such qualms. The plan was portrayed in the public press as an overdue attack on medical avarice and hailed as the harbinger of socialized medicine, a reform expected imminently.[3]

Nor did Flexner have any substantial competition from any other foundation in the expansion of his program. Pritchett was eager to have the Carnegie Corporation enter the field of medical education, but he was frustrated by the cumulative effect of Carnegie's caprice. As long as the steel baron remained active in the management of his benefactions (with the outbreak of World War I Carnegie, who had invested emotions and millions in the quest for international peace, fell into an introverted melancholia which lasted until his death), his prejudice against giving to large schools frustrated Pritchett's desire. When Pritchett took over management of the Carnegie Corporation in 1915 (maintaining his presidency of the Carnegie Foundation for the Advancement of Teaching), he discovered not only that much of the corporation's future income had been pledged but that the trustees, made up of the presidents of other Carnegie benefactions, looked upon the corporation as a common fund to cover the needs of their own organizations. Although Pritchett was able sporadically to make grants for medical education, he could not command anything near Flexner's resources.[4] While Pritchett and Flexner cooperated on many medical education projects, the Carnegie official became increasingly dissatisfied with Flexner's somewhat high-handed style and seeming obsession with the full-time plan and its implications. But without resources at his command, Pritchett would voice little more than a muffled dissent while Flexner formed national policy.

National implementation was an essential feature of the policy Flexner was developing. He saw the efficiency of such a structure as essential for the health of learned disciplines. His model was Germany:

> That vigorous teaching and unwearying research have flourished together in the German university must in the end be largely ascribed to the elasticity characteristic of their organization. No obstacle obstructs the search of a mature student for a stimulating and congenial teacher; and a teacher with ideas can always gain a hearing for them. It is true that men whose productivity has ceased occupy important chairs in some universities; but in the same institutions, docents with more modern views expound the newer faith, which has perhaps already invaded a professorship somewhere else. While organized faculties tend to relapse into conservatism by favoring their own contemporaries, the pressure of the student body and the legitimate competition of universities with each other on a scientific plane, force the filling of vacant posts with men who represent progressive tendencies. Around such individuals, students of quick susceptibility soon gather; a school forms. The speed with which thereupon a novel standpoint travels over Germany is one of the amazing features of its university life. And this quick apprehension and incorporation of demonstrated truth is responsible for what I have repeatedly pointed out—the uniformity of the scientific institutes in respect to type, organization, and ideal.[5]

Flexner sought to produce the same pattern in the United States. The "uniformity . . . in respect to type, organization, and ideal" which he required of members of his network was absolute adherence to his version of the full-time plan. In his vision, systemic uniformity would promote individual career mobility which in turn would be responsible for intellectual and scientific vitality.

In an organizational whirlwind between 1913 and 1920, Flexner saw the full-time plan adopted at Washington University, Yale, Rochester, Vanderbilt, the University of Chicago, and the Columbia University College of Physicians and Surgeons. In all these cases the plan was underwritten by the GEB, and a contract binding the school to the plan on pain of returning the grant was signed. In this effort Flexner employed with telling effect the marginal utility of foundation aid to any school eager to modernize. Some of these reorganizations were easier than others. His task was relatively simple when he had the ear of a powerful local philanthropist such as Robert Brookings, the chairman of the Washington University board (whom he had converted several years earlier to his vision of reformed medical education)—or George Eastman, of camera fame, whom he convinced to endow a medical school for the University of Rochester. Yale and Vanderbilt were desperately in need of funds and met his conditions rather quickly. As Flexner repeatedly observed, clinical reform was most difficult in the larger cities; the reorganizations in Chicago and New York tested his political mettle.[6]

The creation of a new medical school at the University of Chicago was evidence of how effectively Flexner had honed his philanthropic method. In order to avoid the complications which he had encountered in the Harvard episode, Flexner quickly moved to define the situation, foreclose other options, and push his own plan on as many fronts as possible. In less than twelve months he created the groundwork for the archetypal Flexnerian school: geographically and administratively united with the parent university; possessed of its own hospitals and clinics; staffed by full-time researchers drawn from the growing national pool of elite academic medicine. His initial success was rapid, but the implications of his scheme were not worked out until long after his tenure at the GEB.

It was also a measure of his increasing boldness that Flexner created this new school in the face of two active alternative policies. The first was one of consolidation. This tack would have preserved all the local assets while eliminating the worst features of the medical education "plague spot of the country."[7] Northwestern, the University of Chicago, and the University of Illinois would offer the preclinical years on their own campuses, and clinical instruction would be conducted in one large "Chicago Medical School" controlled by the three university boards and using the vast resources of the Cook County Hospital. Flexner worked for this plan while he was surveying schools for his Carnegie Foundation report in 1908 and 1909. By 1910, he felt he had secured the support of the concerned presidents and such local luminaries as Drs. Arthur Dean Bevan and Frank Billings.[8]

Carnegie Foundation president Pritchett supported and pursued this plan, and for the next six years he was the leader of efforts to produce both graduate and undergraduate medical education unity in Chicago.[9] Bevan waxed joyous over the dream of "one really great medical school in this center and one which would of course very much overshadow anything in the Mississippi Valley."[10] This proposal for consolidation was very much in the relatively older tradition of elite reform in which Pritchett was firmly rooted: his goal was to encourage the local schools to act jointly on the higher ideals he felt they all implicitly shared. Such enlightened unity would rid the medical education system of the inferior schools which thrived on elite disunity and competition.

The second possible course was the support of the alliance between the University of Chicago and Rush Medical College. The two institutions had become increasingly unified since 1889, even without the benefit of a Rockefeller blessing. Indeed, Gates's hostility toward Rush was implacable. He had urged Chicago president Harper not to affiliate with Rush. The succeeding administration of President H. P. Judson had been making continual efforts to organize Rush on lines compatible with the university. The goal of having a research as opposed to a practitioner-producing school had been explicitly stated and restated to the Rush faculty by university officials. Despite considerable disgruntlement, especially among younger faculty, the elite leaders—Billings, Bevan, and E. Fletcher Ingals—had maintained control and procured the endowments which were preconditions for further unity.[11]

It was in support of this connection that Judson appealed to the GEB on June 17, 1916, soliciting aid for the introduction of some full-time clinical teaching at the Presbyterian Hospital to which the Rush faculty had ex-

clusive access. That Judson portrayed this move as only a temporary expedient captured the difficulty of his situation. A member of the General
Education Board, Judson was fully aware of how strictly the full-time
ideal had been interpreted in Harvard's case. He had, moreover, experienced both occasional Rush faculty recalcitrance to change and Rockefeller
distrust of Rush. Yet he had little choice. He would have to take up with
the full-time movement if he was to make any headway in medical education, but he could not unilaterally repudiate the Rush connection without
damaging the university's credibility, as well as incurring hostility from
the financially potent community represented by Rush practitioners and
their patients.[12]

During a July visit in response to Judson's plea, Flexner produced a deft
report on the Chicago situation.[13] Using the report to move the debate
toward his agenda, Flexner proposed a new course in face of the older
alternatives. Again, "the uncompromising modern basis of [medical education in] Baltimore and St. Louis" was the standard. But Flexner had
come to believe that "a strictly modern medical school can be most effectively organized in connection with a University which . . . lacks a medical department." The experience of large cities of the East Coast had made
this regretfully apparent. Existing schools were stumbling blocks, and it
seemed that "further salvation in respect to medical education of these,
our largest centres [sic], must be accomplished by a slow and painful evolution rather than by a series of decisive steps taken during a relatively
short period." Chicago was an exception to this pattern since the University of Chicago's pact with Rush was "temporary in character and can be
discarded or reorganized by the University at will." Judson's proposal he
rejected as "two half schools rather than one whole school." "A modern
medical school is a single, organic thing, no part of which can function
effectively except in close physical and scientific relation with all other
parts." Moreover, expectations were a crucial factor, and temporary arrangements were unacceptable in a time of thoroughgoing reform. "To
give to Chicago in order to *improve* a school of defective type in the expectation that someday a school of modern type will take its place might
operate to defer, rather than to hasten the latter day."[14]

While Flexner saw some virtues in building a school around Rush, such
a course also entailed "compromises of doubtful wisdom." The character
of the Rush staff and its close relationship with the Presbyterian trustees

made it impossible that such a school would be "from the start a clean-cut modern organization free from all doubt whatsoever." Flexner feared that the Presbyterian trustees would not long cooperate in a program where "the present staff would necessarily give way to a new set of younger men—men of reputation to be sure, but of a different kind of reputation—men known to scientists, not to the general public—modest workers in wards and laboratories, not personages prominent in the social life of the community."[15]

These conflicts could be avoided if the university were to build and control its own hospital adjacent to its main campus. Such a measure, while costly, was organizationally a Flexnerian dream. "The foreign board of hospital trustees is eliminated; there is no existing hospital staff to conciliate; no tradition to overcome. The University can, in the most favorable atmosphere and the most stimulating environment, create a medical department in complete harmony with the highest modern education and productive ideals." Flexner recommended that the valuable elements of the Rush connection be preserved by creating a graduate school for the retraining of practicing physicians.[16]

Flexner moved forcefully to avoid the type of frustrating delay that had characterized the adoption of full-time at Johns Hopkins. Judson was kept informed, but Flexner preserved command of the initiative throughout the process. The report was submitted to and approved by both Rockefeller junior and Gates before Judson received it.[17] Similarly, Flexner created a Chicago constituency for a new university school. He parlayed a previous connection with Julius Rosenwald, the head of Sears, Roebuck (and a local philanthropist), into a $1/2 million gift. Important beyond its cash value, this gift brought the local Jewish community into the university's medical planning for the first time. Flexner made certain that Rosenwald was committed to the new scheme and its principles, not to the University of Chicago per se.[18] Unable to contain himself, Flexner persistently advised and corrected Judson on the precise wording of proposals and announcements, to the point where even the mild president advised him in a paraphrase of Solomon to "fret not thy gizzard."[19]

With such momentum, the plan was a rapid initial success. The specifics were staggering: $5.3 million was estimated for construction and endowment of the South Side school and upgrading of the West Side school (Rush) as a graduate facility. The GEB and Rockefeller Foundation

(RF) would each contribute $1 million if the university could raise the remainder. That goal was easily met as all the pieces fell into the places Flexner had designated for them. The Billings family gave $1 million for the new hospital. Rosenwald's friend Max Epstein contributed $100,000 to the support of the clinics. Many of Rush's alumni gave to its share of the scheme.[20] Flexner was pleased; he wrote Judson that the university's fund-raising effort was "a campaign worthy of the German General Staff at its best." American entry into World War I put execution of the plan into abeyance, but all seemed to bode well for completion of the paradigmatic Flexner school.[21]

The reform of the College of Physicians and Surgeons of Columbia University and its union with the Presbyterian Hospital to create the Columbia-Presbyterian Medical Center proved to be as tortuous as the reform of the University of Chicago had seemed rapid. The cast and sequence of the two reforms bore striking similarities. In each case there was a university president with substantial philanthropic connections; and independent hospital; and a localist medical faculty. In both cases, these groups sought unsuccessfully to organize until Flexner entered and redefined the situation according to his own policies and the foundation boards enforced that redefinition. However, in contrast to the Flexner cavalry charge in Chicago, the New York case became the organizational equivalent of trench warfare, lasting into the 1920s. Nevertheless, Flexner achieved a not inconsiderable triumph at Columbia. He remained uncompromising even when his old benefactor Pritchett urged him to yield, and he captained a wider coalition through a longer series of negotiations than he ever had previously.

The Columbia University medical school had sought an affiliation with a teaching hospital for some time before Flexner came on the scene. Founded in 1807, the College of Physicians and Surgeons (P&S) was one of the oldest medical schools in the United States, its very name redolent of the medieval guild organization of medicine. Nominally affiliated with Columbia University in 1860, it remained basically an independent school until a stronger union was formed in 1891. This merger was part of a movement which saw donations from the Vanderbilt family for construction of a new school and outpatient clinic on the west side of midtown; subsequent changes included informal use of Roosevelt Hospital and the adoption of a four-year curriculum. When the main university campus

was moved to the Upper West Side, minds turned toward a similar relocation and strengthening of the medical school.[22]

A Roosevelt Hospital trustee interested in such plans was Edward S.
Harkness. Edward's father, Stephen V. Harkness, had been a distiller,
grain merchant, and banker in central Ohio in the 1860s when he was
approached by another food trader for financial backing for ventures in
the Pennsylvania oil fields. Thus the elder Harkness became one of the
original members of John D. Rockefeller's Standard Oil Trust. His marriage childless, Edward Harkness began to turn his mind toward possible
uses of his wealth beyond his established support of Yale, and in 1908 he
offered to construct a new Roosevelt Hospital if it were to formally affiliate with P&S. The Roosevelt board twice turned down the offer, in 1908
and 1910, largely because of loyalty to some members of the hospital staff
who felt a rivalry with Columbia faculty members.[23]

Columbia president Nicholas Murray Butler wasted no time and wrote
Harkness the day after the second refusal that "perhaps you will give me
the privilege of saying to you that I know it to be entirely possible to
carry out, if you are so disposed, at once and in connection with another
Hospital, the purposes and policy which you have in mind to support."[24]
Butler had already conferred with Presbyterian Hospital representatives
and felt that they would be responsive to Harkness. The next month,
Harkness resigned from the Roosevelt board, joined the Presbyterian, and
within a week made the same offer to his new colleagues.[25] Harkness not
only would provide the cost of building and equipping a 150-bed surgical
pavilion and laboratories but also promised on behalf of an anonymous
donor (in fact his mother) $1.3 million to be held in trust "to be use ex-
clusively towards support of the scientific and educational work connected
with the Hospital," the income to be paid to Columbia for its in-hospital
work. The proposal was accepted with alacrity, and on April 25, 1911,
an agreement was concluded with Columbia which provided for all of
Harkness's conditions: hospital staff nomination by the university, increased laboratory facilities, wards to be used for teaching purposes. To
superintend the agreement a joint administrative board was created composed of Columbia and Presbyterian representatives and the keepers of
the flame of medical reform—the presidents of Johns Hopkins and the
Rockefeller Institute or their appointees.[26]

The next step was to give geographical expression to the administrative union, and reconnaissance of local real estate took four years. After the New York Highlanders departed for future glory in the Bronx as the Yankees, the site of their former Manhattan ballpark became available. An option was purchased by Harkness who made clear to Butler "the probable disinclination of the Hospital Managers to the new site without assurance from Columbia . . . to move [the medical school] to this new site." Confident of Columbia's intentions, Harkness purchased a further option so each institution could raise its half of the $1.5 million price.[27]

In August Butler averred that he was having trouble raising money, and as the second option expiration approached, Harkness began to doubt Butler's sedulousness, feeling that Columbia was not taking sufficient initiative in raising funds. P&S dean Walter Lambert expressed to Butler the hope that "the option will not be allowed to lapse and also not be allowed to fall entirely on the shoulders of Mr. Harkness."[28] But Butler did not meet the deadline. "I do not need to tell you," Harkness wrote to Butler, "how distressed and disappointed I am over the present situation." While the philanthropist had not expected Columbia to raise all the money, he had hoped that the university would make the small initial payment and put a mortgage on the property, or secure funds "through the formation of a syndicate of gentlemen" who would carry the obligation for a time.[29]

Harkness let it be known to members of the Columbia faculty that he felt that Butler was not playing fair with him. The philanthropist felt that in an interview the president had given the impression of wholehearted cooperation and willingness to go into debt, then reneged in order to compel the hospital (i.e., Harkness) to purchase the property by itself. Dean Lambert felt that this was not entirely the case, but expressed worry to Butler that the "mutual misunderstanding between two corporate bodies" was "acute" and must be rectified lest Harkness lose interest in the plan and withdraw his offer of donating to Columbia the principal of the hospital's research and education fund of which the school now had use of the interest. "I do not need to emphasize the serious predicament in which Columbia and the College of Physicians and Surgeons would be placed if such an unfortunate result should come to pass."[30]

Butler was indignant and unafraid. Harkness's charges, the president asserted, were "an absolute illusion . . . quite baseless. . . . The position of the University has been perfectly clear and perfectly definite from the beginning, and there has never at any time been any misunderstanding on our part, nor have we given just ground for any misunderstanding."[31] Qualification and understatement were not among Butler's skills, but behind his almost reckless attitude was an accurate analysis of Harkness's determination. The philanthropist would not allow the project to fail and had in fact purchased a third option. Butler approached Pritchett about a possible grant from the Carnegie Corporation and was sufficiently encouraged to arrange a purchase date with the Presbyterian board.[32] It was a logical move: Butler was a trustee of both the Carnegie Foundation for the Advancement of Teaching and the Carnegie Endowment for International Peace and fancied himself an intimate of Carnegie himself. But despite Butler's "confident expectation" and the backing of Pritchett and Elihu Root, the corporation did not take up the proposal.[33] Butler was annoyed; the Columbia trustees, he insisted, "do not wish again to find themselves in the embarrassing position in which they were unwillingly placed during the past few weeks"[34] and would not act again until money was firmly in hand. Harkness and the hospital board were also upset, and since Butler had not informed them of the name of the intended donor, they became more distrustful.

These conflicts and delays frustrated others concerned with the project. "It is not conceivable to me," wrote Presbyterian board member Robert W. de Forest, "that the big, broad men who control the policies of both Columbia and the Presbyterian Hospital should think of each other or act toward one another otherwise than on common terms of confidence in each other's sincerity of purpose and sense of vision. There are probably small men of narrow views, on both boards but we need not open our ears to what they say."[35] Dean Lambert suggested that the negotiations might be improved by including the faculty. "The situation seems to present, not a contract between two parties, but really a three-cornered agreement." Lambert felt that the medical faculty's participation could help settle "scientific" questions. A similar proposal to enlarge the scope of the reform process was to amalgamate into one great medical center the schools of Columbia and Cornell and the Presbyterian and New York Hospitals. This possibility was active throughout 1916 and 1917, and Butler manipulated it just as he did all others.[36] In such an uncertain situation, the more concrete the university's position, the more leverage

Butler had over other parties. His goal was to create a unity in principle and leave specifics for later consideration when he could deal from a stronger position.

The difficulty of achieving a local consensus was the occasion for Flexner's entry into the situation. Rockefeller junior himself approached Harkness "with a view to seeing whether he would be interested in having worked out some comprehensive plan." If full-time were to be included in such a plan, Mr. Junior (as he was known to Rockefeller staffers) felt that the cooperation of both the GEB and the Rockefeller Foundation "was not improbable." Rockefeller suggested that Flexner could prepare "the ideal plan for medical education in New York." Harkness responded that he was "only too happy" to have such assistance as he "was groping in the dark, seeking expert advice."[37] A few days later, Butler, aware of the Rockefeller interest in the prospect, also solicited GEB participation.[38]

Flexner later suggested that in spite of what he felt was Butler's culpable ignorance about the workings of Columbia, he actually had great affection for the university president, whom he characterized as "a Tammany politician,"[39] a sobriquet which accurately captured not only the difference between himself and Butler but also the historical moment they shared. Butler's administrative style had several similarities to that of the municipal political machine: an incrementalist approach rather than a schematized agenda; a reliance on personal trust and deference rather than on abstract rules; and a scrupulous care not to become entangled in extraneous controversies.

In contrast, Flexner's modus operandi, superficially at least, eliminated these factors and substituted "policy" and "program" as the basic forms of discourse. Flexner shifted the question from one of institutional deal making to one of overall policy. Columbia was put on the defensive. Flexner maintained that Columbia should have a simple, unified alliance with the Presbyterian Hospital, which he complimented on its eagerness to reconstruct and reorganize to accommodate clinical teaching and research. The university should, he recommended, abandon all relations with other hospitals and reconstitute its faculty on the full-time basis while reducing enrollment.[40]

Butler and Dean Lambert at first underestimated the deadly importance of the report's specific recommendations and accepted it as already given that Rockefeller support would be forthcoming. As they became disabused of that notion, the difficulty of their situation became apparent. Butler and the Columbia faculty objected to the full-time plan, yet they proved unable to respond to Flexner's challenge in any way except that which tended to prove Flexner's point concerning the need for reform. As the discussions were proceeding, Lambert started a campaign to secure the school's surgery chair for his brother Adrian.[41] This was too much for even the conciliatory Pritchett to bear.

Pritchett had confidentially urged Butler to accept Lambert's offer to remove himself from the deanship. Lambert's efforts to secure the surgery professorship for his brother had made him "one of the hard difficulties to overcome" in changing the practitioner complexion of the school.[42] Butler's reply was typically categorical and obtuse: "My deliberate conclusion is that Dean Lambert is necessary to the complete success of the medical center project, and no one could take his place in it." Particularly important to Butler was the "earnest" support Lambert enjoyed among the alumni and New York medical profession, considerations decidedly irrelevant to Flexner and those who shared his views.[43] The surgery chair was a crucial problem because it highlighted another embarrassing facet of the College of Physicians and Surgeons; the medical faculty retained the right, unique in the university, to elect its members. No presidential or trustee approval was required, as it was for other appointments in other schools and departments. The seeming nepotism and mediocrity of Adrian Lambert's appointment suggested how such independence could be abused. Butler agreed with Pritchett that change of that provision was necessary, but did not seem to understand how singularly upsetting it was to the foundations.

The new format for the negotiations made Butler and Lambert increasingly bitter. The dean felt that the hospital board was "woefully ignorant of all education matters," an ignorance compounded by their misplaced trust in Flexner as "the greatest living expert on medical education."[44] He urged Butler to ignore the report and add a faculty committee to the negotiating process. Butler, however, was in no position to come to Lambert's aid: the Presbyterian committee, of which Harkness was a member, demanded his removal from the Columbia side of the negotiations. In addition, the hospital board, wary of the ruling faculty clique, now demanded that they share in control over hospital appointments. Flexner supported this position, even though it conflicted with his expressed ideal of university control.[45]

Butler was adamant that the university would not yield its (dubious) control of appointments "either as a matter of law or as a matter of policy."[46] As an escape from the confines of the Flexner program, he appealed to Pritchett for Carnegie Corporation support of an affiliation with Lenox Hill Hospital.[47] Pritchett, eager for the foundations to do something for New York medical education, was inclined to go along with Butler despite misgivings about the faculty arrangements. When Butler succeeded in obtaining some modification of the faculty rights, Pritchett urged the GEB to support this new union. It was, he wrote, "not an institutional question, but one rather to be settled upon the fundamental needs of medicine."[48] Flexner, of course, saw institutional and medical questions as complementary rather than dichotomous problems, and the board declined participation. To do otherwise would have meant abandoning Harkness and encouraging end runs around board positions. Flexner, aware of the limitations of the Carnegie budget and of Pritchett's authority, knew it was doubtful that the corporation would act on the Lenox Hill proposition independently.

Pritchett became upset with the board's studied adherence to abstraction. As the negotiations took on an increasingly legalistic character, Flexner submitted formal digests of conferences for Pritchett's approval. The Carnegie president was cautious. While he agreed with the "fundamental notion" of the full-time plan, he did not favor Flexner's absolutism.[49] "I am inclined to think," he wrote, "that when medicine becomes academic it will have weaknesses quite as serious, although perhaps different, from those which it had under the practitioner regime."[50] He himself was "becoming each year more distrustful of educational specifics," he told Flexner.[51] The idea of a contract (such as that which Hopkins had agreed to) bothered him particularly; it was "a questionable proceeding" which he feared "will sometime in the future bring upon all of us a kind of criticism difficult to answer."[52]

But the GEB was the essential lynchpin of any arrangement, and Flexner was unwilling to compromise. Columbia thus returned chastened to the Presbyterian negotiations.[53] As demanded by Harkness, Butler withdrew from the process in favor of William Barclay Parsons, chairman of the university's trustees. Lambert was replaced as dean by William Darrach, a personal friend of Harkness. The Columbia team agreed to the full-time plan, and Darrach drew up a memorandum on the subject in complete accord with the Flexnerian outlook.[54] Only seeming details remained to be worked out. Their resolution, however, would produce further conflict in the 1920s.

Flexner was occasionally distracted from his institution building by the need to rhetorically defend the full-time plan. The initial spate of opposition to the plan was easily portrayed as negative and self-serving. The opposition emphasized three issues: professional autonomy, the danger of creating a special caste, and university integrity. The first had a particularly hollow ring and was quickly driven from the intellectual field.[55] The second and third had more substance, even if they could be manipulated by reactionary premises. The second argument was founded on the "indefiniteness" concept: that the practice and knowledge of medicine had an element which could be only experientially acquired as naturally encountered. Medical wisdom, the argument ran, could not be reduced to abstract data or produced under artificial conditions, i.e., the hospital or laboratory.[56]

As the plan began to be established, an attack came from an unexpected quarter. After a considerable search, Theodore C. Janeway had been appointed the first full-time professor of medicine at Johns Hopkins in 1914. Called from New York where both he and his father had been distinguished clinicians and practitioners, Janeway gave up his community and practice to be part of a new experiment which seemed to promise much. He became partially disillusioned with full-time however, and shortly before his sudden death in 1917 he voiced his unease to a meeting of the Association of American Universities.[57]

Although his presentation was something of a grab bag of positions from the full-time debate, Janeway hit two themes which were at the heart of the Flexner perspective: organization, and the career path. Science was vital, Janeway maintained, but medicine and surgery were "practical arts as well as applied sciences." Since "professors of medicine and surgery are not set to make physiologists or pathologists of their students," any career path in medical education must include an opportunity to obtain mastery of the practical art. Janeway had made the question just the reverse of Flexner's, i.e., not how to guarantee science but how to assure the acquisition of the art. A small private practice was the only way, Janeway answered. Without the incentive of fees, few men would bother to see private patients at distant offices, and the alternative of hospital practice for fees—so called "geographic full-time"—was overly commercialist: "its methods tend to approximate those of successful business and its standards are those of commercial ethics." The chief victims of absolute full-time, according to Janeway, were the younger men. Flexner saw the coming generation as a salvation, growing up as they did uninfected by the gold bug. Janeway wondered how "the younger assistants who grow up in [the plan's] somewhat cloistered seclusion shall became masters of their art."[58]

Janeway's defection from the full-time ranks caused a flurry of concern among the plan's supporters. It was conceded that he had pointed out some real dangers. The full-time head might "be swamped by the details of departmental and hospital administration."[59] There were some distorting effects to hospital practice: Yale dean George Blumer admitted that "there is less opportunity in a hospital to develop a certain kind of skill in handling people which is more quickly developed in private practice."[60] But these problems could be dealt with by having a competent hospital superintendent and careful attention to the nuances of clinical training. It was furthermore agreed that the impact on the rising generation was the crucial issue: "it will not be until younger men uninfluenced by the older traditions have had an opportunity to work under the new system that we shall really know whether it is a success or not."[61]

Conscious of the need to provide for the coming generation of academic clinicians, Flexner lobbied for funds with which to proceed to the next step of his program. World War I provided him with a good opportunity. In a memo of June 1919 he stated that the war had conclusively demonstrated the shortcomings in American medical education, in spite of the "remarkable rapidity with which medical science had advanced in recent years." Moreover, the way to conduct an effective medical school was well known. "Under conditions, the time is ripe for an organized and progressive effort to bring medical education throughout the United States to the level made possible by the recent progress of medical science. . . . The General Education Board is in a position to direct a large work of this kind." It would be costly work. Flexner estimated that the minimum cost of a modern medical school and hospital was $6 million, and in all $200 million was needed to raise the fifteen likely schools to passable levels. If the board were to receive $30 million to be used—principal and interest—in this effort, Flexner was confident that its judicious application would stimulate the remaining $170 million.[62]

The energizing effect of the war on the Rockefeller boards provided Flexner with an organizational as well as a rhetorical advantage. The plight of the Belgians, the Armenians, the doughboys, and others caught up in the cataclysm occasioned a quantum leap in the size of gifts by both the Foundation and the Rockefellers personally. After the war, Rockefeller senior continued this pattern with a series of large presentations to his boards for specific purposes: $50 million to the Foundation for public health and medical science; $50 million to the GEB to aid salaries in higher education; and, in September 1919, $20 million (later increased to $50 million) also to the GEB "to be used for the advancement of medical education in the United States in the discretion of your Board of Directors."[63]

In a memorandum to the board of December 1919, Flexner proposed that the gift be used for the purpose he had outlined in his earlier memo: a more general improvement of medical education than the board had been practicing. Again, there was a combination of dogmatism and apparent flexiblity. The United States was diverse and, for the time being, "the same type of medical education cannot be everywhere realized"; thus the funds should be used for "improvement rather than standardization," and the board should "vary the form and object of our cooperation, according to local conditions." On the other hand, Flexner reiterated that "modern medicine is . . . a definite logical conception," and the board's actions should always be informed by ultimate goals.[64]

This novel broad-mindedness on the subject of school organization was not a retreat from the conceptions which underlay the full-time plan, but rather an effort to gird the scheme. The top schools, Flexner asserted, were turning out more teachers than could find places. "That is, we have and are developing teachers, but we have too few well-equipped and well-financed institutions to utilize them." The system of medical education that Flexner had so far helped create was incomplete, an apex without a base. The reform of the elite schools had fostered a new career ethos and training pattern. Flexner now wanted to assure that there were sufficient career opportunities: a second tier of schools in his network would provide them. In a crucial policy change, Flexner sought to aid public as well

as private institutions. "It is evident . . . that if Mr. Rockefeller's benefaction is to be made generally effective, cooperation with state and
municipal universities is necessary." The "local conditions" he had in
mind referred to the predominance of tax-supported schools in the South
and West.[65]

Flexner's proposal for the accommodation of regional diversity was
consistent with the stand he had taken against the AMA's Council on
Medical Education. Both he and Pritchett had advocated that the council's
grading standards should take account of the educational underdevelopment of the South. Flexner had excoriated the "folly and unwisdom" of
the council's inflexible policy, which he felt was based on "complete ignorance of the real facts of the situation." Feeling his power, he had threatened to "organize a revolt which will practically detach the south from
your field of operations at the present" if the council did not change its
policies.[66]

That his proposal in no way represented a withdrawal from his
staunchest support of the full-time plan was indicated by a memo Flexner
composed for George Vincent, the president of the Rockefeller Foundation.[67] Vincent had urged that "to attempt to impose a single and inflexible standard upon institutions which vary widely in their stages of development and environments would be a serious mistake."[68] Speaking of
both the GEB and the Rockefeller Foundation, Flexner agreed that "these
boards are above all things practical and they realize that conditions in
this country . . . are not sufficiently far advanced to make it possible to
standardize medical education or to press forward too fast towards the still
distant ideal."[69] However, to Flexner, ideals were not idle metaphysical
speculations but vital organizational tropisms:

> First, ideals are valuable because by contrast they make administrators and
> teachers conscious of defects and stimulate them to remedy their shortcomings.
> Second, ideals are valuable because they can be approximately attained by the
> most highly favored institutions and from these institutions can go forth teachers
> and practitioners of medicine who can improve and still further stimulate institu-
> tions with which they may be connected and communities in which they reside.[70]

Elite schools were therefore essential, and Flexner felt that there was "no
danger that these schools or resources . . . can be created too rapidly" and
"no reason" why the elite schools "should not be held to the severest

standards from every point of view."[71] These elite schools would then supply the second tier of upgraded schools with idealistic scientific teachers.

Flexner made such an elaborate argument because he was certain that extending his program to cover public institutions would provoke conflict. He was conjuring with one of the basal problems of the American polity: the relative limits of public and private authority. The original ideals of scientific philanthropy partook of the antigovernment prejudice of many progressive reformers who decried the corruption and inefficiency of public agencies. But as private organizations began to help redefine the public agenda and staff public agencies, the dichotomy became problematic.

Foundations were among the most prominent of all private agencies, and their potential power made the problem particularly keen. Within the GEB the conflict was both generational and ideological. Gates had been reared on Manchesterian economics, and he saw public and private as mutually exclusive categories. For him, the necessity of maintaining a rigid distinction between the public and private spheres defined the philanthropic role: foundations were to strengthen private institutions and not to stray into the growing thicket of tax-supported enterprises. Flexner saw the issue as just the other way around: the integrity of foundation policies (in this case the development of a new elite in scientific medicine) demanded the involvement of both public and private agencies. To him, public and private were adjoining faces of the same process of social development. If his program for the national reconstruction of medical education was to achieve its aims, he would have to overcome Gates's opposition.[72]

Flexner therefore made sure the ground was well prepared before he made a specific proposal for the support of a public institution. In December 1920, he inspected the Medical Department of the University of Iowa in Iowa City. Eleven years previously, during his tour in preparation for the Carnegie Foundation report, Flexner had found a dismal picture: "facilities were inadequate, personnel inferior, administration loose and inefficient, terms low, and fee-splitting practically universal." By 1920, conditions had improved considerably, particularly the leadership of the school. The new university president, Walter Jessup, was "a perfectly corking fellow, solid, hard headed, averse to expansion, determined to improve what the university now has in strength." A new state board of education with "absolutely no trace of politics" had been appointed. Localism in the appointment of clinical heads had ended, and the laboratory men and women were on a full-time regime.[73]

Despite these favorable omens, the lag in adjusting the plant to the intellectual and idealistic resources of the school worried Flexner. The university planned to develop a new site for the medical school piecemeal, but the GEB secretary worried that this "very unfortunate policy" might "destroy team work and impair the momentum which the reform movement has gained." Given the depressed state of agriculture, the Iowa legislature was reluctant to put up at once the entire $5 million required for new construction. "I raised the question as to whether an inducement in the shape of an outside contribution would do the trick." The university authorities agreed that it might.[74]

Flexner was tentative in bringing such a proposition before the GEB and the Rockefeller Foundation (which would have to cooperate in a project so large). The Iowans were edgy. W. R. Boyd, chairman of the finance committee of the state board of education, did not want "to even seem to overurge you on any matter," but wrote in November 1921 that the "out of plumb" business situation made it "an exceedingly critical time . . . if this College of Medicine ever needed help it needs it now."[75] But arranging the strongest possible case for Iowa took time. While not requiring the school to adopt the absolute clinical full-time policy, Flexner urged the medical school dean to avoid any implication that the board's proposed gift would support private practice. This and other measures would assure the GEB of the state's sincerity with respect to carrying out the board's intentions.[76]

On May 24, 1922, the executive committee of the Rockefeller Foundation pledged $750,000 to the project provided the GEB would pledge an equal amount. The board met the following day but "was unable to conclude its discussion of the matter," and consideration of the question was put off until its October meeting.[77]

Gates had been accustomed to playing the role of devil's advocate in questioning proposed gifts, but on this issue his opposition was genuine and thoroughgoing. Flexner hoped to resolve the question in a "quiet discussion" before the next meeting. He assumed, incorrectly, that Gates was opposed only to the lack of complete full-time at the Iowa school. Flexner was anxious about confronting someone "for whose wisdom and achievements I have the profoundest possible admiration," and so he painted the issue as "merely one of procedure," i.e., how to ensure the agreed goal of "clinical development on educational lines." He tried to persuade Gates that "full-fledged full-time" could come to Iowa only after the development of the physical foundation.[78]

Gates's opposition, however, ran deeper than the question of the full-time plan. The October meeting of the GEB was held at the Gedney Farms Hotel in White Plains, N.Y., one of the favored spots for periodic philanthropic retreats from the workaday distractions of Wall Street. Aware of the coming confrontation, some Rockefeller advisers with divided loyalties tried to avoid the meeting, but Gates specifically requested attendance at what he himself prophetically termed his "swan song." At the meeting, Gates made a "strong and moving appeal" in his best homiletic style.[79] His composition was a medley of scientific philanthropy, scientism, and political economy, all grounded in the common-sense philosophy he had imbibed as a college student at the University of Rochester. Since he detected in the Iowa proposal "a drift . . . far from our original policies," he wanted to review the GEB's "fundamental principles . . . to force us to take our bearings anew." His bedrock premise was the dramatic promise of science: "universal in scope, all embracing, eternal." Since the promotion of science was difficult and costly, bold leadership was necessary. "It is our mission, a heaven sent opportunity reserved now to us alone, to increase the light which will ultimately illumine all mankind, light which once got, will shine we hope forever, and render the earth a more tolerable place for the countless myriads of our future." Gates felt that the only way medicine could become a science was through the creation of "creative schools" of national and international prominence which "will constantly work along the boundaries of medicine."[80]

Iowa, Gates maintained, could in no way be one of those creative schools. "To call it national, to speculate on it as prospectively national is to take a gambler's chance with our money." The location of the school was unpromising: the town was small even for Iowa, and the new site was removed from the heart of the university. The faculty was in a poor position: "the laboratory men are so shamefully ill-paid that one blushes to read the salary list," and substantial practice by the clinical men was still permitted—"the State being unwilling to buy their whole time." Moreover, Gates doubted that the school was even necessary. The Uni-

versity of Iowa was surrounded by schools which already supplied a portion of the state's doctors and could easily supply them all.[81]

The core of Gates's brief against the proposed appropriation was "the
fundamental constitution of the school and the nature of its control." The
GEB was being asked to fund a project for which Iowans were unwilling
to tax themselves. "If the old women in their sunbonnets who gather the
fruit of the Iowa henroosts, were to lay aside one chicken and one egg,
from each 13, for the great medical reconstruction in Iowa City, that
project would be financed, not in ten years nor in two, but less than one."
Gates accused the state and the university of conspiring to conceal from
the GEB their true purpose. The new site was made necessary not by the
requirements of medical education but by the expansion of other parts of
the university into the old building and by the need of a new hospital to
accommodate county welfare cases from around the state which law mandated be sent to Iowa City. To Gates, the university was not in any way
autonomous but merely an arm of the state. He conceded that while the
university president "knows reasonably well what a modern medical
school ought to be," he and his associates, "however high their ideals, are
perfectly helpless to carry them out." Legislative and popular control
meant that the school would always be overenrolled and never able to
organize itself with the rigor and selectivity which marked the creative
schools.[82]

In response, Flexner stood Gates's reasoning on its head. A grant such
as he was proposing "does not weaken the reliance of the state university
upon taxation, but really increases it," since levies would still provide the
operating expenses for the enlarged university. Gates's objection that
Iowa could never be a "national" school was founded on a notion of
nationalism the frame of reference of which was the institution's functions rather than its representativeness: his was the nationalism of the
metropolis. Flexner held no brief for prideful localism, but he accepted
that his national system would reflect the nation's diversity. The practical
result of limiting foundation cooperation to private institutions, he pointed
out, would be to focus exclusively on the East. By including state institutions in the program, "we not only escape bureaucratic uniformity but we
obtain a wholesome competition."[83] Whereas Gates conceived of the state
university as a dependent creation of the legislature, Flexner saw the

foundations, universities, and the state as distinct but functionally related institutions:

> Cities and states are all rich enough to do these things without foundation aid, as far as mere wealth is concerned. They don't do it, because they haven't been educated up to it, and the most effective way to educate them is to stimulate them by a conditional gift. This strengthens the university authorities whether they deal with individuals or states.[84]

However painful the conflict, all other members of the board in attendance supported Flexner.[85] The alliance between foundations and universities which Flexner was promoting was already reflected in the careers of the board members. Eleven of the sixteen board members in 1922 were or had been employed by the Rockefeller philanthropies: an overlapping seven of the sixteen had had substantial careers in higher education. Men like Jerome Greene, Harry Pratt Judson, Anson Phelps Stokes, and Edwin A. Alderman had seen in their lifetime both the transformation of colleges into universities and the growing homogeneity of state and private institutions. To their ears, Gates's Dickensian views must have had an antique ring. Gates's conception of philanthropy as the patron of worthy enterprises gave way to Flexner's view of foundations as the entrepreneurial force in the creation of new policies.

The Iowa university authorities also solicited support from the Carnegie Corporation, but with less success. On the Carnegie board, Elihu Root held views similar to Gates's. Pritchett also shared that attitude to some extent and, as always, was also worried about the legitimacy of the philanthropic foundation. He feared that the act of making a conditional grant to a sovereign state was "capable of by-products quite different from those that are intended."[86] More practically, the corporation was without any spare funds.[87] The Iowans were "sick at heart" at being unable to get the additional funds they had counted on but resolved to go ahead.[88] "Our faith and credit are involved, just as yours are," Flexner exhorted them, "so that we shall sink or swim together."[89] He urged them to adopt clinical full-time so that "Iowa will take the lead among state universities just as the Johns Hopkins has taken it among the endowed universities." Toward that end, he urged the authorities to consult with Hopkins experts in regard to building and personnel plans.[90]

Gates remained unreconciled. Flexner offered to keep him informed of

Iowa developments, knowing that "you will rejoice if Jessup and his associates succeed in their determination to reach a new level in state supported medical education."[91] Gates was still astonished by the change which had taken place: "It is amazing. How could you! You have never squarely met one of my arguments."[92] At subsequent board meetings, Gates futilely reiterated his stand against gifts to public institutions, and the episode became the filter through which he began to conceive of the history of the boards. While always accorded a respectful hearing, he could no longer dominate the boards.[93]

But in freeing his program from the drag anchor of Gates, Flexner was in danger of losing some of his own moorings. The program he was constructing rested in part on the pro-science, anticommercialist perspective which Gates and Flexner shared. While the younger generation did not comprehend Gates's fear of the state university, they also did not fear the university's redescent into commercialism as Flexner did. This was an attitudinal gap which would become more apparent throughout the decade.

Flexner's victory over Gates was the zenith of his effectiveness as a manager of organized knowledge. He had nationalized his program and demonstrated his authority. By 1922 he had put in place almost all the essentials of a network of reformed medical schools which he hoped would create a new discipline of clinical science. Even in an age of reform, professionalization, and national networking, his was a spectacular achievement. Flexner saw his work as vindication of American democracy. As he wrote to his wife in 1916:

> We have no considerable experience of culture except in connection with a leisure class. For culture in the sense above described/music, art, and literature/has needed two conditions—(1) sympathy, (2) support; & both sympathy and support have been forthcoming from people of leisure, who were able to be patrons of culture,—sometimes very directly (as at the Court of Weimar or in Florence), at other times indirectly, but not the less essentially.
>
> Does it follow that unless this relationship can continue, culture will fail? I think not necessarily. The instincts & needs that have blossomed in art, literature & music are still *there*. They are going to crave and find expression & satisfaction, like other forms of energy. How they are to be expressed—is another matter. What is to be substituted for the support & sympathy of a leisure class, I do not know & cannot be fairly expected to tell. For democracy is an experiment; democracy leaves unlimited leeway for innovative & invention. And among other forms that democracy must try to furnish is a form under which the profoundest needs of the human spirit may be satisfied.

It is conceivable that a hundred years ago someone might have said: Higher education and pure science cannot be prosecuted without a leisure class, for masses cannot be expected to sympathize with & to support either. Well, democracy is finding not one, but several ways to support higher education and science, because they are profound needs that simply *will* be recognized. In the same way, democracy will experiment with other forms of culture. We have no right to predict the downfall of culture or to assert its entire dependence on a leisure class, until democracy has had a fair chance to show what it can do.[94]

That someone who was associated with the wealthiest man in the world should be worried about the absence of a leisure class might seem ironic, but Flexner was concerned with social leadership and not just the bulging purse. He was vigorously and single-mindedly trying to use Rockefeller's money to provide that leadership in medical education. His characterization of his work as part of the democratic process was premature. The management of his now-nationalized structure of medical education would be the real test of the viability of his type of leadership in a political culture which demanded representativeness and distrusted power.

Frederick T. Gates, 1923

William H. Welch

Simon Flexner

Henry Smith Pritchett

Charles W. Eliot

Wallace Buttrick, 1919

Raymond B. Fosdick

Alan Gregg

4 The Perils of Management

Abraham Flexner entered the 1920s with a mixture of satisfaction at the growth of academic medicine in the United States and zealous resolve to nurture that growth further. "The developments in the field of medical education are little short of phenomenal," he wrote to Charles W. Eliot in 1921. With the $50 million that John D. Rockefeller, Sr., had earmarked in 1919 specifically for medical education, it would be possible to continue the momentum of reform. But difficulties lay ahead. Clinicians, it seemed, were not "made of quite as stern stuff as the men who made academic Physics and academic Chemistry and academic Pathology." Accordingly, Flexner vowed to be a "ringing and persuasive voice . . . raised in behalf of academic ideals in the field of clinical medicine and research."[1] He did not, however, anticipate a merely oratorical program. "These are critical times in medical education," he wrote to Rockefeller junior the same year, "for the effort to bring medical education up to the level of medical research involves extension of facilities and elevation of ideals, which can be accomplished only as larger means are available."[2]

Flexner was in a strong position to carry out his campaign, as he effectively dominated the private system of support for medical education. Not only did he have full control of the resources of the General Education Board, but he had also tailored the medical education program of the Rockefeller Foundation to dovetail with his. Together these two foundations provided 60 percent of the foundation aid for medical education. No other foundation could provide a significant alternative to Flexner's program. The young Commonwealth Fund (founded in 1918) was not eager to compete with him. On the Carnegie Corporation board, Pritchett still had hopes of mounting a medical education program but was unable to match Flexner's resources or his organizational agility.

Flexner's very success had changed the nature of his task: he now had the responsibility of administering a system as well as extending it. The schools Flexner had reformed required continual financial assistance and oversight. Opponents sharpened their criticism of his plans, and new agendas for medical education were put forth and required response. Even the enthusiasm of his allies in the clinical science elite occasionally bedeviled him. His rhetorical skill and political instinct were sorely tested by his new burdens. Flexner's conception of the proper organization of academic knowledge did not prepare him for these managerial demands. The single-minded determination he displayed in the founding of his network was something of a liability in the adminstration of it.

Flexner's administrative trials had an important audience. At the headquarters of the Rockefeller boards at 61 Broadway, the withdrawal of John D. Rockefeller, Jr., from the presidency of the Rockefeller Foundation after the Ludlow incident and the quantum leap in philanthropic giving during World War I had opened up new opportunities to a rising generation of managers within the boards. Men such as George E. Vincent, Trevor Arnett, Edwin R. Embree, and Raymond B. Fosdick were struggling to define their roles amid a thicket of inherited programs and commitments which reflected the naive hopefulness of their predecessors' Progressivism.

Flexner had an ambivalent relation to this group—a relation which expressed his position on the generational cusp. He had molded the predispositions of the founding generation—the Rockefellers, Gates, Pritchett, and Buttrick—to his particular plans, but he was not their full partner. When Buttrick retired as president of the General Education Board, Flexner was, somewhat surprisingly, not chosen as his successor. Neither, however, was he of the new generation: his experience was dramatically different from theirs. His career was one of reforming institutions. The members of the new generation made their careers through institutions. At the offices of the boards, he was respected for his achievements and feared for his sharp tongue. The Rockefeller program staff met for lunch, usually each Tuesday. This was one of the few occasions where there could be freewheeling exchange and discussion of ideas instead of the cramped position-paper format of the boards' formal decision making. It was clear to his companions at these affairs that Flexner did not suffer lightly those he took to be fools. Those wounded at lunch were unlikely to cross him later in committees.[3]

Although Flexner could be openly contemptuous of the abilities and ideals of the younger managers, in avuncular moods he would subject them to his waspish tutelage. In 1921, he began a "correspondence course" on "this game which I have had the opportunity to play with other people's money this last ten years or more," with Embree, then the Rockefeller Foundation secretary.[4] Flexner sketched for Embree what he felt was the crucial role of foundations as planners in a democracy: "the soundness of reform can never be left to the mercy of majority vote, else the human race would still be in the state of cave men . . . votes must be weighed not counted." Revealingly, Flexner was impatient with the very mechanism which had lifted him to national prominence: the fact-laden survey of the Progressive Era. "*Discipule* [sic] *carissimo*," he addressed Embree, "you can't settle such questions [as the worth of the full-time plan] on the basis of evidence, because nobody has ever studied the evidence and no sensible person would take the time to do it . . . a decision must be reached on a rational basis."[5] Flexner felt that such decisions should be reached quickly among the like-minded: "I know perfectly well that in medical education, as in theology, souls are saved in twenty minutes if at all."[6]

Flexner cautioned Embree that in 1921 American medical education remained a "complex, uneven, hopeful thing, needing stimulus and assistance, now here, now there, but requiring above all constant and wise leadership." Thus, he felt, the full-time system had to be carefully nurtured "in the few medical schools that are going to lead in medical investigation, in the creation of hospital standards and in the training of teachers." If such a new elite could be constructed, it could gradually be expanded beyond the "inner group" through fellowships and support of selected individuals at other schools.[7] In doing all this, Flexner resolved to maintain a distinction which was clear to him at least, if not always to others:

> We [the foundations] have no right to criticise what institutions do by way of objecting to it. They are absolutely free to do as they please. But we are in duty bound, as rational beings, to criticise in the sense of appraising what they do.[8]

Over the previous decade, the founding philanthropic generation had come to prize Flexner. Charles W. Eliot, in spite of earlier conflicts, praised

Flexner to GEB president Wallace Buttrick: "it is of the utmost importance considering the potentialities of his future career that he be encouraged."[9] Buttrick had developed considerable affection for Flexner. He noted that while Flexner's "moral earnestness" was evident to all, only those closest to him knew that he was actually quite "timid," with "that timidity which is so closely allied to real modesty."[10]

But the rising generation was not so appreciative. To Embree, Flexner's most striking feature was his "all consuming zeal" which brought to mind the Old Testament passage "The zeal of thy house hath eaten me up."[11] Unstated was the possibility that this managerial zeal would consume Flexner as well.

In the early 1920s, Flexner was the administrative master of all he surveyed. With his victory over Gates on the question of aid to state institutions of medical education, he administered GEB funds for medicine with unquestioned authority. He also maintained effective control over Rockefeller Foundation funds spent in the United States. The Foundation's Division of Medical Education was set up in 1920 under Richard M. Pearce. An administrative concordat among the Rockefeller boards gave exclusive initiative in American medical education to the GEB, but the Rockefeller Foundation cooperated in GEB projects.[12] Thus the Rockefeller Foundation became reluctantly embroiled in the full-time conflicts with Columbia and the University of Chicago. The Foundation's European program was roughly congruent with Flexner's. The development of full-time clinical units was the major aspect of the Foundation's gift of £1,205,000 to the University of London between 1920 and 1923.[13] But while Pearce was in favor of clinical full-time as a general idea, he was not as rigid as Flexner in its enforcement. Relations between the two directors were not easy. While Flexner would suffer no intrusion on his administrative territory, he felt an obligation to criticize Pearce's handling of his European bailiwick. On a European tour in 1924, Flexner was outraged to discover what he felt was Pearce's neglect of German medicine and upon his return mounted a campaign to have more Rockefeller Foundation aid sent in that direction. (Just the opposite of Flexner, Pearce had a personal distaste for the German academic style.) Flexner made it obvious to other members of the Rockefeller office that he was contemptuous not only of Pearce's views but also of his ability.[14]

Another medical philanthropy of the 1920s, the Commonwealth Fund, was also dominated by Flexner, albeit with curious results. The fund had been created in 1918 by Mrs. Stephen V. Harkness, the mother of Edward S. Harkness. Medical education was a logical interest for the new board: Edward Harkness, the board chairman, was already involved with Flexner in the development of the Columbia-Presbyterian Medical Center. In a very self-conscious review of possible programs, Max Farrand, the Yale historian and the fund's first director, noted that medical education and research was an area where public approval was assured and lines of procedure were clear. But it was also felt that it would be difficult for the new agency to work out an institutional definition in a field already so identified with Rockefeller work.[15] Flexner underscored that problem by suggesting to the new board, only partially in jest, that the GEB would gladly hand over its other programs to its new colleague so that the Rockefeller organization could concentrate on medical education and research.[16] Accordingly, the fund started a program in child welfare and public health, leaving the institutional support of medical education to Flexner.

Flexner's former sponsor, Henry S. Pritchett, the president of the Carnegie Foundation for the Advancement of Teaching and acting president of the Carnegie Corporation of New York from 1921 to 1923, provided the only philanthropic alternative to Flexner's policies—and it was a weak one.

Pritchett felt strongly that medical education and medical problems formed one of the few areas in which the corporation should work intensively, but the foundation's work in that line was never more than sporadic. The relation of the corporation to the other Carnegie boards remained an unsolved problem throughout the 1920s, absorbing both adminstrative energy and the corporation's scarce funds. The problems resulting from the constitution of the corporation persisted and were compounded by executive personnel difficulties. James R. Angell was chosen to be the second president of the corporation in 1920 but was in office only a year before he answered a call to assume the presidency of Yale. It was another two years before Frederick P. Keppel assumed the Carnegie presidency. By then the drastically limited resources of the corporation were the overriding issue in its management. Keppel's interest in medical programs was not equal to Pritchett's, and the corporation soon started to withdraw from that area. As the new president commented to his senior, "There is nothing more useful for humanity [than medical research and education], but there is nothing more expensive for a foundation."[17]

While Flexner reasoned downward from the lofty heights of a learned discipline, Pritchett reasoned upward from what he felt was the lowest common denominator of the problem of medical education: the average doctor. "The primary purpose of the medical school," he stated unequivocally, "is to train practitioners of the medical profession." Pritchett felt that the other medical school activities, including research, were "by-products" and that it was "essential that the professional school shall keep in view its primary purpose." Pritchett even felt that research had been overemphasized to the point where "the thing which ought to be the greatest inspiration toward good teaching, has become only too often an excuse to escape the primary duty—to teach."[18]

Pritchett was convinced that "it is clearly not possible to solve the problem of medical education in the United States by building up a small number of richly endowed and highly equipped medical schools," and so he was determined to attempt to "strengthen weak schools that sincerely seek their own improvement."[19] As was noted earlier, the impulse to aid smaller schools had both personal and principled origins. Andrew Carnegie had been partial to the efforts of smaller, less prestigious institutions, and Pritchett's father had supervised a struggling Missouri college. Pritchett was concerned that the new standards of medical education would leave many areas institutionally underserved. Pritchett had long been enthusiastic about the leadership of the University of Cincinnati, and $500,000 was given for its development. The Carnegie official swallowed his distaste for Roman Catholic education to aid in the improvement of the Marquette Medical School. The corporation aided both Vanderbilt and Tulane as a way of ensuring a southern presence in the ranks of modern medicine.[20]

But even this, the most ambitious of Pritchett's programs, was overshadowed by Flexner's campaign. Before 1920, the Carnegie Corporation made roughly $10 million in grants to medical schools; during the same period, the GEB granted almost eight times that amount. Flexner followed a Carnegie gift to Vanderbilt with several from the GEB in an attempt to build Vanderbilt into one of the "small number of richly endowed and highly equipped medical schools." Tulane and Cincinnati also figured in Flexner's program as part of his second tier of schools. Most of the corporation's $10 million went to other schools in Flexner's nascent elite: Yale, Hopkins, and Columbia.[21]

Whereas Flexner was given to occasional outbursts of hostility and threats when dealing with the organized medical profession, Pritchett tried every possible avenue of cooperation. Although he sometimes grappled with the AMA over certification of medical schools and hospitals, Pritchett was careful to give that organization liberal credit for its reform efforts. At his direction, the corporation supported the work of the American College of Surgeons in hospital upgrading and that of the National Board of Medical Examiners in fighting what he labeled the "medical tariffs" of the several states.[22] Under Pritchett's leadership grants were also made to such groups as the American Child Hygiene Association, the American Society for the Control of Cancer, and the National Health Council. Unlike Flexner, Pritchett was not interested in the promotion of a fixed policy but rather saw continuing reform as a "matter of medical and social statesmanship," and toward that end he supported the development of independent agencies in the entire medical field.[23] Pritchett wanted existing elites to cohere; he did not want to create new ones.

Pritchett was keenly interested in the vexing question of specialism. The Carnegie official realized that while specialization was an avenue for the rapid diffusion of medical advances, the proliferation of free-standing specialists was both costly and inefficient. "It seems clear," he wrote in 1922, "that the problem of graduate instruction must in the future take its place alongside the problem of instruction of candidates for the medical degree."[24] In contrast, Flexner could not sustain any significant interest in this issue, which has continued to preoccupy medical education planning since the 1920s. At one point he even suggested that it would be better to leave the support of mechanisms for specialist training to the grateful patient than to allow them to take up valuable foundation resources.[25]

However, when such gratitude came to his attention Flexner responded to it with alacrity. The founding of the Wilmer Ophthalmic Institute at Hopkins was an instance. William Holland Wilmer was the leading ophthalmologist of Washington; his practice had included several presidents. In 1922 one of his grateful patients, Mrs. Aida de Acosta Root, initiated a campaign to build and endow an institute to better accommodate Wilmer's work. This effort was meant to be a personal "tribute to the character, professional attainment and service to Humanity of Dr. William Holland Wilmer," as much as a vision of the scientific possibilities. Mrs. Root canvassed Wilmer's former patients and approached Rockefeller junior, who in 1923 directed her to Flexner. Flexner seized the opportunity to aid Hopkins, suggesting that the plan put forward by Mrs. Root (who had since become Mrs. Henry Breckinridge) was "inadequate" and what was needed was to install Wilmer in "a medical school with facilities, colleagues and students who would form a body of disciples."[26] After convincing Wilmer and his wife to move to Baltimore, Flexner began a philanthropic full-court press. With the aid of Welch, $3 million was raised, including $1.5 million from the GEB and donations from Edward Harkness, Harry Payne Whitney, and J. P. Morgan.[27]

The agreement negotiated between the Wilmer Foundation and Hopkins reflected the eagerness with which Flexner and Welch wanted to capitalize on the movement to honor the ophthalmologist. The Wilmer Institute was semi-independent, and special arrangements to benefit Wilmer himself were taken over by the university. The fees obtained from private patients were to be kept by Wilmer up to a certain limit and beyond that went to the institute and not to the university, as was the case in other departments. Opportunistically, Flexner approved in this case arrangements which he would condemn elsewhere and which would later cause friction within the medical school.[28]

Flexner was aware that the solidification of past reforms was placing new issues on the national agenda which were potential threats to his system. One such question was the distribution of physicians. The felt decline in the number of rural practicioners was blamed in some quarters on raised admission standards which, it was claimed, altered the pool of medical students. In 1924, the GEB published a study which attempted to defuse this issue. The study's authors, Lewis Mayers and Leonard V. Harrison, asserted that the lopsidedly urban distribution of physicians was related more to changing social and economic patterns than to the sheer number of medical graduates. The study contended that changing the requirements for medical school matriculation would not alter these trends but would simply produce inferior graduates. Mayers and Harrison suggested practical measures by which rural communities could lure physicians. The establishment of local hospitals, a program which the Commonwealth Fund would adopt in the 1930s, was one such measure.[29]

Another frequently made complaint was that Flexner's program aimed too high and demanded too much of both instructor and student. According to Harvey Cushing,

> Those unknown people who set the fashions and who determine the proper number of pupils that are to be taught, and the distribution of their hours, and the way they should be instructed, and how they should be examined and graded, expect something else than instruction; some of them, indeed, wield a big stick labelled "Research," which strikes terror into the rabbit-heart of many a hard driven and underpaid teacher.[30]

Drawing a metaphor from the other rapidly developing area of American life, Cushing suggested in a letter to Flexner that one could perfectly well drive a motor car without a detailed knowledge of its internal workings and that medical schools should not strive to make every student an expert mechanic.[31]

Flexner could not accept the suggestion of a two-track system of medical education akin to the English model of general practitioners and specialists. His views on the proper organization of scientific knowledge were more easily grafted onto the American social pattern of contest mobility. He replied to Cushing that his concern was for the freest possible recruitment of medical scientists for the educational elite:

> Are the large majority of doctors to be of the chauffeur type or are they to be men who can repair defects, understand fundamental theory, so as to be more than mere tinkerers and really keep up with the advance of a rapidly growing profession? I know the limitations of the human ability, human energy and time. Yet I confess I hesitate to admit that an overwhelming percentage of men practising medicine are by their training doomed to be mere chauffeurs in medicine. . . . A poor education is apt to check the development of men who under favorable stimulus might have gone on growing. In other words, there is no way of realizing who is the average man, a man that is of meagre ability who won't grow in any event. A scheme of higher education ought surely not be largely determined by his limitations.[32]

Flexner's policy was grounded in a coherent, if limited, theory of the interaction of knowledge and organizational structures. One of the chief characteristics of his vision was its fearful symmetry: it so fully justified both his goals and his methods that he could not question any aspect of it. It was this vision which gave his thought and actions the adamantine quality which made him so daring as a philanthropic policymaker. It also served as a way for him to reconcile the bureaucratic management of knowledge with his own "modest" self-image.

His policy was premised on a straightforward and comprehensive view of science:

> We do better, taking an historical view, to consider science as the persistent effort of men to purify, extend, and organize their knowledge of the world in which they live. . . . For our purposes, science may safely be treated as a developing conception, moving at different rates and with varying degrees of confidence towards the entire comprehension embodied in the mathematical formula. And in this sense we are entitled to assume not only the science of mathematics and the science of physics, but also the science of agriculture and the science of medicine.[33]

Two obvious corollaries followed when this postulate was applied to medicine: "no distinction can be made between research and practice," and there was properly "no difference in the intellectual attitude between the laboratory and the clinic."[34] To define medicine otherwise, he maintained, would be to forswear the potential of its development:

> If medicine is classified as an art, in contradistinction to a science, the practitioner is encouraged to proceed with a clear conscience on superficial or empirical lines; if, on the other hand, he is acutely conscious of a responsibility to scientific spirit and scientific method, he will almost inevitably endeavor to clarify his conceptions and to proceed more systematically in the accumulation of data, the framing of hypotheses, and the checking up of results.[35]

The proper conception of medicine was what Flexner meant by "ideals," a subject the importance of which he stressed at every opportunity. Flexner's idealism was not so much a philosophical construct as a combination of moralistic behaviorism and faith in scientific rationality. It was also a rhetorically valuable minimization of foundation influence:

> Progress depends, in the first instance, on neither money nor machinery, but on ideas,—or more accurately, on men with ideas. Men with ideas have rarely been entirely defeated—though they have been hampered or retarded—by lack of money, or the things money can procure. . . . On the other hand, lacking men with ideas, money and the things money can buy, produce little.[36]

This behavioristic idealism was the axis on which Flexner located all institutions relevant to his policies. Organization was to him at best a neutral variable and at worst an impediment to the immanent force of scientific knowledge. His goal was so to organize the universities, the professions, and the foundations that they could be frictionless conduits of "ideals."

Flexner idealized the university as "essentially a free society of students, professors, and pupils mingling naturally in the pursuit of intellectual aims."[37] The university succeeded in its aims precisely to the extent that it allowed its inhabitants to "work their own way . . . without fettering them with the deadly paraphernalia worked out for the proposed standardizing of higher degrees."[38] Similarly, he defined the professions as basically systems of organized knowledge. "A free, resourceful, and unhampered intelligence applied to problems and seeking to understand and master them,—that is in the first instance characteristic of a profession."[39] The professions were thus essentially dynamic propositions, powered by the growth of scientific knowledge. "They [the professions] need to resort to the laboratory and the seminar for a constantly fresh supply of facts: and it is the steady stream of ideas, emanating from these sources, which keeps the professions from degenerating into mere routine, from losing their intellectual and responsible character."[40] If the knowledge base was continually cultivated, Flexner predicted that the professions would shed the aspect of commercial guilds and become "increasingly altruistic in motivation."[41]

Flexner completed his triptych of idealistic social progress with a complementary definition of the role of the foundation:

> Assuming possibilities in the outer world, what Foundations can accomplish depends upon their having in them men with ideas—definite, sound ideas, based on wide and thorough knowledge of our own and other countries in different fields of interest. . . . Foundation officers, who are to be constructive contributors to social progress, need then to be forceful, analytical, imaginative and well-informed, if Foundations are to be fertile, rather than sterile, and fundamentally productive, rather than superficially helpful.[42]

It was only seemingly paradoxical that Flexner would use the stress on ideals to insist on the technicalities of the full-time regime. It was because ideals were the vital spark of progress that Flexner did not feel that it was inconsistent to insist on full-time restrictions. As he wrote to Rufus Cole:

> You say rightly "full-time occupation is only the material sign of spiritual rejuvenation," and it's the spiritual rejuvenation that we want. But doctors and lawyers who have been spiritually rejuvenated are peculiarly exposed to financial seduction. By insisting on the full-time limitation we rule out that possibility.[43]

Full-time was not "itself the thing" but a prophylactic measure. Conversely, Flexner consistently assumed that opposition to his full-time program was cynically motivated. "It is somewhat amusing to say that the real difficulty with the full-time scheme is that it is not applicable to 'our generation,' *our generation* of course meaning people who have gotten used to a scale of living which they prefer not to change." Flexner wanted to see to it that the next generation of clinical teachers was not "spoiled."[44]

This idealistic focus was also Flexner's solution to the problematic combination of organization, democracy, and expertise. Even though the basic medium of his career was organizational politics, Flexner lamented bureaucratization, particularly its effect on the university:

> America has its answer to this question how to develop higher education in the form of the word: by means of "organization." Magical word! Complex, interlocking, ramifying, varied, expensive enterprises have to be "organized"; thus railroads, trusts, department-stores are made to work and to pay. Precisely the same is true of a modern university with its complex, interlocking, ramifying, varied and expensive activities; they have to be "organized," else chaos and bankruptcy will inevitably result. A president [with] large executive powers, a squad of deans who serve as his lieutenants in charge of separate departments, schools, and activities. . . . Meanwhile somewhere, more or less sheltered from the traffic, real thinkers—not a few—are also at work with groups of worthy disciples.[45]

Flexner also feared that "the alluring title of executive work" was distracting foundation officers from their creative reflections with a "hodgepodge of feverish and indiscriminate activity."[46]

Like bureaucratization, democracy was to Flexner an ambiguous element in American institutional life. On the one hand, democracy held forth the possibility of a consensus around ideals which could be the basis of the sort of educational meritocracy Flexner was striving to construct. On the other hand, democractic ideals occasionally promoted egalitarian attitudes which could be destructive of the very idea of an elite. Flexner bemoaned that the notion "every individual is entitled to his chance" tended to freight American educational institutions with a surfeit of goals and impediments.[47] In this way, the hurly-burly of democracy was likely to call bureaucratic organization to deal with democratic demands.

The task Flexner set himself was to assure the proper orientation of democracy; like William James he saw the "social value of the college bred" in their ability to "scent out" the difference between the first-rate and the mediocre.[48] With his belief in immanent scientific standards, Flexner wanted to educate American democracy to that distinction.

> Will America finance institutions whose services are not local, institutions that have outgrown their collegiate alumni; finance them, too, on a salary scale that will make teaching and research—what they are rarely now—bearable careers? . . . Assuredly, as democracy needs intellectual distinction, it would be fatal to prejudge the issue by exhibiting too timorous a spirit.[49]

Flexner's beliefs were put to the test in the management of his network. Even as he was successfully expanding his program to include a second tier of schools, the apex of his network—Johns Hopkins—was plagued by two problems which required his attention. On the one hand, Eliot's 1916 indictment was somewhat accurate: the school was small and weak, located in a community where it was difficult to garner support. There were obvious deficiencies in facilities which had to be rectified if the full-time reform was to have any meaning. A second problem was the smoldering resentment and distrust with which the part-time faculty continued to regard the new full-time regime. Still doing much of the patient care and teaching work, the part-timers were excluded from any organizational authority in the school. After the death of Theodore Janeway in 1917, William S. Thayer, Osler's protégé who had been passed over in 1905 and 1913, was finally appointed to his old chief's position as professor of medicine. Recognizing that the school was becoming dangerously incestuous, the full-time leaders brought a group down from Columbia to help staff the department. Led by Walter Palmer, this contingent also included Adolph Dochez, Robert Loeb, and Dana Atchley. But the ex-New Yorkers soon chafed under the barely muted hostility of their part-time colleagues and the limited facilities.[50]

In January 1920, the boards of the university and the Johns Hopkins Hospital jointly petitioned the GEB for aid in a $9 million expansion program they had devised. Buttrick delayed consideration of this proposal until other appeals could be taken up in order that the board might "remove the charge of playing favorites."[51] The following year, Flexner went to Baltimore to direct personally the organization of a new appeal. Apprehending the severity of the internal divisions in the school, he urged his interlocutors to keep all conversations confidential and to commit as little to writing as possible.[52] But even though Flexner was showing his old vigor, the planning process was becoming a little less joyous. As he wrote to hospital director Winford Smith:

> I read very carefully your letter in which you implicate the teaching staff and a certain reformer in the responsibility for the huge sums now being demanded. There is doubtless force in this remark and we must all take it to ourselves. Nevertheless I cannot wholly acquit the architects and their advisers . . . these huge demands for funds come to us daily and leave me stunned and helpless.[53]

Palmer and his associates were growing restive, and Flexner hoped that his implications of increased aid might induce them to stay in Baltimore. Palmer was a particularly vital figure since Thayer was preparing to resign. Since his appointment Thayer had been caught up in war work, and when he returned to Baltimore in 1919 he found adminstrative duties distasteful.[54] Palmer was the logical successor, and the full-time leaders of the school labored to give him the strongest start. Drafts of Thayer's resignation were circulated so that it could be worded to "aid rather than harm the full-time movement."[55] A resolution adopted by the Advisory Board of the Medical Faculty (the ruling council of the school, controlled by the full-timers) announced that no appointments to the department of medicine would be approved or continued until a new professor had been chosen and then would be limited to those in sympathy with the full-time movement. "This will simplify procedures," Hopkins dean J. Whitridge Williams wrote to Flexner, "and enable us to cope much more effectively with the commercialization of the Hospital by some of the part-time men."[56]

In a memorandum urging the GEB to support the Balitmore school, Flexner put the case squarely: "If the development of medical education of high quality is to go forward with all possible momentum, the Johns Hopkins Medical School must not during this generation be allowed to decline, relatively or absolutely." As the very pinnacle of the new academic medical elite, the school was a vital feeder to the newly reformed institutions in St. Louis, Chicago, New York, Rochester, Nashville, and New Haven. At that moment, even those schools were "liabilities" since they needed scientific teachers and were producing none. With German training no longer a viable alternative, the only trustworthy sources of academic clinicians were Hopkins and the Rockefeller Institute. "It is a pity," Flexner wrote, "that one cannot confidently add the Harvard Medical School to the list of institutions which produce men who have both the training and the ideas needed for the further development of academic medicine . . . but the Harvard Medical School is not pursuing a policy calculated to make its graduates satisfied and happy in academic life and with academic rewards." If men were to stay at Hopkins with full-time restrictions on income and not be lured to such competition as Harvard, facilities would have to be increased and endowed beyond their present "meagre" state. Even though the GEB had already been generous with the school, a further grant was merited, Flexner urged, in view of the essential role Johns Hopkins played in "the general program which the General Education Board, the Rockefeller Foundation and the Rockefeller Institute have so much at heart."[57] Accepting Flexner's reasoning, the board approved a grant of $3 million at a meeting on May 26, 1921.[58]

The Hopkins authorities then turned to the Carnegie Corporation. Flexner was aware that the corporation was hard-pressed by its accumulated earlier commitments, and he urged Johns Hopkins president Frank Goodnow to make clear to the Carnegie board that Hopkins would not require actual payment of any gift for some years.[59] Even so, the corporation could not see its way to granting the requested $4 million, a sum which would have meant that the entire plan was to be funded by New York foundations.[60] But Carnegie officers were eager to honor Welch and expressed interest in contributing $2 million to construction and endowment of a new dispensary, the largest single item in the university's plan.[61] A feature which particularly commended the dispensary plan to the corporation was its intention to serve patients of "moderate means who are now admittedly ill-served under the present medical regime." The corporation's acting president, Pritchett, felt that "no more important problem is before medical science today than this [extension of service]."[62] Moreover, the new dispensary arrangements would mollify the part-timers who did most of the dispensary work and could thus extend their practices to paying patients.

These grants came too late, however, to dissuade Palmer, who had concluded that Baltimore was not the promised land of medical education, from resigning to return to Columbia. To keep his program's engine from stalling, Flexner found it necessary to raid one of the rear cars. At his urging, Vanderbilt agreed to a leave of absence for its chief of medicine,

G. Canby Robinson, to serve as temporary head of the Hopkins department. Robinson brought about an armed truce between the full and part-time faculty and after a year was succeeded by Warfield Longcope. Longcope, a Hopkins graduate, had been particularly influenced by Mall and was an assured full-time partisan.[63] But Flexner did not rest easy. As he wrote to Welch, the fact that Longcope was called from Columbia, which Flexner was also striving to reconstruct, "emphasizes our problem—we must train more men." The institutional shell of his system was growing faster than its human content. "The leadership of the world has been forced upon us," he moaned, "and we are not ready for it."[64]

Such problems as the Palmer episode made Flexner realize that the strengthening of American institutions of medical education was having unintended effects on elite training. "As matters now stand," he warned in 1923, "medical education in America is in danger of becoming more or less provincial." The custom of postgraduate medical education in Europe had dropped off. The generation trained solely in America lacked the seasoning of its predecessors who, Flexner felt, "knew at first hand the best that was done and thought in the world."[65] Accordingly, the GEB funded two fellowship programs for overseas study in the 1920s. The first, with matching contributions of $250,000 from both the board and the Rockefeller Foundation, was administered by the National Research Council. As a safeguard against the pursuit of lucrative specialist credentials, this program was restricted to basic science work even if the fellow intended a career in clinical medicine. A second program, created in 1922 and administered directly by the GEB, was designed specifically to nurture Flexner's cadres. Funds were set aside to be "distributed in grants to persons who have attained academic and scientific recognition, without having enjoyed the largest opportunities for training."[66] Flexner used this program to give those whom he had placed in institutions he was developing a *tour d' horizon* which he hoped would ensure their idealism.

Flexner was also concerned with the broad intellectual context of the reconstituted discipline of medicine. He wanted scientific medicine integral to, not abstracted from, higher learning. He regretted that "scientific medicine in America—young, vigorous and positivistic—is today sadly deficient in cultural and philosophical background."[67] To help initiate Americans into the glories of the medical past, the GEB authorized publishing arrangements for and translations of Theodore Billroth's *Lehren und Lernen der medizinischen Wissenschaften* and Claude Bernard's *Introduction à l' étude de la médecine expérimentale.*

But this history lesson required careful framing. In his treatise, Billroth endorsed the idea that clinical professors needed to maintain a private practice in order to hone their skills and noted that he had declined "to undertake the martyrdom of an exclusively classroom professorship."[68] In a carefully worded introduction, which Flexner praised for its "propagandic value,"[69] Welch tempered his praise for Billroth by noting that these "startling" sentiments had to be understood within the contexts of the "strong sense of responsibility and the high scientific ideals" of the German university of Billroth's time which "kept within bounds for the most part their outside private practice."[70]

Flexner soon institutionalized this effort to give historical ballast to his new elite. Programs in the history of medicine have generally been seen as good for whatever ails the field of medicine at large. During the nineteenth century, when the prestige of medicine was sinking, medical students were urged to study medical history as a way of proving that they were indeed learned gentlemen; an "antitoxin for medical commercialism."[71] But for Flexner, medical history was an instrumentalist effort; he had no desire to create or subsidize a field which might have an outlook of its own. When, in 1923, the Hopkins committee suggested Fielding Garrison as a possible occupant of a chair in the history of medicine, Flexner scorned the idea. "What we lack in this country is not courses in the history of medicine but interest in the subject on the part of our newer scientific workers. . . . I am skeptical enough to doubt whether a professor of the history of medicine would make very much difference."[72]

Flexner reversed himself in 1925, however, when he was assured of the proper historicism. As Welch's seventy-fifth birthday approached and he began contemplating stepping down from the directorship of the Hopkins School of Public Hygiene, associates began urging him to become a professor of the history of medicine. Welch's occupancy of such a chair would ensure its rapid endowment. Welch was hesitant. "For me to take such a chair at my age would merely emphasize the spirit of dilettantism in which the subject is regarded and pursued generally in this country."[73] However, the honorific tide overwhelmed him and he accepted the post. With Welch in the picture, the GEB not only got behind the professorship but also donated $1.2 million to construct the William H. Welch Medical Library which would house an entire institute of the history of medicine on the model of the institute at Leipzig.[74]

Allied with but occasionally diverging from Flexner in his struggles to define a new discipline in medicine was the increasingly self-conscious vanguard in clinical science. Rufus Cole and Alfred E. Cohn of the Rockefeller Institute were leaders of this movement.[75]

The founding in 1923 of the *Journal of Clinical Investigation* was their declaration of the rights of clinical science. In the inaugural editorial, Cohn declaimed that it was "clear and unequivocal" that medicine was a science and that "learning must be pursued for its own sake."[76] But his movement was not simply an echo of Flexner's views. Flexner's latent expectation was that scientific clinicians would simply recapitulate the form of the scientific development of the basic sciences. Cohn in contrast looked to a more organic development of the new discipline:

> For there has never been a time either in the ancient or in the modern world when medicine was far removed from the influences of neighboring disciplines. It has, in point of fact, often benefited by importing for its own guidance the conceptions which prevailed in other domains of inquiry. . . . But it has also suffered from this habit. . . . The record of the history of medical progress gives us no assurance that, without constant watchfulness, we shall escape in the future enticements from the proper direction which thought and activity ought pursue in the study of human disease. . . . Medicine must, like the other sciences, be properly credited with having specific objects of interest on its own account. . . . For it cannot be the object of medicine or of any other discipline to "apply" the methods of other sciences to itself. . . . Medicine, in the light of its history, might properly pause at each new stage of its development and make the attempt to define for itself its legitimate scope and objects.[77]

Cohn concluded with this purpose:

> This, then, is the task which academic medicine in the United States, now become self-conscious, has set itself: it is the task of clinical investigation. Its business involves a legitimate interest in learning, as well as a means of furthering the methods which lead to the cure of disease. It is vitally concerned with the success of both projects. It ought, as it has been, to be concerned with the arrangements both in education and in organization for accomplishing its ends. We must appreciate the fact that there is perhaps no single road to salvation open, the search for the single road has often led hunters far afield.[78]

In his ardent desire to underscore the integrity of the new medicine, Cohn could go to the extreme of claiming that medicine "has nothing to do with physiology, bio-physics, bacteriology, or anatomy, or indeed any other discipline." [79] He felt that the independent pursuit of each discipline—independent in terms of premises, methodology, and support—would advance science faster than would feverish cross-applications. Flexner thought that such comments were "of a somewhat irresponsible, though suggestive, character." Most of all, Flexner resented backseat policymaking. "Fellows like Cohn are in a simple position," he wrote to his brother. "They can be very radical, because they can ignore whatever factors in the situation they don't like." [80]

One beachhead of the clinical science vanguard was the University of Chicago medical school, and developments there illustrated just how fragile the reforms of the previous decade were. Under Flexner's guidance and with pledges of support from both the GEB and the Rockefeller Foundation, the university had committed itself to the construction of a new full-time facility on its South Side campus. The university's troublesome affiliation with Rush Medical College and, via Rush, the Presbyterian Hospital had been dealt with by announcing intentions to transform Rush into a postgraduate school for practicing physicians, the only function of which Flexner thought Rush worthy. It had been a neat trick at the time, but it had by no means defeated all opposition to the full-time plan. The irony was that even though Flexner had succeeded in orienting the university's medical ambitions according to a national standard, local support was still essential for any university, especially one which aspired to national prominence. In return for its allegiance to the full-time plan, the university administration received the support of the Rockefeller boards and of the still relatively small band of zealots for a new clinical science. That relationship would be put severely to the test over the next two decades.

The difficulty of transforming an abstract plan into a living organization was soon apparent. In January 1920, Flexner urged Chicago president Harry Pratt Judson to begin staffing the school. [81] Judson was reluctant to do so without a completely worked out financial plan, but gamely tried to entice Francis W. Peabody to take the deanship and chair the department of medicine in the new school on the Midway. [82] Peabody was a Hopkins graduate who had taught at the Peking Medical College and in 1920 was a Harvard professor serving at the Boston City Hospital.

Peabody expressed to Judson great hopes for the Chicago enterprise, but the very novelty of the plan made it an unattractive career choice. "I do not feel tempted to give up the next few years of professional service for a life that must be largely devoted to administrative matters and that is at the present time contingent on so many uncertainties."[83] Perhaps overcompensating, Judson interpreted Peabody's unease as anxiety over the university's commitment to full-time, and hastened to reassure him that it was "not merely a policy in which the General Education Board is interested but is one of our own deliberate choice."[84] Just the opposite was in fact the case: despite his Hopkins and Peking experience, Peabody was hostile to the full-time plan. (Upon learning of Peabody's hostility, Flexner expressed disgust that "the influence of the Harvard crowd" had "spoiled him for purely academic purposes.")[85] Aside from Peabody's opposition, the paradox was clear. The new school had to be placed securely in the hands of individuals so committed to the new movement in medical research and education that they were willing to forego those activities for a significant period. Representatives of the new clinical science were in limited supply and were needed as both researchers and administrators.

The full-time movement, which aspired to educational leadership, was finding itself, in the early 1920s, short of leaders. With the retirement of Judson from the Chicago presidency in 1921, the task of finding a dean for the prospective medical school fell to his successor, Ernest Burton. The new president rejected the suggestion that "it will be a great mistake if you start in by Johns Hopkinizing your school" by appointing outsiders.[86] Instead he continued a national search, made another offer to Peabody, and was rebuffed.[87] Eager to see an unquestionable full-timer in the position, Rufus Cole in the Rockefeller Institute nominated his colleague, Alfred E. Cohn. Burton found Cohn to fit the requirements of the position "except for his Jewish name and physiognomy."[88] Francis Blake of Yale was a more appealing possibility, even though pillaging another full-time camp embarrassed Burton.

"If in this we have violated inter-university ethics, you have my apology," Burton wrote to Yale president Angell concerning his approach to Blake. "The situation is critical with us," he went on; "I am discovering that there are astonishingly few men in the country who can fill the position."[89] Evidently agreeing, Flexner urged Angell to let Blake go.[90] Sympathetic but unyielding, Angell noted that Yale, too, was at a critical pass in establishing the plan, having implemented it more extensively than any other school including Hopkins. At Yale, Blake was a keystone whose removal "would be to strike a blow at our progress which we cannot face with anything but the deepest misgivings."[91] Blake agreed; he turned down Burton on the grounds that the crucial test of full-time was taking place at Yale and he could not desert his post.[92]

Once again disheartened, the Chicago leaders began considering expedients. Burton floated to Flexner the possibility of appointing Peabody as a consultative dean, pending construction of the school.[93] After waiting until Burton had presented the idea to Peabody, Flexner vetoed it as impractical and unnecessary. "It is a funny thing—this medical business," he wrote Burton seemingly without reference to himself. "Legends very rapidly grow up about people . . . I have the feeling . . . that at the moment Peabody looks bigger to you than he is."[94] Seeing "no use of a struggle with Flexner," the Chicago adminstration set aside the interim proposal and searched further.[95] The ultimate choice, Franklin Chambers McLean, agreed to accept appointment as professor of medicine and acting chairman, leaving further questions of authority in abeyance. McLean was clearly a second choice, reflecting the dilemma of the construction of the plan. He was "excellent for the immediate future," one informant commented, "experienced and skillful in organization." But he was "not a good clinician. . . . Not self-directing as an investigator. . . . Does not seem much interested in teaching."[96]

The administrative detours in McLean's once-promising research career illustrated how the movement for a new science was in some ways devouring its own young.[97] An Illinois native, McLean had received both a Ph.D. in physiology from the University of Chicago and an M.D. from Rush Medical College. After European study, he was taken in by the Rockefeller Institute where he became a favorite of Rufus Cole and the special protégé of Alfred Cohn. McLean interrupted his work at the institute on the biochemistry of edema in 1917 to answer a call to help organize the Peking Union Medical College which the China Medical Board of the Rockefeller Foundation was establishing.

Peking Union was the most exotic application of the philanthropic faith in science. It was one more twist in a long and tangled relationship between the United States and China.[98] Many Americans, especially the eastern elite with a clipper-ship heritage, were fascinated with China, which they considered to be enveloped in the desiccated husk of an obscurantist civilization, yet about to burst forth as a dynamic Oriental exemplar of American values. This missionary zeal took on an increasingly scientific cast as the nineteenth century progressed. That Sun Yat-sen, the "George Washington of China," was a physician rather than a surveyor reflected the ascension of medicine to a place in the ideological constellation surrounding Sino-American relations. Similarly, the roofs of the Peking Union Medical College would be peaked and tiled in Eastern fashion, rather than gabled and cupolaed, but within its walls the "Johns Hopkins of China" would help construct the same clinical science as that in Baltimore. McLean believed that to be "efficient as a Christianizing force a medical institution must be efficient from the professional standpoint," and he labored to achieve his ideas against considerable opposition from within the Rockefeller Foundation over the costliness of his objective.[99] The same problem would plague him in Chicago.

By 1922, McLean had decided to return to the United States and resume his research career. Alfred Cohn applauded the decision:

> Your decision to come back to work is distinctly pleasing to me. There's no other real salvation. The management of men is after all a silly business; it coats you over with an armour designed to prevent the sort of person you really are from breaking through and wards off from you the possibility of what men really want,—what they are really like. . . . We pretend to select the professor because he can investigate and immediately he is in his post, we rob him of the opportunity to develop his calling. Truly the "efficiency" of America is a wonderful thing. . . . Come back to science Mack while there is yet time. You may then succeed in saving your soul.[100]

With his acceptance of the Chicago offer, however, McLean was committed to the "silly business."

The construction and organization of the new school were complicated by the full-time standards. Dean Lewis had been appointed professor of surgery to the new school, but McLean reported to Burton in early 1924 "growing dissatisfaction, not peculiar to myself, with respect to the attitude of Dr. Dean Lewis, and a growing doubt as to his availability for the purposes of the University in medical education."[101] Lewis, it seemed, would not keep appointments, was carrying on a substantial private practice, and was reported to be considering offers from other schools. Burton sent Lewis a copy of the regulations which the university was adopting to meet the full-time requirements of the Rockefeller contract and asked that he conduct himself accordingly.[102] Lewis replied that he would not abandon his practice since he felt that full-time "tends to isolate the hospital from the community" and interfere with the professional development of younger men.[103] Burton tried to adjust the situation, but was dismayed when Lewis unexpectedly resigned in August.[104] Consternated, Harold Higgins Swift, chairman of the university's board of trustees, urged Burton to inform Flexner of the turn of events. "I think it is quite important that it cannot be said that we proceeded without his knowing it."[105] The president wrote to Flexner that he feared that Lewis' leaving "will perhaps injure us to some extent in the eyes of his friends in Chicago."[106]

Flexner's reply was typical of his style of philanthropic management: abjuring any direct authority while implying his approval of both the action and its being brought to his attention:

> It is very kind of you to write me as fully as you do regarding your surgical situation, though you must not feel that we are in any wise entitled to be consulted on these intimate matters. However, I do confess that I am flattered to be taken into your confidence. I do not believe that there is any reason to regret the outcome.[107]

The next candidate for the surgical chair, Dallas B. Phemister, was also critical of the full-time plan. He wrote to Burton that he was certain that he could obtain a much better staff if some fees could be charged. Phemister buttressed his argument with an unvarnished Social Darwinist logic: "Curing one capable patient may mean more to the world than curing a hundred of the average charity type."[108] The university stood firm, and Phemister finally accepted absolute full-time as the basis for organizing his department. Burton, however, was wearying of these struggles: "the clouds do not roll away as fast as the negro melody might suggest," he lamented.[109]

Flexner's strict management tended to rupture the university's connections with the local elite. Printing magnate and university trustee Thomas Donnelly urged trustee chairman Swift to consider a proposal that the Chicago Memorial Hospital be built on university land in hopes that the university would eventually absorb it into its medical center. Swift reported that Donnelly believed "that something might be worked out on it and if we did not try further we might be very severely criticized by prominent Chicagoans."[110] The one "irreducible minimum" condition of the Memorial trustees was "loyalty to the men who had stood by them."[111] The hospital would turn over to the university $1.2 million for construction and endowment if in exchange its present staff could conduct private practice for fifteen years in a sixty-bed unit in the university hospital. "It was distinctly intimated that the acceptance of this proposal by the University would carry with it the interest of certain men in the University of Chicago that would undoubtedly be of value."[112] But upon doing the necessary checking, Burton discovered that Flexner was unalterably opposed. "You have a clean proposition," he advised the president, "Now keep it so."[113] In turning down the hospital's proposal Burton made the rather weak offer that if the Memorial Hospital would relocate in the university neighborhood, its staff would be granted use of the libraries and the faculty club. Full-time was the issue, as he wrote to the Memorial officials:

> May I make it clear that we are compelled to this conclusion by the fact that having committed ourselves to a policy in some respects new and dependent for its success on a strict adherence to it, we must, we judge, hold consistently to it and, in any case such as the present one do only what we can also do in any other case.[114]

Spurned by the University of Chicago, the hospital eventually affiliated with crosstown rival Northwestern University.[115]

With many avenues of local support foreclosed by "strict adherence" to full-time, the university was forced to a more complete dependence on "our Eastern friends."[116] This situation produced the misunderstandings likely in such inequitable relationships. The inflation of building costs after World War I had already obliged the New York boards to alter the terms of their earlier gifts so that money previously earmarked for endowment could be used for actual construction. McLean reported optimistically on a February 1924 conference with Flexner that the foundations were prepared to aid in a building scheme which would set up all the basic sciences as well as medicine and surgery. "I personally feel that Mr. Flexner's imagination is fired by the attitude of the University in this development, that it represents the kind of progress he is at present interested in."[117] Such news gratified the university administrators since it freed them to devote their upcoming fund-raising campaign to the still-incomplete arts and sciences campus. Perhaps, they even dared to hope, the Rockefeller philanthropies would bankroll the projected medical construction entirely.[118] When he realized the cavalcade of expectations he had aroused, Flexner announced that he was "a little aghast" that his "decidedly speculative" comments were intoxicating the Chicago officials.[119]

"I am anxious that these vaporings should not become the basis for any calculations."[120] Burton excused his enthusiasm with the perhaps half-sarcastic comment: "You see I am so accustomed to take your lightest word as gospel truth that what you say for me is as good as done."[121]

The Chicago planners were advised by third parties that Flexner "is keen on a small beginning."[122] McLean accordingly felt that rather than start the Department of Medicine full-blown it was best to seek out only a few unquestionably qualified men as they became available.[123] This would mean of course that clinical teaching could be only slowly inaugurated on the South Side and that the conversion of Rush into a postgraduate school would have to be delayed. Such a prospect distressed Flexner as much as did grandiose schemes. Max Mason, who succeeded the deceased Burton in 1926, tried to resassure the GEB secretary that the university was still committed to his 1916 plan of eliminating Rush as an undergraduate school, although it would have to continue to take some students since the South Side school could not as yet accommodate all the students who finished the preclinical course.[124] Flexner's testy and condescending reply begged the question of how the school could be maintained in line with his principles: "The Medical School is *yours*, not *ours*, not *mine*. . . . It is, I know, not easy to hew the line, but it has been done, and is being done in Baltimore, New Haven, Nashville, and elsewhere."[125]

Rush remained an important factor because of its valuable connection with the Presbyterian Hospital. Any refurbishment of Rush to form it into a postgraduate school would be expensive, an expense that seemed increasingly less attractive as the costs on the South Side continued to mount. A possible economy would be to bring the Presbyterian to the South Side and use it for undergraduate clinical teaching so that all the hospital expense did not fall on the university. Flexner admitted to the university officials that this was an alternative he would have favored in 1916 if it had been possible and would favor now if the full-time plan would not be compromised.[126] But any agreement with Presbyterian would certainly have involved some provision for current Rush professors in the new amalgamation, and the Presbyterian board was loath to compel the veteran staff to go on full-time. Flexner had put the university in a double bind. He constantly urged university officials to pass the maintenance of the hospital on to another agency while ruling out any concrete possibility of such a step.[127]

Despite these difficulties, the opening of the University Clinics in 1927 was celebrated by the clinical science vanguard as the materialization of their ideas. Rufus Cole spoke hopefully of "the inauguration of a great experiment" which he confidently predicted would be a "world situation . . . a true university department of medicine."[128] Alfred Cohn was also enthralled with the possibilities, but he worried privately to McLean that the university might be sidetracked:

> If I am correct in believing that the future at Chicago depends on following the plan, it follows almost that it depends on your retaining the helm. . . . No one who is not intimately acquainted with the movement & who cares for it, can know how much the prosecution of the plan at Chicago means. The issue is intellectual. You may need to round out the departments to an extent commensurate with the requirements of professional education. But making the place large and full of a multitude of unnecessary specialties . . . may tend to obscure the core, the main interest.[129]

Cohn had confidence that McLean's ideals would make it possible for the Chicago dean to separate the scientific wheat from the organizational chaff; but, to his frustration, Flexner had discovered that even the reformed clinicians could lose sight of essential principles. Even as he struggled to staff the Chicago school, he found that some "reformed" clinicians were pursuing an academic specialization away from his ideal. In an appeal from Hopkins to the GEB in February 1923, a committee composed of John Howland, Howard MacCallum, and Lewis Weed suggested that to "improve in a radical way some of our methods of teaching and training . . . we must improve our facilities and equipment and enlarge in special directions our teaching staff." The proposal envisioned the recreation of the school's departments as "institutes" with independent laboratory and clinical facilities. The committee maintained that "it is clear that much is gained in the efficiency of any department when the greater part of its more intimate work is provided for within itself without necessary dependence upon other departments." The new "institutes" would be "well organized divisions rather than the present idea of departments which implies rather excessive interdependence."[130]

These proposals struck Flexner as "a reactionary proposition," impracticable, and educationally not to the point. He felt that further development of the school was desirable, but only so long as it was conducted "unambitiously" and with a reasonable end in view. "Schematic completeness is an utter impossibility. . . . There are nowhere in the world any such things as complete medical schools or complete research institutes, any more than there is such a thing as a complete university." Schools should be "susceptible to growth,"[131] but he did not want such growth to rend the seamless web of knowledge:

> Team play is more important, not less important, than it used to be; the congeries of laboratories and clinics make an organic whole . . . the committee appears to lose sight of the fact that the Johns Hopkins Medical School is a medical school, the various organs of which should be developed with a view to harmonious cooperation toward a certain end. The institution is not an "Institute," nor is it a collection of institutes.[132]

Having prescribed bureaucratization to reform medical education, Flexner was now obliged to limit it.

Flexner was not nearly as successful in the bureaucratic management of his network as he was at its founding. This was partly a matter of his personality, but the more important failure was conceptual. He was caught in his own ideological trap. For all his skill at organizational politics, his distaste for bureaucracy required that he discount the power of organization and take refuge in overarching idealism. "The men who have ideals and who are determined not to be separated from them simply won't allow the details to swamp them," he confidently asserted.[133] That conviction made it difficult for him to understand the development of his system. He had grounded his network on the premise that individual scientific ambition would, if properly channeled, produce an almost self-regulating learned discipline. But when his new elite began to demand more—more money, more institutional resources, more independence—Flexner became frustrated, insisting even more strongly that his dictates be followed precisely.

The question might be asked: Why was Flexner so unremittingly inflexible and so insensitive to the political exposure this inflexibility produced? His history provides some clues to what is essentially a matter of psychological speculation. His success in the emerging philanthropic community had been based on the elegant simplicity of his ideas and their expression. Clarity, not ambiguity, was his stock-in-trade. That success had come late in life and must have been somewhat unexpected even to him. To have deviated from the formula which had served him so well would have required of him a tolerance for uncertainty which itself would have made his earlier achievements impossible. Moreover, his moralistic stress on the necessity of fidelity to academic ideals was no doubt re-inforced by the displaced evangelicism and pietism which several scholars have noted as characteristics of the early Rockefeller boards.[134] A habit of didacticism may be another answer. Before coming to New York, he had spent his adult life almost entirely in the supervision of adolescents. He was perfectly comfortable in referring to negotiations with hospital and university trustees as "lessons" in which he was the patient but conde-scending instructor.[135] In sum, it must be remembered that his life course was characterized by uncertainty: an unsteady father who never recov-ered from his failure in the Panic of 1877; a penurious childhood; the indeterminacy of his acceptance by a society which felt anti-Semitism was only bad taste. His need to be self-assured must have been too great for him ever to have considered the alternative.

But whatever its cause, this rigidity achieved just the opposite of his goal: the political and not the idealistic aspect of his management was em-phasized. Criticism of his program increasingly focused on the legitimacy of his authority. In 1927, Francis Peabody bemoaned the "overorganiza-tion" of clinical medicine. "What we want," he asserted, "is less of the system and law that kills and more of the spirit that gives life."[136] When that criticism converged with the ambitions of the rising generation of philanthropic managers, Flexner would be in difficulty.

5 The Reorganization of Philanthropic Management

Abraham Flexner had set out in 1911 to reorganize medical education from a system of professional training to the institutional setting of a learned discipline. In that process he had helped to transform Rockefeller philanthropy into the organizing center of transinstitutional networks. By the mid-1920s, he was trying to manage his medical education network in an altered organizational landscape. To his peril, he disregarded the implications of the very changes he had caused.

The 1920s in the United States represented the culmination of organizational developments of previous decades. Progressivism had built institutions and national networks of influence and expertise. In the twenties, the institutional development of many fields became much more self-conscious and bureaucratic (although the term itself was despised) as a new generation of managers sought to rationalize the functions and structures which the ferment of the previous decades had wrought. These changes involved not only further reorganizations but reconceptualizations of organizational purpose. Using the terms "strategy and structure," Alfred Chandler has described how new forms of business enterprise were created and a new cohort of managers was developed.[1] Similar changes took place in government and in the areas of public life overlapping business and government. These new managers were working out mechanisms whereby modern America could be managed by constellations of institutions linked hierarchically by budgetary lines and laterally by professional expertise.

A political formula needed to be developed since many of these trends were in profound tension with inherited democractic political discourse.

The idea of "associationalism" was one response to this need. Associationalism promised that the shakeout of the early twentieth century was over; that the rationalization and the absorption of institutions so typical of the period between 1890 and 1920 was finished and that national organizations were to be partners and not threatening competitors. Older ideas of "efficiency" continued to be employed, but there was a dedicated effort to make managerialism congruent with democracy. This subculture was clearly not democractic in any classical sense, or even in the nineteenth-century sense of party government, but it did mean that forms of representativeness and pluralism could apply on an institutional scale. The periodic conferences called by Herbert Hoover as commerce secretary and as president to consider such questions as unemployment and housing policy were examples of the new polity: an organizational federalism where representatives were drawn from professions and institutions rather than from states and localities.

The same process was going forward in the Rockefeller boards and in the nation's medical schools. A rising generation of foundation managers (they even coined a name for themselves: "philanthropoids") was chafing under its subordination to the generation of institution builders. Eager to experiment with new mechanisms of social management and influence, they looked upon universities and other adjacent institutions as necessary partners in the management of society and not (as Flexner did) as sick patients who themselves required management. These philanthropoids found natural allies in the new administrative class which had been produced by the institutional strengthening of the nation's medical schools. This new class of deans viewed Flexner more as an oppressor than as a liberator. Flexner was profoundly out of sympathy with these developments. Even though he had opened up new vistas of managerial capacity, he saw the sort of reforming management he engaged in as only a temporary expedient which would wither away once the scientific discipline of medical education had been assured. Like Sinclair Lewis in *Arrowsmith*, he celebrated the lone scientist, even if he would house him in a reformed university and not in the back woods.

It is therefore not surprising that as the 1920s drew to a close criticism of Flexner's policies from organized medical education increased and found a greater hearing within the Rockefeller boards. That criticism focused more and more upon questions of institutional efficiency and legitimacy on which the philanthropic and medical managers could agree. By 1928 an alliance between these forces culminated in a reorganization of the Rockefeller boards which resulted in Flexner's ouster. The program of research produced by the reorganization was grounded in the conviction that the age of institution building was over. All of what Flexner despised about American democratic culture—uncritical representativeness, logrolling, organizational boosterism—were part of this new system. His defeat was a dramatic illustration of the problems of bureaucratic planning in a democratic society.

Renewed negotiations over the Columbia-Presbyterian Medical Center provided the occasion for a display of just the sort of Flexnerian intransigence which sorely frustrated his colleagues. In 1916, Flexner had demanded full-time as a condition of Rockefeller participation in plans for the creation of the new medical center. Many-sided negotiations involving the university, the hospital, the Rockefeller and Carnegie boards, and Edward S. Harkness had seemingly culminated in 1919 in an agreement which Flexner could support.

Implementation of that agreement proved problematical, however. In April 1920, the dean of the Columbia College of Physicians and Surgeons, William Darrach, submitted a tentative budget to the GEB. Darrach felt that the salaries of the full-time positions "must be such that the choice of appointment will not be limited to men without families or with independent means, and it should be possible to attract men from other cities." He felt that the salaries of the clinical chiefs should be $15,000 annually and that those of their assistants and of the preclinical staff should be a substantial fraction of that figure.[2]

Such generosity did not fit into Flexner's national plan. Darrach's figures were half again and sometimes double what the other full-time schools were paying. "Columbia ought, of course not, be asked to reduce the proposed salaries merely because other institutions cannot afford to pay them," Flexner noted, "but to the extent that the proposition is really an extravagant and dangerous precedent, we ought to consider its effect on the probable future of medical education and medical research in general."[3] He felt that the high salaries for junior men would congeal the required fluidity of the system. Flexner put the case to Darrach with unusual candor:

Academic medicine can succeed in America only if those entering it are so keen for its opportunities that they are not only willing but eager to play what I may fairly describe as the "academic game." It cannot succeed if this particular group demands for itself conditions and advantages that lift its members completely out of the academic class. . . . The number of men available for full-time clinical posts is as yet so small and the relations that exist, personal and academic, between these departments in the several institutions are so intimate, that whatever is done at one place at once reverberates elsewhere. The development of full-time staffs is therefore what may be called a team game and, until the personnel is very greatly increased, it is necessary to look at questions that arise from the standpoint of a group of institutions loyally and cooperatively engaged in the effort to develop in this country a new and higher type of medical teaching.[4]

But Columbia did not accept Flexner's ideas of collective responsibility and was determined to go forward without Rockefeller aid. Columbia president Nicholas Murray Butler pronounced himself "greatly relieved" that the GEB would no longer be involved with his institution: "They have already done what I conceive to be so great damage to the cause of medical education in this country by the conditions attached to their several gifts that Columbia will occupy a favored and distinguished position in seeking and in securing elsewhere the funds needed for Medical School development."[5]

Pritchett was distressed by this turn of events and again urged Flexner and his associates to compromise "not only for the sake of medicine but for the salvation of your souls."[6] He chastised Flexner that "with your clearly formed notions on such matters I think your tendency is to go a little too far in laying down the rules."[7] Pritchett also tried to cajole GEB president Wallace Buttrick noting that even though "our friend Flexner" had "the best intentions . . . the [unhappy] outcome [of the negotiations] was not entirely due to other people."[8] Pritchett knew that Rockefeller participation in the effort was essential. When Columbia petitioned the Carnegie Corporation in early 1921 for aid in its $5 million campaign to build and endow its share of the medical center, Pritchett turned them down, noting that "it will be clear to you that no one of these foundations can, unaided, devote so large a sum of money to a single project as would be necessary to carry it through in its entirety."[9]

When it was apparent that Flexner was unyielding, Columbia retreated and scaled down its salaries. A new agreement was reached in May 1921.[10] The three foundations—the GEB, the Rockefeller Foundation, and the Carnegie Corporation—would each contribute $1 million to the $5 million needed by Columbia. Rockefeller junior was particularly pleased. "At last the impossible has been accomplished!" he wrote to Flexner.[11]

But this agreement soon faltered also. After one year on the absolute full-time basis, a medical school committee in 1923 recommended that a version of geographic full-time be adopted, a proposal which the president and the board of trustees of the university approved.[12] Columbia officials tried to portray the change as one within the full-time movement, "just as one can be a Davis Democrat or a Bryan Democrat and still satisfy the party's nominal claim without subscribing to every plank in its plat-form."[13] This unfortunate reference to the 104-ballot 1924 Democratic national convention accurately captured the wearisome quality of the situation. Flexner was cagey in dealing with the predictable dangers of this now-familiar negotiation. Aware of the impatience of Pritchett, Harkness, and his Rockefeller colleagues, he was careful not to preemp-torily cancel the university's grant. Fortunately for him, the Columbia authorities once again exhibited what he saw as the "fatal lack of team work" which continually plagued their efforts.[14]

When the Columbia treasurer requested from the General Education Board payment of their pledge, it was discovered that the university had never formally accepted the grant. Even though this seemingly strength-ened Flexner's hand, other Rockefeller officials were reluctant to stand on legalisms. Board counsel Debevoise officially ruled that the GEB was in no way legally bound to pay on its pledge.[15] However, in a second letter the same day Debevoise expressed the hope that this was "a case where informal, unofficial conversations might lead to adjustment." He had been surprised upon reading the record to discover just how much the board had had to do with the adoption of the plan in the first place, and "it seems to me it would be very unfortunate now for the Board to insist on changes as a condition for gifts which have been dangling just out of the reach of the University for the past seven years."[16]

In the course of efforts to reach an understanding, Columbia board chairman Colonel Parsons proposed that rather than readjust the earlier grant, the boards consider a new petition from Columbia which com-passed the creation of "the greatest and biggest medical school in the world."[17] Other hospitals along with Presbyterian would participate in this splendid medical acropolis. The two boards were requested to donate $4 million to this great work. Parsons' intention in making this proposal was to obviate the full-time problem by presenting the foundations with a proposition they would be embarrassed to reject. Flexner, however, had no qualms about opposing what was a very poorly thought out scheme. As he wrote to his brother, it was to his tactical advantage that "the issue turns upon these questions and not upon the full-time organization regarding which a difference of opinion would be controversial."[18] At a joint meeting of Rockefeller, Columbia, and Presbyterian officials he peppered the university representatives with pointed questions about financing for which they had no answers.[19] "I have never seen any such performance in my life," he wrote afterward. "They had not the remotest ideas of what they had gotten themselves in for."[20]

Despite Columbia's misfires pressure was building on Flexner for a compromise. Pearce felt that the boards should give money for construction of the new laboratories and should ignore the unpleasant features of the Columbia design.[21] Rockefeller Foundation president Vincent, Flexner sensed, was "frankly nervous about the attitude of the profession and the public towards us, and fears that while our position is technically and legally sound, in effect we are in the position of offering and influencing policy. I can of course see his point, though I am not as sensitive about the thing as he is."[22] Pritchett again urged the Rockefeller officials to vote the money upon which so much had been premised.[23] Harkness's associate Dean Sage wrote to Flexner that he could see "no difference in principle" between geographic and absolute full-time.[24] The idea in many minds was summed up by Buttrick's theory that it was occasionally necessary to "give them the money and tell them to go to hell."[25] Debevoise put the issue squarely:

> The Board has taken steps to get rid of the full time bogey in other cases but the Columbia situation bids fair to make a record which cannot be overcome for a long time. The more I think of the matter, the more I feel that it will be better for the Board if some way can be found to let Columbia have the million and thus to end the talk and leave the Board in a position where no one can say that it has broken faith.[26]

But Flexner remained inflexible. He informed the Columbia authorities that only if they agreed to undertake absolute full-time in the new hospital would the Board appropriate its original $1 million pledge.[27] The authorities agreed to that condition in December 1925 and the board voted the appropriation.[28]

An aggregation like the Columbia-Presbyterian Medical Center was the physical representation of the organizational development of American medical education. More than perhaps any other system of training, medical education requires the interaction of a broad range of individuals, institutions, and services. This is particularly true of the clinical phase. A large part of the appeal of medical education reform and of Flexner's full-time version of it was that they held out both an ideological and a practical framework which ordered the various functions. But with his continuing insistence on the particularities of his plan, Flexner had become just the opposite, a force for disorder, disrupting the flow of support which the growing complexes of institutions needed.

The emerging administrative class of academic medicine felt this problem most keenly. The growth of this class is best seen in the changes in the medical school deanship. What had formerly been chiefly an honorific post, often connoting the lengthiest service in an affable collegiality, had become by the 1920s the juncture of several organizational networks. The growth of research, intern and residency programs, and new forms of outpatient service all meant that it was increasingly necessary for the medical schools to maintain stable relations with agencies which could offer support and facilities for the new functions. As organizational and financial resources became more crucial to individual career advancement, the necessity of the dean as an intrafaculty mediator also increased.

The increased responsibilities and relative power meant a growing and improving self-image for medical administrators. The Association of American Medical Colleges, basically an organization of deans and self-selected academic activists, began in 1923 to hold meetings separate from the AMA with which it had been meeting jointly since 1911. Perhaps the leading figure in this trend was Ray Lyman Wilbur, who during the course of the 1920s went from dean of the Stanford Medical School to president of the parent university to Secretary of the Interior in Hoover's cabinet.[29]

Another archetypical figure was Willard C. Rappleye; the advice concerning his career which he received throughout the decade illustrated the changing status of administration in academic medicine. When in 1920 Rappleye was considering a post with administrative possibilities, Roger

Lee of Harvard warned him about the cost to his research potential. "Organization work always takes a great deal longer than one expects. As a rule, there are only about ten years of active, productive work, and it always seems a pity to me when a man loses several of these years in creating an organization."[30]

But as Rappleye progressed further along the executive pathway, reports became more glowing. In 1921, Edsall assured Rappleye that if he took a proffered post with the Committee on Training Hospital Executives (a new efflorescence in the increasingly complex medical organization), he would not "be left stranded or without opportunity for valuable work."[31] Rappleye's performance in that position elicited praise from Hugh Cabot, then dean of the University of Michigan Medical School:

> You are extraordinarily well fitted for an executive position in connection with a large teaching machine, and I feel sure that in this work you will make an enduring reputation. I am further of the opinion that opportunities of this kind are becoming increasingly available and that it will certainly be possible for you to obtain a commanding position within a relatively short time.[32]

Finally, when Rappleye contemplated the offer of the Columbia deanship in 1930, Hans Zinsser urged him to take on what would be "a life job and one in which in the present development of medical education it is of the greatest necessity in the interests of stabilization to have a man who can keep his head."[33]

Flexner's ambivalent attitude toward the evolution of the deanship was indicative of an unwillingness to confront certain implications of the reform process. Flexner had too much regard for the intricacies of organizational power to dismiss administration as simply a "silly business," but neither would he consider it a "life job." Flexner felt that administrative talent was necessary only at the point of institutional reconstruction: after reform the governing power of scientific idealism would reign. The GEB secretary often keyed his medical school reconstructions on a local "C-in-C" like Welch or Milton C. Winternitz at Yale, but his ideological distaste for organization led him to the wishful prediction of the withering away of the deanship:

> It is, in the first instance, not easy to find in the medical faculty a person who possesses at once executive talent, fine appreciation of scientific achievement, and the requisite contacts with scientific leaders. Once found, men so highly endowed ought not to be lightly sacrificed to executive routine, to which, unfortunately, the

American is a singularly easy victim. On the other hand, conditions being what they have been and are, American faculties would, in the absence of competent and continuous leadership, either stagnate or flounder. Perhaps as university ideals become clearer, faculties more homogeneous, support more generally adequate, and preliminary education more efficient and more truly selective, the executive duties of the dean may be devolved upon a secretary, to whom will be left the operation of the machine, itself, let us hope, greatly simplified; under such circumstances, the dean may be saved to science, without wholly surrendering the principle of effective representative leadership.[34]

For Flexner and his allies such as his brother Simon or Alfred Cohn, executive authority was legitimate only insofar as it was grounded in scientific ability. Among themselves, they tended to excuse with a deprecating condescension the actions of opposing administrators on the grounds that those antagonists' scientific abilities were exhausted.[35] That attitude obscured the transition taking place. A certain level of scientific credentials and rapport with current scientific developments remained a necessary aspect of administrative equipment, but the new deans were forging a perspective independent of Flexner's vision of medicine as a learned discipline.

The conditions which brought about the growth of the deanship accelerated a reconceptualization of the aims of medicine which the new administrators turned rhetorically to their advantage. Just as fifteen years earlier Pritchett had expounded on the public responsibility of medical schools to goad them out of commercialism, the new medical leaders parried the particularist claims of the profession and their own faculties (Flexner's erstwhile constituents) with references to comprehensive obligations of medical education. But while Pritchett's preaching had been largely ethical, the new theme was more sociological, stressing that changing conditions required the medical school to be a mediating force in the welter of clashing social forces.

The organization in 1924 of the Commission on Medical Education was an attempt by the deans to become a collective force in medical education policy and compete with Flexner in setting the policy agenda. Like its contemporaries, the Committee on Recent Social Trends and the Committee on Recent Economic Changes, the commission was an effort to take stock of developments and, implicitly, assert the role of expertise in setting a future agenda. Rappleye was the director of this study, and the commission was studded with Flexner's adversaries: Harvard president A. Lawrence Lowell was the overall chairman, Harvard dean David L. Edsall was the chairman of the committee on clinical teaching, and Columbia dean Darrach was a commission member. The commission was supported by the member schools of the American Association of Medical Colleges, the AMA, the Carnegie Corporation and the Rockefeller Foundation. Its basic charge was to "establish certain fundamental relationships which, if accepted, would allow the universities greater freedom in their endeavor to modify the rigid, overcrowded and overstandardized curriculum and to conduct medical training on more sound educational lines,"[36] but its reports encompassed broader issues. Flexner's version of full-time was condemned in terms which all disputants would recognize: if "clinical teaching is to attract and hold teachers of the caliber and ability which it requires, there must be a fuller recognition of the freedom and dignity which such work should command."[37] The commission's reports laid more stress than Flexner was wont to on the "problems of medical practice and community health" and less on research.[38] The commission's *Final Report* announced the eagerness of the administrators of academic medicine to participate in the formation of new policies:

> The rapid growth in knowledge and the changes in social organization in recent years have greatly complicated the problems of medical service. . . . Medicine must be looked upon as a form of public service. . . . The training of students adequately to meet the newer conditions and the new philosophy of medical responsibility can only be brought about through a shift in the interests and point of view of those in charge of medical education, who must be convinced of the vital importance of these newer influences.[39]

Among these deans, Edsall was Flexner's most tenacious opponent. Despite Flexner's antipathy to Harvard, Edsall had succeeded throughout the 1920s in prying loose from the GEB small grants for his institution. But the dean's negotiations with Flexner were only the more open skirmishes of an ongoing guerrilla struggle which Edsall waged throughout the decade against Flexner's program. Edsall specifically insisted that some private practice be allowed to the heads of any Harvard departments the GEB aided. One result of this conflict was Harvard's relatively pathetic share— $635,000—of the $78 million distributed to medical education during Flexner's tenure with the GEB.[40]

Just as Flexner felt that Harvard's policy toward full-time threatened the medical education structure he was attempting to build, Edsall felt that Harvard was caught in a bind Flexner had created. The school was unable to compete with the relatively lavish full-time salaries which the board funded at competing schools, but also was unwilling to allow unrestricted private practice as a compensation. As Edsall pointedly wrote to Flexner, the "danger of instability here is due solely, so far as I can see, through contrasts with things offered elsewhere."[41]

Although alienated from Flexner, Edsall was not without contacts at 61 Broadway. Pearce and Edsall had been colleagues at the University of Pennsylvania, and Alan Gregg, Pearce's assistant, had been one of Edsall's students at Harvard. Edsall repeatedly complained to these friends about what he felt were Flexner's stubborn prejudices.[42] That Edsall was elected a trustee of the Rockefeller Foundation in May 1927 was a sure indication that his complaints were registering and that Flexner's dominion over Rockefeller medical policy was waning.

Relations between Edsall and Flexner reached the breaking point when the Harvard dean attempted to secure more than token support for his school. In late 1925, he outlined to Flexner the design of a large joint fund-raising campaign by the Harvard Medical School and the Massachusetts General Hospital in which he hoped the GEB would participate. The $2 million the school hoped to secure from the board would round out the clinical upgrading of the school "without friction" and "without violence."[43]

Edsall hoped for a prompt response, but Flexner began to cavil that the number of institutions involved in the campaign raised "complex and novel" questions which would delay consideration.[44] Edsall was infuriated:

> If your Board maintained the requirement that they would aid only medical schools and hospitals that were absolutely under one control that action would, it appears to me, be entirely opposed to the best prospects or progress of medical education throughout the country for there is not now and will I believe not be in the future any instance in which the enormous costs of adequate clinical facilities with all their diversity can be carried by a University and it seems to me a wrong social and economic principle not to take advantage of the interest of the communities in hospitals in aiding the progress of medical education.[45]

In April 1927, Edsall took up the cause again, this time determined not to give Flexner any tactical advantage. He sent a copy of his proposal to Pearce to see if he or his Rockefeller Foundation associates had any objections "that would act as a direct and influential further argument by Mr.

Flexner against taking up the plan." Edsall felt that his influence within the university would be harmed by a rejection, so he would drop the matter if there were any possibility of one. "That is not mere irritation on my part," he wrote Pearce, "though I confess that I do have very great difficulty in avoiding a constant sense of injustice in the way that we have been treated."[46]

When it became apparent to Edsall that Flexner was "fencing to avoid giving anything except a trivial sum" he requested that the proposal be withdrawn. To Pearce he again expressed his anger:

> I am quite unwilling to accept a little sop and let Mr. Flexner or the General Education Board feel that they have absorbed thereby any conscientious feeling that they ought to aid us. . . . I am awfully tired of this specious argument that the money is rapidly vanishing when it is obviously rapidly vanishing wholly for the things he [Flexner] is actively interested in and used in very large amounts for those purposes. . . . I would far rather have an entire bread and have no sense of any possible dependency in the future upon such aid than to be trifled with in this way as compared with the manner in which various other institutions are treated.[47]

A more public attack on Flexner's program came in an article by Hans Zinsser entitled "The Perils of Magnanimity: A Problem in American Education," published in the February 1927 *Atlantic Monthly*.[48] Zinsser was logically a Flexner ally: he was not only a preclinical scientist but a bacteriologist, the very field most exalted by the revolution in scientific medicine which Flexner felt he was championing. But Zinsser (from positions at Columbia and Harvard) had watched Flexner's maneuvering and had not approved. Flexner thus became the target of Zinsser's plea for university autonomy.

In his article Zinsser, in a perhaps backhanded compliment, praised "the golden fertilizer scattered over our medical schools" but, mixing his metaphors, detected a "threatening centre of the cloud with such a golden lining." He was wary that "the guidance of medical education is to a considerable extent passing out of the hands of the universities themselves into the hands of a permanent or, at any rate, self-perpetuating body of gentlemen who, by the very force of the established relations, cannot help extending their influence over all important centres of American education." Zinsser decried the asymmetry of power in the situation. "The expert and his board have opinions. They also have money. The universities, too, have opinions; but often no money; never enough." With

Columbia's humiliation clearly in mind, Zinsser rhetorically asked: "Have any of the leaders of individual schools put their pride into their pockets, reconsidered their own decisions, and wandered like Henry the Fourth to Canossa to say, 'Father, I have erred; give me the two millions?'"[49]

Zinsser was not criticizing philanthropy per se. He specifically complimented the International Health Board of the Rockefeller Foundation for avoiding these overbearing tendencies. In a suggestion which was soon reflected in the reorganization of the Rockefeller boards, he noted that

> it would appear to the observer a simple matter to eliminate them [the abuses of philanthropic power] completely from the educational programme of the foundations by a relatively slight adjustment to recent changes in the management of medical schools. . . . Is it not reasonable to hope that future donations may be determined purely on the basis of demonstrated needs and bestowed for definite purposes, leaving the details of procedure and organization entirely to the governing bodies of the beneficiary institutions?[50]

Distressed at the broadside, Chicago's McLean considered replying to Zinsser in print. Flexner wisely dissuaded him on the grounds that the close relationship between the University of Chicago and the Rockefeller boards would weaken the credibility of any rebuttal. "Moreover," he haughtily added, "on general principles, I think it hard to beat Disraeli's maxim: 'Never Reply!'"[51]

Despite the mounting criticism, Flexner began to extend his plan in the latter half of the decade by expressly or implicitly implying hefty commitments to his favored schools. He was restless with ideas for the future. He wrote his brother in May 1926 of his feeling that for the last few years "I have been busy with minutiae, I have, as far as large undertakings are concerned, simply marked time." He was determined to strike out on a bold path again despite "puerile suggestions" from his office colleagues that he take up projects which he considered "second-rate work of second-rate importance." He had not grown fonder of his colleagues over the years. "Whether the office group has done any real thinking I don't know."[52]

The starch in Flexner's administration of his policy was beginning to chafe this group. Although the Rockefeller Foundation was committed to promoting full-time in Europe, Vincent refused to adopt "the awkward position of forcing a hard and fast plan" in the face of local objections.[53] Other philanthropic officials reasoned from the standpoint of the recipients. One such was Anson Phelps Stokes. In many ways the intermingled history of American business and philanthropy converged in the figure of Stokes. The Phelps colonial merchant house developed into the Phelps-Dodge Corporation, a mining and industrial enterprise. The intermarrying Phelps and Dodge families were for generations active in religious, educational, social and even radical political movements. Anson had spent his life in the service of a variety of elite institutions: Yale, the Episcopal church, and several foundations. The distrust implicit in Flexner's full-time regulations irritated Stokes. "In the long run the difference between Mr. Flexner and myself, is largely this: That I have more confidence in our Universities administering the money for medical education in a wise way, than Mr. Flexner has."[54] Stokes's sentiments were widely shared. As General Education Board counsel Thomas M. Debevoise worried to Gates:

> Some day the power of the dead hand will again be the subject of political, if not popular, discussion, and if at that time the Board can show that its only purpose has been to give wisely and not, through the power of its wealth, to control the institutions on which the public depends for its medical men, I believe the Board will stand on safe ground.[55]

With this logic in mind, Stokes proposed in 1924 that the board retroactively liberalize the provisions of some of its grants so that full-time was not a binding condition on the recipient universities. When Stokes informed Flexner of his misgivings about the enforcement of full-time, the latter was "annoyed" but ready for the fight: "I shall skin him alive!" Flexner anticipated with relish the "dressing down" Gates would deliver to his weak-kneed colleagues. But in September 1925, the board approved the liberalization with only Gates and Flexner opposed.[56] Flexner was apparently unaware that in helping to destroy Gates's authority he had both weakened an ally and prepared the way for his own downfall.

The discomfort of the philanthropoids with Flexner went beyond the issue of binding contracts. The distance he had put between himself and them proved fatal to his program; beneath his notice the transition to new policies was gaining force. When his views collided with those which his despised office mates hammered out in a reorganization of the Rockefeller boards, his carefully articulated program in support of institutional networks was rejected in favor of a policy of support of particular research directions. That reorganization, which began in 1925 and culminated in

1928, was the first general review of the Rockefeller philanthropic agencies since their creation. As such, it was the occasion for consideration of organizational and theoretical issues to a fuller extent than was possible at the level of quotidian decisions. The outcome of the reorganization represented the full ascension of the new generation of philanthropic managers.

The captain of the reorganization process was Raymond Blaine Fosdick. In the late 1920s, Fosdick was well on his way to becoming Rockefeller junior's most trusted friend; but it was a typical Rockefeller intimacy: in their entire lives they never addressed each other as anything but "Mr. Rockefeller" and "Mr. Fosdick."[57] Fosdick's background rehearsed the Progressivism which his managerial class was rapidly transcending. Born in western New York of New England stock, he escaped his boyhood "preoccupation with the solemn issues of theology" at Princeton, where he formed a lasting devotion to Woodrow Wilson.[58] After college he worked in the Henry Street Settlement House and later became city chamberlain in the reform administration of New York mayor John Purroy Mitchell. During World War I, Fosdick headed the Commission on Training Camp Activities, one of the mixed public/private efforts produced in the organizational fever of the war. In that capacity, he catalyzed the merger of separate charities into the first national war relief drive.[59]

Fosdick had become associated with the Rockefellers through his brother, Harry Emerson Fosdick, the leading Baptist modernist whom the Rockefellers had brought to head the Fifth Avenue Baptist Church. Raymond performed a variety of tasks for several Rockefeller agencies and had been Rockefeller junior's first choice in 1920 to head the Laura Spelman Rockefeller Memorial, but Fosdick preferred to remain in the less conspicuous background of a law practice at 61 Broadway which permitted him ample time to serve on the several boards.[60] While serving on the Memorial board, Fosdick was an ally of Memorial director Beardsley Ruml in urging a more active role in the social sciences, despite the misgivings of such elders as Gates and Simon Flexner.[61] But Fosdick's focus was not particularistic. He was to serve Junior as a generalist whose first concern was the integrity of the philanthropic organization.

Just as the first waves of organizational activity among the philanthropic elite corresponded to the institution building of the early Progressive period, this reorganization process was congruent with similar changes in other fields. The "associationalism" of the 1920s was a reflection of the maturation of American institutional life to a stage where renovation and coordinations were more characteristic than the mere creation of new agencies.

The transition which took place in the Rockefeller boards was the same in form but radically different in content from the changes Alfred Chandler describes. Fosdick worried that the foundations were going about the reorganization process incorrectly. "Program must always come first and organization second," he wrote in 1926. "Perhaps in our zeal for efficient machinery we are making the mistake of trying to adapt our programs to our organizations instead of our organizations to our programs."[62] His misgivings proved correct. Although it was never acknowledged, the basic goals and concepts of the reorganizers were informed by their organizational positions in the Rockefeller hierarchy; the policies they developed were secondary to the preservation of the organizational integrity and legitimacy of the foundation. Structure determined strategy.

The internal administrative difficulties which confronted the Rockefeller boards in the late 1920s were the cumulative effect of their haphazard evolution. The situation was particularly acute in the Rockefeller Foundation itself, and it was there that the reorganization process began. Under the umbrella of the Foundation, subsidiary boards such as the China Medical Board and the International Health Board had been created to provide technical expertise and representative legitimacy. These subsidiaries reflected divergent paradigms of philanthropic activity. Whereas the China Medical Board reflected a combination of Jerome Greene's missionary heritage and Gates's bias toward strong central institutions, the International Health Board maintained the more evangelical style of the hookworm campaign, scattering fragile seedlings of public health organization as widely as possible but not necessarily planting them deep. In contrast, the International Education Board (tied to the GEB) reflected the idea that further growth of scientific knowledge was a more urgent task than the social application of existing expertise.

While nominally in charge, the Foundation president had little control over these subsidiaries which spent half its income. The diffusion of authority had become the occasion for internal empire building, a situation which naturally irenic president George Vincent found difficult to deal with. F. F. Russell, the director of the International Health Board, was so flagrant in pursuit of his own ambitions and so heedless of attempts by the central administration to restrain him that he finally provoked Vincent to request that the trustees resolve the issues. Vincent complained that it was no longer possible "to maintain unity of administration and co-ordination of effort solely by conference and mutual understanding," but that "the only satisfactory basis for the future is to be found in a clear definition of status, powers and duties" of the various officers.[63] Pearce echoed that "the most important change of all is to give the President of the Foundation a real job."[64]

Vincent and Pearce were natural allies. Both were part of the generation of disciples to the pioneers in their disciplines: Vincent in sociology and Pearce in pathology. Both had given up significant academic careers to join the Rockefeller Foundation, only to become frustrated by the difficulties of dealing with colleagues like Russell and Abraham Flexner. Unassuming to their admirers, neither was a particularly forceful personality in the give-and-take of daily policymaking. But that very ineffectiveness redounded to their benefit in the reorganization: respect for their conciliatory natures gave their views extra weight. This was particularly evident once the Rockefeller Foundation presidency had been strengthened and the process focused on revamping all the boards on a functional basis.

The reorganizers diagnosed the boards to be suffering from three interrelated sets of problems: disunity of purpose, a decline in the quality of personnel, and a disruption of the chain of administrative authority. It was felt that the several boards frequently worked at cross-purposes, sometimes giving mixed messages to a single recipient agency. The inability of the trustees to intelligently exercise any oversight was a frequently mentioned problem. The complexity and variety of the boards' operations induced officers to promote their own operations without reference to higher direction. These problems became especially acute when combined with the felt decline in the quality of philanthropic executives. Fosdick wrote to Rockefeller junior of the danger of the boards' "dying from the neck up," because of a lack of "first-class men." Fosdick felt that most American foundations were "wobbling" under "mediocre leadership" and that if the Rockefeller group were to set an example it would have to solve the problem of "brains."[65]

The specter of "bureaucracy" haunted the reorganizers. By their very American use of the term they meant to connote a circular pathology of confusion, inefficiency, and incompetence. "Bureaucracy" functioned for them as a convenient symbol upon which could be focused the accumulated tension of trying to promote reforms which would be both efficient and congruent with democracy. The concept was a foil which permitted redefinition of proximate goals without exploring the source of the tension. Rockefeller junior discerned a general pattern:

> Any human institution tends to get into a rut, to confuse motion with progress, and to exalt machinery and organization above work and objectives. This is certainly true in the business world, and it is equally true in philanthropy. . . . Machinery and personnel are merely the instruments by which objectives are reached, and unless we keep ourselves clear-eyed and fresh and keep machinery elastic, we run the risk of dry rot.[66]

Memoranda warned against "the tendencies towards setting up under private auspices administrative machinery which takes on some of the aspects of governmental bureaucracy."[67] Vincent, in a revealing juxtaposition, echoed transatlantic concerns over the "parliamentary inefficiency" of a possible "pseudo-bureaucratic system." "I wonder whether, after all, we do not need a benevolent despot, somebody big enough to dominate the entire situation," he speculated. "I for one am ready to put myself at the disposal of any leader of imagination, courage and will power who may be discovered and put in authority."[68]

The reorganization process put Flexner on the defensive. He shared the prevailing dissatisfaction with the quality of personnel and the growing absorption with administrative problems, but much of the reorganizers' litany read like an indictment of his style. In dealing with the University of Chicago, Flexner had displayed an obstructionist commitment to fixed notions and attitudes which frustrated more general goals. His conduct in the Columbia episode was an illustration of the problem of division of responsibility among the boards. His behavior toward Harvard had been characterized by a dissembling formalism. Flexner now had to defend in principle the structure and tactics which had given him so much power.

The conflict between Flexner and the reorganizers became apparent as the reorganization focused on two overlapping issues. The first was the extent to which the Rockefeller philanthropic efforts were to be unified. The second was the conceptual design of a program for whatever new structure was decided upon. These were interrelated insofar as the greater the functional unity decreed, the greater the need for a synthetic program which would accommodate the previously disparate enterprises. On the question of administrative unity the two polar positions which emerged for consideration were "one big union" of all existing lines of work in one corporate body or, conversely, separate endowment and organization of each activity.

Flexner tended toward the second position. His contributions to the reorganization discussions stressed his view of education as a system which required strong leadership from an enlightened elite. "Education broadly conceived necessarily involves organizations, systems, institutions, as well as individuals: hence, if you are going to deal broadly with education, you must have contacts with, knowledge of, and influence over, institutions and systems."[69] He rejected the notion, which he associated with Vincent, "that foundations dole out money to deserving organizations or institutions without attempting leadership of any kind."[70] He emphasized that foundation officers must face the fact that vital decisions were implicit in the grant-making process. In exercising "indirect leadership," foundation officers should promote within their fields a "cooperation [which] means not only the giving of money but placing at the disposal of persons dealing with local problems a broader experience and wider outlook than they usually possess or can acquire."[71] This was exactly the role Flexner had attempted to play over the past several years. He claimed that "the intimate, informal relationship" he had built up with the American medical education system was "the source of the strides that have been made in this field partly through the use of our funds."[72] However, as if to concede the tenuous public legitimacy of his view, he agreed that Vincent's was "doubtless the proper line to take in talking to the public" and that his own theory should not be "trumpeted from the housetops."[73]

Flexner recommended to the reorganizers that the Rockefeller boards be consolidated into two foundations. "The organization of the General Education Board must parallel the educational organization of the country," and thus it should absorb the domestic educational activities of the Laura Spelman Rockefeller Memorial and of the Rockefeller Foundation. The Foundation, in his proposal, would continue to be mostly an overseas operation.[74] Flexner saw such a geographical division as a virtue, at least in the case of the GEB:

> Now an American board dealing with education in the United States enjoys certain great advantages. It is at home; it can know people; it can understand the organi-

zation and spirit of those administering it. It is therefore in a position to deal with educational problems intimately, thoroughly and systematically. The moment you leave the United States, you are under enormous disadvantages—disadvantages so great that cooperation with *educational systems,* such as is possible and necessary in the United States, becomes at once impossible. Even in a country as close to us as Canada, no American board can deal with the system as a system.[75]

Flexner's view of educational unity had a vertical dimension as well. "You cannot undertake to develop science in a college or university as a thing by itself apart from other college and university activities." Similarly, medicine could not be abstracted from the area of higher education as a whole.[76] "To be really helpful," Flexner asserted, "foundations must be expert in aiding the men, the institutions, the ideas that will determine the future," and these much be treated not as three discrete problems but in "systematic interrelation."[77]

The reorganizers did not find the sort of leadership Flexner endorsed appealing. They rejected the idea of geographic division between two boards as conducive to bureaucratic mischief. Pearce felt that the division of responsibility for medical education between the GEB in the United States and the Rockefeller Foundation overseas had been a failure and should be abandoned.[78] While reluctant to lock horns with Flexner, Vincent cautiously averred that with proper staffing a transnational organizational was possible.[79] Wickliffe Rose put forward and Fosdick took up the slogan that such a geographic division was "like trying to maintain a body without a head."[80] Flexner's power was to be slowly eclipsed: all plans circulated among the in-group of reorganizers in 1927 and 1928 placed medical education exclusively in the Rockefeller Foundation. In those scenarios Flexner would supervise from a withering GEB the remains of Rockefeller senior's 1919 endowment.[81]

The degree to which Simon Flexner used his influence to try to maintain his brother's position is unclear. He did favor keeping domestic and foreign medical education organizationally separate but did not force the issue. Simon had lost some enthusiasm for the full-time plan. Whereas Abraham understood science through the framework of education, Simon was more oriented to the process of discovery. In his view, even full-time had proven an insufficient reform since teaching and patient care still impinged on time for experiments. (Abraham, in contrast, saw the three functions as synergistically related.) By 1926, Simon had come to feel that there was a worldwide "famine of ideals in medicine" following the wave of discovery associated with Koch and Pasteur. He did not see salvation coming from academic medicine, but rather looked to more concentrated efforts at experimental biology organized along the lines of the Rockefeller Institute or Woods Hole.[82]

Not only was Flexner's organizational base to be eliminated, but the policies compassed by the new structure were to be incompatible with his program. If the boards were not to be reorganized as Abraham Flexner had proposed on the basis of symmetry between the foundations and educational structures, then the reorganizers had to define a program which would preserve managerial authority over a new enlarged Rockefeller Foundation and prevent slippage into the bureaucratic slough. The new program was to be conditioned by the worldview of the reorganizers. Administrative control of the foundation was but one requirement of their managerial ideology. The new generation of managers, viewing the construction of modernity as yesterday's work, was preoccupied with the need for social control of the dynamics of modernity. Society was becoming more specialized and fragmented and by reason of the same forces more interconnected and liable to internal disruption. As pioneer sociologists, Vincent and Albion Small had tried to construct a discipline which could produce strategies for social stability based on that understanding.[83] As a foundation officer, Vincent wanted to direct foundation energies and funds toward that goal.

Fosdick shared this view. He wrote to Rockefeller junior that the era of entrepreneurial institution building was over: there was already a sufficiency of universities and foundations in the United States. What was needed was strategic management which would efficiently focus the capabilities of those institutions.[84] Such a management was vital since the very technological and organizational power of modern society was fraying the strands of social connection.

One of Fosdick's informing themes was the dangerous difficulties of modern life:

> We . . . are projected into a world so complex, into an environment so baffling, that few individuals can understand it at all, and fewer still can control it. We are tested with burdens in a way our grandfathers were never tested. We must carry responsibilities that would have broken the backs of our forebears a century ago.[85]

World War I in particular had led Fosdick to realize that "evolution may mean retrogression as well as progression, and that there is little in the past to encourage millennial expectations." He discerned an "abyss upon the edge of which the race is immediately standing," and foresaw "the inevitable doom which lies ahead unless we can achieve a measure of social control far greater than any which we have hitherto exercised."[86]

A program like Flexner's made no sense in the context of this view. Science was no longer seen as the facile solution to contemporary problems. "Science is neither the upbuilder nor the destroyer," wrote British scientist Frederick Soddy, who was influential in Fosdick's thinking. "It is the docile slave of its human masters. It will appear as the one or the other, according as the moral outlook of the latter is derived from a progressive and deepening sense of responsibility."[87] Science, and the universities which supported it, could be a tool for wider social management, but not ends in themselves as they were for Flexner.

The new program which the reorganizers devised for the Rockefeller Foundation was tailored to this attitude. This yearning for stability suggested that foundations should function as the crucial social lubricant which could keep the gears of science, social change, and mass politics from grinding. This worldview was a mandate for just the sort of management the rising generation of philanthropoids was eager to supply.

What strategy to pursue remained a problem, however. Anxious though the reorganizers were to avoid the depth of institutional entanglements of the Flexner program, they were uncomfortable with the notion of retail philanthropy. Vincent asserted that there was "no ground of dispute" that the foundation should not aid ad hoc research projects. Vincent was also worried by the "danger of over-simplification and suggestions of grandeur" in the use of sweeping phrases to define programs. But the employment of such rhetoric was already established in philanthropic tradition.[88]

In November 1927, Fosdick suggested (in a phrase originally put forth by Beardsley Ruml) that the solution to the reconstruction of the Rockefeller Foundation was "to think of it as an organization that for the time being is interested in the advance of human knowledge."[89] Under that rubric the foundation would be made up of divisions concerned with the physical and social sciences, the humanities and the arts, medical education, and agriculture and forestry. This "advance of knowledge" formula justified centralization of philanthropic power in one foundation while giving play to Fosdick's vision: the smaller units could selectively fund programs which promised to advance social integration. All other "miscellaneous functions unrelated to our central objective" were to be relegated to smaller boards, such as the GEB, which would be slowly liquidated in the foreseeable future.

But even if Flexner's program had been eliminated, the problem of his personality remained. The reorganization also turned on questions of personnel, and the choice to head the reorganized General Education Board was Trevor Arnett. Arnett had felt the sting of Flexner's lash both as a colleague at the General Education Board and as an administrator at the University of Chicago. He and the other reorganizers realized that having Flexner, forceful and active as he was, in a reformed structure alien to his ideas and his methods would be a recipe for disaster. As plans were firming up, Fosdick wrote to Rockefeller junior on February 21, 1928, of a complication:

> Arnett gave me to understand yesterday that he could not consider the Presidency if Abe were left in the picture. He said his situation would be impossible, and I think Rose would concur. Consequently something will have to be found for Abe or he will have to be retired. [90]

At lunch on March 29, Rockefeller junior informed Flexner of the decision to gradually terminate the General Education Board and concentrate work in medical education in the Rockefeller Foundation. Rockefeller delicately put it that Flexner should not have to serve under a younger man (Arnett) and suggested that Flexner resign from the board and join his personal staff. Flexner responded that he would not be "happy or useful" in that capacity and that he thought the plans to eliminate his program were a serious error. [91] But whatever his anger, Flexner later assured Fosdick that it was "perfectly plain to me that the one course for me to pursue was to retire in order to leave a free and unembarrassed situation for the new regime." He declined Rockefeller's offer of employment, but even so Rockefeller pledged to personally pay Flexner's salary ($20,000 a year, one-third higher than any salary Flexner would approve for full-time clinicians) and fund his pension until Flexner reached retirement. [92]

The reorganizers were eager to make Flexner's departure seem like a natural culmination of his work rather than a summary execution, so they decided not to name Pearce his successor as director of medical education in the GEB. They counted it a piece of good fortune that Flexner

would be leaving the country in the spring of 1928 to deliver already scheduled lectures at Oxford.[93] In publicly praising Flexner when his resignation
was announced, Rockefeller junior assured him that "while it never seems
as though one's work had been completed, to a marked degree the tasks to
which you have set your hand have been established in a way which en-
sured without question their permanency and further growth."[94]

The dismissal caught Flexner in a passionate dilemma. He was tem-
peramentally against public protest, yet sufficiently angry to want his
position made clear. "Now I accept with perfect good humor and good
faith a decision adverse to my own opinion," he wrote to Fosdick after his
resignation was announced, "but I do not wish the Board to get the impression given in Mr. R's letter to me, that I concur in the solution arrived at. How can my opinion be protected without raising any unnecessary discussion?"[95] Fosdick assured him that he would make the situation
clear to the board and mute any public controversy.[96] For his part, Flexner
sent out a typically apophasic circular letter "to my friends" which assured them that while he retired "with the most cordial and friendly personal relations" with his colleagues, he felt that "my presence under the
new conditions might prove an embarrassment to those who had the responsibility of conducting the new organization."[97]

The private management of this dispute concealed from the wider public the generational transition within the boards. Flexner, never fond of
the press, kept his silence even though reporters dogged him. The only
possible intimation of any conflict came from the *New Republic* which
commented, "as he [Flexner] closes one career . . . he will find his usefulness unimpaired and perhaps augmented by his new independence."[98]

The appearance of cordiality in Flexner's departure did not mislead
those most directly concerned, including the clinical science vanguard. Alfred Cohn felt that "one's worst suspicions in respect to the motives and
behavior among the greater gods are realized." Cohn acknowledged that
Flexner may have exhibited "awkwardness and tactlessness," but felt
that his "intellectual contribution" more than offset this. Cohn also felt
that Flexner's circular showed "a kind of habit of subservience to the
powers that be which seems to me altogether undesirable." Now that it
had seemingly turned against him, Cohn resented the power of the philanthropic elite. "It is entirely unnecessary," he wrote to McLean, "that
the opinions of a person like him [Flexner] should be pleasant or agreeable

to any lot of lay people who have nothing to recommend them from his point of view except the vastness of their financial resources."[99] Cohn's resentment was misdirected: it was not the plutocrats but the bureaucrats who had displaced Flexner. To Flexner, Cohn was more encouraging: "Without any obligations you may now become our sage . . . I congratulate you and rejoice heartily that you are a free man."[100]

But Flexner was far from rejoicing as that spring and summer he privately vented his spleen. To his brother Simon he wrote that the "sudden guillotining of a life's work,"[101] had left him stunned and angry: "my mind has not ceased to marvel at either the folly or the brutality of what has been done."[102] He was particularly distressed at the "dismay throughout the groups I have worked with," and worried that without New York support the teams that had been assembled would disperse.[103] While in England, Flexner found himself "wondering more and more what on earth Fosdick, Mr. R., Vincent etc., think or why."[104]

Upon his return to America in the late summer, the sources of his frustration became clearer. Flexner came to feel that he had been the only honest player in the intrigue of the reorganization. He concluded that Charles Howland, of the GEB reorganization committee, had led him to believe that they were allies when in fact Howland was too timid to object to Flexner's ouster since Rockefeller junior was bankrolling Howland's work with the Council on Foreign Relations. "Hence, that's his bribe!" Abraham indignantly announced to Simon, "And how is intellectual freedom to develop in America under such conditions inside and outside universities, etc.?"[105] Howland tried to appease Flexner by describing how it was Fosdick who had determined the reorganization, an intelligence which Flexner felt "compromises the candor and straightforwardness of R.B.F." Aghast at the ascendency of the new managers, Flexner despaired that "there are no boards any longer at 61 [Broadway]."[106]

In December 1928, eight months after his ouster, Flexner still lamented not only his personal rejection but also that of his paradigm of planning leadership:

> I confess I do not see far ahead as far as America is concerned. Prosperity has swept the country off its feet and all the echoes one gets come from the stock market. Doubtless in quiet corners, men and women of ideas and ideals are working, but they are not running the show,—and will not, I assume, for a long time to come. Time was when guidance of a sort came from one or two institutions,—the Hopkins for a generation, the Foundations when Mr. Gates' vision ruled. All that

has for the time being disappeared. No University represents Gilman's ideals: and the Foundations are at sea. I have been favored with a copy of the Pearce-Edsall medical program. It does not strike me as sound or hopeful. The Hopkins-Flexner regime is to be summarily replaced by a Pearce-Edsall-Harvard regime. No more institutions to be established and financed: that day is over. . . . "Knowledge is to be extended" through furthering projects and selecting men—and who is to judge: persons who every day get further from the realities. . . . In my view, institutions must be built up,—as at Yale, Chicago, Cornell, and let alone. If they do not furnish conditions in which ideas, ideals and men will sprout, no fellowship can do the job.[107]

Simon Flexner tried to reconcile his brother to the new order: "The great constructive period may indeed be eclipsed. . . . There is, however, a vast consolidation needed."[108] But Abraham was only partly mollified. "I have no doubt they will do some good things," he wrote of the new managers to another of his brothers, "even Mr. Carnegie could not spend hundreds of millions and waste them all, but they are timid and they are trying to buy popularity, both of which I abhor."[109] Still, though he wished to "explode and tell the world," he remained publicly silent.[110]

The course of Flexner's tenure with the General Education Board was an indication of the limits of philanthropic reform. He was undone by the very forces he had set in motion, in a fate that had elements of classic tragedy. Surely he had more than his share of flaws: he could be arrogant, stubborn, and occasionally dishonest. Moreover, his program was a top-heavy and expensive system which he force-fed into overrapid growth. This policy compassed the organization on fixed principles of a network of medical schools with internal hierarchy and collective similarity. He reserved to himself the authoritative interpretation of those principles. Flexner conceived of this structure as a vindication of democracy in that it would produce collective excellence and individual opportunity. But in order for that structure to achieve its democratic end, Flexner insisted that it be uniform and centrally directed.

In that unyielding attitude, his usually acute political instinct had failed him. His portion of authority was too large: it threatened the political legitimacy of the philanthropic foundation. However, it is important to note that the telling attacks on Flexner's authority did not come from a neo-populist movement but from a bureaucratic class within the foundations and the medical schools which was frustrated in its projects by his regime. That those attacks deliberately employed an idiom borrowed from the wider democratic political culture suggests both the impoverished vocabulary of the organizational revolution and the survival of an independent political structure in the face of that transformation.

To his frustration, Flexner realized too late that his model of foundation management rested on a shifting combination of ideals, perceived organizational needs, and personal ambitions which was far too unreliable for a program as carefully articulated as his. As he ruefully noted after his dismissal: "contemporary America . . . does unwittingly two things—gives such opportunity as no other country does, and then denies opportunity as perhaps no other country could."[111]

His success at promoting the idea of philanthropic policy as an integral entity made possible the career of his successors and the means of his own overthrow. This was the irony of his fall. Indeed, it was his tenacity as a policymaker which meant that he had to be swiftly extirpated from an organization whose goals he would oppose. Not sharing Flexner's underlying belief in immanent scientific rationalism, the succeeding managerial generation perceived his style as a niggling persnicketiness that threatened both their organizational efficiency and their institutional legitimacy. By focusing on Flexner's undeniable liabilities, the new managers were able to pass over, initially at least, more substantial problems (such as the necessity of hierarchy in the social organization of knowledge) which Flexner had frankly faced.

The reorganization which Fosdick led was not entirely the cynical operation which it seemed to Flexner but founded on a large amount of wishful thinking. The problems of the bureaucratic management of knowledge could not be easily reorganized away, particularly by the plan that had been fixed on. In the following years, the combination of the vague formula of the "advance of knowledge" with an inherently competitive divisional organization produced frustrations which vexed both the foundation officers and the trustees. Nor could the responsibility for leadership be fulfilled in an organization the size and importance of the Rockefeller Foundation without producing friction which would eventually find political expression. But these were lessons each administative generation would have to discover for itself.

6 "Administrative Tabes"

Abraham Flexner never groomed a protégé in the Rockefeller boards, but the man chosen to be his successor, Alan Gregg, could logically have been his own choice as well. Gregg, director of the Division of Medical Science of the Rockefeller Foundation from 1930 to 1951, shared many of Flexner's ideals and abilities, but none of his flaws.[1] Flexner and Gregg held to the same formula for social leadership: a belief in the university as the incubator of a vital elite and in the foundations as the institutional buttress of the university. Gregg was a man of great insight and was skilled at putting his insights into compelling expression. Unlike his cocksure and irascible predecessor, Gregg was enormously self-reflective and possessed a broad sympathy for human variety. Indeed, when in 1936 Flexner surveyed from a distance the foundation managers who had succeeded him, the only one who passed his stringent muster was Gregg.[2]

However, Gregg's attempts at enacting the formula of institutional leadership met with continual frustration, a frustration which testified to the singular moment of Flexner's career. That moment had passed, and Gregg was caught looking backward. Flexner's regime cast a shadow on Gregg's in two ways. First, Gregg was obliged to spend a great deal of energy pacifying Flexner's abruptly weaned network of medical schools. Even more difficult was Gregg's struggle to cope with the consequences of the reorganization which ousted Flexner. Raymond Fosdick had intended the 1928 reorganization to strengthen the Rockefeller Foundation's capacity for philanthropic leadership by obviating "bureaucracy," his catchall designation for arbitrary action, administrative futility, and petty empire building. From Gregg's standpoint, just the opposite took place. The results of reorganization—the divisional structure of the foundation, the policy of giving only small grants, and the determination of the trustees to maintain control over the officers—all produced what Gregg, applying a medical term, labeled "administrative tabes": a progressive withering of the Rockefeller Foundation's leadership.[3]

The withdrawal of the Rockefeller boards from the role they had played under Flexner coincided with the growth of government funding for medical research and education. In spite of government's increasing role, however, there was by the 1950s as little capacity for strategic leadership in the formation of policies for medical education as there had been before the rise of private philanthropy. The centrifugal tendencies of American political culture had reasserted themselves, but on a bureaucratic plane. Moreover, the new policy stalemate was likely to be more intractable than the Jacksonian deadlock of a century earlier.

At a meeting in January 1929, the Rockefeller Foundation trustees resolved that "concern with the development of medical schools as institutions be lessened and the principle of aid to individuals, groups and departments in relation to research and advance of medical knowledge be emphasized."[4] This change in policy was portrayed as "obviously an adjustment to changed and bettered conditions, an adjustment in fact to alterations that the activities of the Foundation itself have been in very noteworthy degree responsible for bringing about."[5]

The new policy held that the Rockefeller Foundation would no longer play the sugar daddy to the universities. "If the purposes that the individual academic institutions themselves have in view in their own work are to be determining factors in deciding upon aiding or not aiding further the general developments, these general matters will be endless and will absorb certainly far the larger proportion of the Foundation's resources." The trustees were intent on devoting those resources to purposes of their own determination.[6]

This "departure from the policy of multiplying well-organized and complete schools" was consistent with the thrust of the previous year's reorganization of the Rockefeller boards.[7] In order to achieve greater control over the various Rockefeller philanthropies, Fosdick centralized most activities in the Rockefeller Foundation. A new set of personnel had been brought in to administer the new organizations. After an attempt to hire Ernest Hopkins, the president of Dartmouth College, failed, Max Mason, the departing president of the University of Chicago, was selected to assume the Foundation presidency. Richard M. Pearce was the head of the Medical Science Division. As part of the effort to strengthen administrative control over the Foundation's actions, grants for endowment were prohibited and no grants were to be made for longer than two years.[8]

These revised policies posed problems for the network of schools which Flexner had been nurturing. The new managers invited Flexner to a meeting in May 1929 to discuss those schools. It became apparent that Flexner had implied significant support for a number of years and that the Rockefeller boards would not be able to gracefully back out of his commitments. With ironic understatement Flexner said he hoped the trustees would not feel that he had subverted their authority; but whatever suspicions the new managers had held of Flexner's tactics could only have been increased by this glimpse into the workings of his previously privately managed system. Pearce agreed that some aid to the schools would have to be forthcoming, but he was determined that the connection between the schools and the New York boards would have to be definitively tapered off.[9]

However, Pearce died in 1930, and the task of righting Flexner's program fell to Alan Gregg. Like so many of the early philanthropoids, Gregg was the son of a clergyman. He was born in Colorado Springs, Colo., to a Scotch Presbyterian minister and his wife. Gregg grew up in the vortex of the "age of industrial violence," and he later recalled that his first, no doubt unflattering, introduction to the Rockefeller name was at an Industrial Workers of the World meeting. At Harvard College, he was deliberately a C student, not out of social pretension but "so that I could cover a lot of ground and fields of interest." He later recollected that the most important event of his college life was a stay at James Jackson Putnam's summer camp in the company of Freud, Ferenczi, and Jung who were then touring America. Gregg considered attending the Johns Hopkins Medical School but, worried about the prospect of obtaining summer employment in Baltimore, decided instead to continue his education at Harvard where he was one of David L. Edsall's pupils.[10]

Gregg never practiced medicine. After graduation from medical school, he joined the International Health Board of the newly formed Rockefeller Foundation and was assigned to work in Latin America fighting hookworm disease and organizing public health departments. When the Foun-

dation's Division of Medical Education was created in 1920, Gregg became
Pearce's deputy in the Foundation's New York office. In 1924, Gregg undertook Rockefeller Foundation work in Europe where he eventually became head of the Paris office. He remained in that post until Mason, with
the offhanded diffidence which characterized his unsuccessful Foundation
presidency, belatedly informed him that he had been appointed Pearce's
successor as director of the medical sciences: Gregg himself had already
read of his appointment in the newspaper. [11]

Gregg had harbored a personal devotion to both Pearce and former
Foundation president George E. Vincent, but those sentiments did not
preclude a certain admiration for their old antagonist Flexner. Gregg felt
that Flexner had some disagreeable traits, but recalled him fondly as one
of the "giants" of the Rockefeller philanthropies. After his ouster from
the Rockefeller boards, Flexner had begun to organize the Institute for
Advanced Study at Princeton, but he still kept his eye on medical education. Soon after Gregg assumed the directorship, the two men met for
lunch. Flexner was emphatic that Gregg should pick up where he himself
had left off. He beseeched the new director to concentrate Rockefeller
money on a few selected schools and admonished him not to let the Foundation's new policies drag him into what Edith Wharton called the "thick
of thin things." [12]

Gregg shared Flexner's misgivings about the exclusive focus on research which was the mandate of the Foundation's program in the "advance of knowledge." He felt it was "unwise to ignore the conservation
and propagation of existing knowledge." [13] He worried that the gains of
earlier medical education reformers would be lost if the Rockefeller Foundation did not exercise a watchful guardianship. Gregg knew that the economic and administrative position of the schools Flexner had reformed so
recently was not so strong as to easily withstand the abrupt termination
of support from New York.

Indeed, those schools where Flexner's influence had been the strongest
were in the most difficult positions. In the early 1930s, Rochester, Vanderbilt, and Chicago all confronted the deepening depression with insuffi-
ciently endowed schools, incomplete plants, expensive hospitals, and little
community support. Gregg's problem was how to reconcile efforts to aid
these schools with the Foundation's shift away from institutional support.
One expedient was the fluid research fund—a mechanism whereby the

Foundation made a substantial grant to a school for internal distribution to fund research projects. This device strengthened the hand of the school's administration, which could select the ultimate recipients, and also freed up some of their own resources for other uses. Gregg secured significant fluid research funds for Vanderbilt and Rochester, although some within the Foundation wondered aloud where Vanderbilt ever got the notion that it could be primarily a research school.[14]

But the problems of the University of Chicago needed more than a fluid research fund for solution. The tangled situation there showed how the Rockefeller Foundation's new policy tied Gregg's hands. Flexner's achievement in creating a new medical school for the university in 1916 was in danger of becoming undone. The relation between the university and Rush Medical College, the school with which Chicago had been exclusively affiliated before 1916, was still unresolved. The resulting uncertainty was heightened by change in the university's administration. After Max Mason resigned in 1928, a long interim ensued under acting president Frederic Woodward until the summer of 1929 when Robert Maynard Hutchins took office.

Whether the new administration was committed to Flexner's original 1916 plan to concentrate all undergraduate clinical teaching on the university's South Side campus, and convert Rush into a postgraduate school where practitioners could "brush up," was not at first clear. A complicating factor was the desire of the university administration to have the Presbyterian Hospital, which had always had a relation to the Rush faculty, move to the South Side so that some of the financial burden of maintaining the clinics could be lifted from the university.

In 1929 the university administration repeated an offer to turn over the Billings Hospital (which it had constructed) to the Presbyterian board and expressed its desire "that the [Presbyterian] hospital shall fully retain its identity with the same degree of independence and control of its affairs which it now enjoys." Woodward did not want to make an issue of the full-time plan but wanted to stipulate "that so far as practible our medical faculty and your hospital staff should be made up of men, whether 'part-time' or 'full-time,' who are qualified both in medical science and in the art of healing." This meant, in effect, that present members of the Rush faculty would either be excluded from the merged faculties or be in clearly subordinate positions.[15]

The Presbyterian trustees rejected the offer as incompatible with the hospital's purpose. The board president stated that he and his colleagues did not want to "change the Hospital from a public hospital primarily for the care of the sick under the care of a staff of practicing physicians and surgeons, to a hospital primarily a department of the University's school of medicine." Moreover, there was the problem of institutional loyalties: Presbyterian had been in large part founded by the Rush staff members, and the hospital trustees did not feel that they could sever that relation.[16]

The university was thus in a bind. The full-time plan had been premised on the assumption that a charitable hospital would underwrite the maintenance of beds for nonpaying indigent patients who would be the clinical material for the full-time staff. Without that charitable support, the clinics were too expensive for the university to maintain. The solution which Professor of Medicine Franklin McLean and other leading members of the South Side faculty turned to was the admission of patients to the Billings Hospital on the basis of their ability to pay. The fees for professional service which those patients paid to the full-time staff could then be devoted to the support of the clinics. This was a desperate innovation: it had not been previously thought that paying patients would submit to being used as teaching material. But the slow and cautious implementation of the system was eventually successful; the increased prestige of medical science had made the alliance between hospital care and research seem desirable to patients.[17]

When Flexner, then writing his book *Universities: American, English, and German* (a defense of his education views in general and the full-time plan in particular) heard of this scheme, he was livid. He saw the move to accept paying patients regularly as a retreat from the university idea.[18] McLean managed to assuage Flexner, but the university administration, unsure of the extent of Flexner's influence, was distressed. After a visit to New York, Hutchins assured his colleagues that they need not worry about Flexner anymore. "Neither Mr. Mason or Mr. Day expressed any sentiment but amusement" at Flexner's opinions, and Mason said "explicitly" that Flexner's attitudes would have no effect on Foundation or GEB decisions. The New York boards were happy to let the Chicago administration work out its hospital policies and its relations with Rush in any way it saw fit.[19]

But pressure was exerted from other quarters. University trustee

Thomas E. Donnelly wanted to continue undergraduate teaching at Rush. "What I am afraid of is that we are altogether too theoretical," Donnelly wrote Hutchins, "and because Rush Medical College does not quite measure up to our theories, we are scrapping a real asset, and when we look back upon what we have done ten years from now, we will realize that we have been guilty of both an educational and an economic blunder." He was willing to continue the South Side school as an "experiment," but he was convinced that full-time "was more of a hobby of Dr. Flexner's than the result of a conservative development in medical teaching." Donnelly felt it was important that Rush cost the university little and was producing far more graduates than were the University Clinics.[20]

To help plan its course, the university asked David Edsall to make a survey of the situation. Not surprisingly, he recommended that the university organize its various medical departments as his colleagues had done at Harvard. Edsall proposed that "both the Presbyterian Hospital and those associated with Rush move out to the immediate neighborhood of the University; not coalescing the departments fully, however, but running as two separate units, any two departments handling the same subject in a different way, and let them cooperate with each other and, so to speak, compete with each other, but leaving them in a situation where they are in control of their own activities in a way that would not be very different from the present." Edsall discounted the jealousy which might ensue from having two groups of widely differing incomes cheek by jowl, seeing it as a "theoretical rather than actual" objection. Rather, he thought, Rush would be stimulated to higher academic standards. Such a solution would be far superior to the "serious misfortune of having any definite conflict with Rush Medical School [*sic*], and those associated with and interested in it, and the great harm of having actual separation."[21]

A memorandum on the situation was also solicited from Alan Gregg, and his response was indicative of both his values and his methods. In contrast to Flexner, Gregg did not desire to be "contentious or particularly argumentative," but he was forceful nonetheless. He laid out the costs and benefits of each possible move the university and Rush might make. While he considered the Harvard option as a possibility, he felt the comparison with Chicago was "fallacious" since there were no full-time clinical chiefs at Harvard. The general thrust of Gregg's argument was that the university had embarked on a course which was too promising to abandon. Gregg laid particular stress on the importance of preserving the South Side organization in its original form. From Harper on, he maintained, the university had been closely associated with a "continuing preference for the advancement of knowledge." While Edsall had stressed the value of Rush's clinical resources, Gregg was confident that "more and more clinical facilities will be given to the University of Chicago and that in twenty five years the West Side beds will be quite superfluous to the needs of the medical faculty." A university was the most durable of human institutions, Gregg pointed out, and he averred that "were the Presbyterian Trustees familiar with the history of European hospitals I am confident they would consider more seriously the ultimate unwisdom of a new building anywhere except the South Side when the time comes for rebuilding."[22]

Gregg's comments on full-time were insightful. "The full time plan has been too much fathered and too little mothered: after a vigorous and incisive initiative the plan now needs a wise, patient, and solicitously protective attention to the details of a favorable environment." He hoped that the university would be able to protect the fragile growth since he was unable to provide any significant aid from the Rockefeller Foundation.[23] But increasing financial pressure put the university's commitment to full-time in danger. In April 1932, McLean wrote to the dean of the biological sciences that "the clinical departments of the Division of Biological Sciences are entering upon a critical period, and one which threatens their whole existence as university departments" as they were planned. The problem was that full-time had been adopted "during a period of prosperity, when it was assumed that almost any financial needs could be met," but the university still needed at least $5 million more in endowment if the clinics were to be stabilized. The need was particularly acute since the Julius Rosenwald Fund was no longer able to pay on its pledges to the University Clinics because of the severe drop in the value of its endowment.[24] McLean asked Gregg if the Rockefeller boards would be receptive to a plea from the university, especially in view of the fact that the purposes for which they had invested over $10 million were threatened. Gregg regretfully predicted that the boards would be unwilling to make any large grants to Chicago. He pointed out that he disagreed with that policy and hoped that it would be changed, so he urged the university to try to hold off any such requests until it would meet a friendlier reception.[25]

Because of the tight financial situation, the university was especially loath to take any action against Rush that would alienate potential donors. As Thomas Donnelly did not fail to remind Hutchins, "If we abandon Rush, it will hurt the standing of the University with the substantial people of the city. There will be an impression that we are theoretical and perhaps high-hat and are not a practical institution to which to leave their money."[26] Hutchins was too much an educational purist to abandon the full-time school; but at the same time he was leary of losing local support by cutting Rush loose. In his inaction, rumors flew that the schools would be merged, and relations between the two faculties became increasingly acrimonious. Writing to Hutchins in 1936 the director of the University Clinics urged actions to strengthen his school's morale, noting that "sitting about for another ten years is not going to promote sweetness and light, nor heal the breach that now exists."[27]

Hutchins did sit about, however, and time was on his side. Rush had traditionally drawn many transfer students from two-year schools in the Midwest, and as those schools shrank in size or lost their accreditations, Rush's enrollment dropped dangerously. By 1939 it was clear that since Hutchins would oppose a merger with the South Side school, the only effective choices for Rush were to become independent or to transform into a graduate training school as Flexner had urged in 1916. The Rush faculty was neither qualified for nor interested in graduate teaching, and accordingly, in 1941, Harper's impulsive affiliation between Rush and the university was formally dissolved.[28]

The Chicago full-time school was thus saved by Hutchins, a somewhat Flexnerian figure in his conception of the university's unique mission and his stubbornness in maintaining it. Without such dedicated leadership, other schools in Flexner's network—Columbia, Rochester, Vanderbilt, and Yale—abandoned the scheme as Flexner had outlined it and as Gregg supported it. Because of the limits placed on him by the Rockefeller Foundation's new policies, Gregg was powerless to shore up the full-time system. This inability to take critical actions in support of projects he felt were important was a continual vexation to Gregg during his tenure as director of the Medical Science Division.[29]

Another problem was his relationship with Warren Weaver, the director of the Foundation's Natural Sciences Division from 1932 until 1955. Weaver was a classical physicist who had collaborated with Max Mason on a textbook on electromagnetism. In 1932, Mason asked Weaver to come to New York to join him at the Rockefeller Foundation. Weaver was anxious about city living, but since he had become alienated from his chosen field by the ascendancy of quantum mechanics, which he considered a passing fad, he was willing to launch a new career. Unfortunately, the program of the Natural Sciences Division was totally outside Weaver's expertise. The trustees had mandated that Foundation programs should enhance "man's understanding of himself," and so the Natural Sciences Division had developed a program in the life sciences which Weaver further refined according to the theme of "psycho-biology." This brought him into intramural competition with the program of the Medical Science Division in psychiatry.[30]

The activities of the Medical Science Division in psychiatry cannot be explored in detail here, but several points are relevant to the interrelated problems of the organization of the Foundation and Gregg's administrative style. The program in psychiatry represented the transition from broad social reform to more scientifically focused studies: "mental hygiene" (an interest of the Foundation in the 1920s), gave way to psychiatry. There was also a personal dimension: as Gregg later recalled, it was possible to gain support for an often esoteric program because "many of the trustees had personal reasons to know the ravages of mental illness."[31] Both Mason's and Fosdick's first wives had suffered from mental illness and committed suicide, Mrs. Fosdick also killing her two children.[32] Gregg's administration of the program gave evidence of his breadth of mind and his devotion to institutional leadership. Rather than try to promote a single point of view in a shifting and contentious field, Gregg tried to promote ideological and scientific diversity in the university departments and subdepartments of psychiatry which the Foundation supported. He strove to promote cooperation among the professionally jealous psychiatrists, psychologists, neurologists, and psychoanalysts. He wanted the departments he help found to explore every aspect of the problem of mentation from basic research in neuroanatomy to the application of various talking therapies. In addition to supporting psychiatry departments in medical schools, the Rockefeller Foundation under Gregg supported such organizations as Yale's Institute for Human Relations and the Chicago Institute for Psychoanalysis.[33]

Gregg's desire for breadth in research brought him into conflict with

Weaver. Weaver's aggressive promotion of "psycho-biology" preempted many of the basic sciences which Gregg was interested in and confused recipient institutions. Because of the competition, Weaver became increasingly aggressive in his promotion of his program. This tended to alienate the trustees and produce just the sort of problems the 1928 reorganization had been designed to avoid. Weaver later recalled "a definite atmosphere of well, conflict is too strong a word, but contest is not—between the officers and the trustees." To the officers, the board loomed as "a somewhat hostile audience" which held "an orthodox and restraining attitude toward the ideas which the officers brought in." Meetings thus became "rather violent and sometimes rather unhappy and unpleasant."[34]

Another problem was Mason's unsuitability for the strong presidency which the reorganization had created. Even by the testimony of his friends, Mason's "mercurial brilliance" was not suited to the task of administering a foundation with varied concerns. He had neither the patience nor the desire to be the essential link between the officers on the one hand and the trustees and the public on the other. Unlike Gates, Flexner, Vincent, or Fosdick, he made little effort to produce the sort of guiding concepts and documents which were essential to the rationalistic procedures of scientific philanthropy.[35]

In order to clear up this administrative quagmire, a "Committee on Appraisal and Plan" of the trustees with Fosdick as chairman was formed to review the Foundation's work. As historian Robert Kohler has pointed out, the committee was designed to give Fosdick an opportunity to reinforce the consensus which lay behind the principles of the 1928 reorganization.[36] Like so many such operations, the form of the committee's procedure was wide-ranging, but the conclusions were preordained. Despite the long odds, Gregg made every effort to bend the committee's recommendations in a new direction away from the narrow focus of 1928.

Echoing Flexner, Gregg made clear to Fosdick his concern "that programs in the RF tend to get small, scrappy, numerous and diffuse." The trustee-imposed limitation of grants to one year pushed the officers "toward numerous . . . inconsequential undertakings." Gregg felt that there had been a "tendency towards too rigid an interpretation of research and concentrated teaching." He maintained that such an emphasis was shortsighted since "in the long run research can be aided better through some attention to teaching facilities than through ad hoc Simon pure research grants." Like Flexner, Gregg saw teaching and research as inextricably linked in the institutional form of the university which it was the task of private philanthropy to maintain. "One might as well insist," he pointed out, "that the tree has nothing to do with the fruit as to say that assistance to the stability and healthiness of education has nothing to do with the quality of research." Gregg wanted the Foundation to turn its attention to the "general husbanding, stimulation, protection, and support which will make the permanent difference which I understand to be our best objective."[37]

Gregg proposed several methods by which the Foundation should reassert its institutional leadership. In his reports to the committee, Gregg suggested that "the best programs during the past ten years in the field of medical education and medical science have been buildings and endowments at strategic points, fellowships local and foreign, and long-term research grants-in-aid of capable investigators."[38] Gregg also extolled to Fosdick the virtues of fluid research funds. He maintained that such a fund "sharpens the critical judgment of professors and the university administration since it repeatedly posed the question of relative merit or probable excellence of performance in research of a number of applicants." Gregg saw the funds as a means of institutional strengthening without the domineering supervision which Flexner had exercised. Gregg was certain that such funds "would meet the greatest institutional needs in the U.S. in the years 1934–36 almost regardless of what faculty is involved."[39]

However, Gregg's pleas went unheeded, for while the committee endorsed his management of the Medical Science Division, it turned down every one of his suggestions for new departures. Although the report of the committee expressed some "uneasiness" over the rapid growth of the "small and scattering type of gift," it still took refuge in the notion that a carefully defined program could eliminate the problem. The committee refused to change the policies which prohibited endowment and general institutional support. It urged that fluid research funds be dispensed with since they tended "to blunt the force with which the Foundation might strike at problems of pressing moment." The report also airily asserted that the universities would take up where the Rockefeller Foundation left off.[40]

Since the committee's report did not address the fundamental problems, the tensions within the Foundation persisted, increasing Gregg's frustration. In 1936, he privately complained to his former mentor David Edsall, who was then a Foundation trustee, about the devastating combination of a faulty policy and Mason's flawed personality. Since the committee's report, acrimony between the trustees and the officers had continued unabated. Gregg was sympathetic that "the trustees want some handles, guiding lines and general programs and some limits," on what the officers were trying to do, but he felt that hewing closer and closer to an abstractly defined program only increased the disagreements within the Foundation. Since the trustees, Gregg felt, did not "understand the projects submitted nor entirely trust the results of Trustee-Officer collaboration," further concentration on small projects only made the projects more esoteric and thereby widened the gulf between the two groups.[41]

Weaver remained a problem. Gregg professed a personal liking for the "sincere, conscientious and hard working Weaver" even though he felt the natural sciences director was "pretty naive in dealing with people" and "quite simply not at home in dealing with the biological sciences." But Gregg was certain that a program in biology "could be put in hands far more competent internally and far more acceptable externally" than those of Mason's protégé. Referring to Mason, Gregg complained of the absence of "a kind of leadership which has emphasized the exchange of opinion, the suspended judgments, and the reflections of the officers . . . and most of the others don't go in for that sort of thing anyway."[42]

Gregg suggested to Edsall that the basis of the divisional organization was itself foolish. Making the same point that Flexner had made during the reorganization, Gregg thought that the Foundation should organize its activities along lines symmetrical with educational organizations rather than according to the abstractions of its internal program. "It seems to me," he wrote, "that either the NS [Natural Sciences Division] or the MS [Medical Science Division] should be fused or that the line between them should be on the basis of the recipient institution being a medical school, hospital, or medical institute, or other than that, the NS taking all others than the medical schools."[43]

Gregg came close to resigning at several points during the early 1930s over what he felt was Mason's incompetence and consistent favoritism of

Weaver in any dispute over administrative turf. He eventually became so frustrated with the president that in 1935 he complained directly to Fosdick.

Fosdick acknowledged a "growing lack of confidence" in the Foundation president, but was not sure how to get the trustees to handle it: "I dread it like a toothache," he commented when he contemplated the possible confrontation. He hoped that Mason might still "change his spots" since he was not at all certain who would be a good successor. But when he was convinced that the situation had become impossible, Fosdick stepped into the breach and in 1936 assumed the presidency. [44]

Gregg was pleased with this change, but remained wary. In a trenchant and prophetic analysis he noted to himself that Fosdick was an "active and restless man . . . quick in his estimates and essentially partisan in his sympathies and attitudes." The new president, Gregg felt, was "intelligent but not intellectual" and more concerned with means than ends. Gregg was confident that he would be emotionally and intellectually compatible with Fosdick and hopeful that Fosdick would resolve the conflict with Weaver in a way that would probably see the subordinate officer's departure "on the basis of lack of knowledge of his field." But while Gregg was convinced that Fosdick was someone who "presses hard for what he wants" and who would even "employ various and perhaps devious means to obtain it," he worried that Fosdick had a tendency to "countenance expediency" and favor "temporary and inconclusive makeshifts if these be necessary to avoid decisions he dislikes." [45]

Gregg's insights soon proved correct. The administrative concordat Fosdick worked out in 1937 between Gregg and Weaver was just one of those makeshifts. The program of the Natural Sciences Division was defined as "modern experimental biology": biochemistry, cellular biophysics, cellular and general physiology, developmental mechanics, genetics and cytology, nutrition, and radiation biology. The physical sciences which "seem likely to furnish results of importance to biology" were also to be supported as were items of "unquestionably outstanding quality" which fell outside those disciplines. The Medical Science Division was to be concerned with psychiatry, broadly understood, and other challenging opportunities in medicine which might be presented to the Foundation. [46] The demarcation between the divisions was made on the basis of program and not recipient.

Fosdick weakly addressed the question of institutional demarcation by urging the Natural Sciences Division "regard as out of program requests which have to do with specific applications in medical schools of the results of fundamental research." In making this distinction, Fosdick was putting forth a lawyerlike abstraction which was untenable in daily practice and which repudiated the Foundation's heritage. Not only was the line between fundamental and applied research ultimately indistinct, but the entire thrust of Rockefeller activities in medicine had been to bridge the chasm between clinical and preclinical research. Fosdick had transferred the programs in the physiology of sex and endocrinology from the Natural Sciences Division to the Medical Science Division because they were largely "clinical." Perhaps aware of the futility of the exercise, Fosdick admonished Gregg and Weaver that "an unusual degree of cooperation and understanding between the personnel of the two divisions is essential."[47]

Gregg was dismayed at Fosdick's action and once again considered resigning. He did not want to "share responsibility with a man whose knowledge of biology and medicine is not what the RF could command and whom I would not choose as a subordinate or superior for the work." He did not feel that cooperation with Weaver in a field divided "along lines of vagueness" was workable. "Directors can and do help each other by general and solicited suggestions or information but to require approval of one for the judgment and work of another challenges the meaning of the word director." Gregg maintained that "all the experience since '29 and the present trouble shows that much of what we help as biology is medical science or medical in import."[48] Still, although "heavy hearted at the prospect of continuing in a plan that has shown its basic illogicality," Gregg stayed on. He felt he could rely on Fosdick's sympathy if not his conviction, and he knew that a great deal of work remained to be done. As he sometimes "with great regret" lamented to himself: "All this money and good will and free opportunity . . . and we fall to bickering! No! The work is too important for that."[49] Finally, Gregg's dislike of factious self-seeking made him distrust his own frustration.

The deteriorating position of the nation's medical schools was one area of important work to which Gregg wanted to turn the attention of the Rockefeller Foundation. Gregg was frustrated that the financial timidity of the trustees made it difficult to deal with these problems in any more than a stopgap fashion. By pleading the desperation of schools in which the Rockefeller boards had substantial investments, he did win some sympathy, and the fluid research fund mechanism was resurrected. Substantial funds were given to Johns Hopkins in 1939 and Rochester in 1941.[50]

The financial and organizational problems of Washington University in St. Louis were indicative of how far Flexner's system had unraveled with the withdrawal of his philanthropic leadership and support. The shrinkage of the productivity of the school's endowment funds had meant that many of the junior men had gone off full-time and were thus not engaging in the sort of research which would qualify them to succeed their chiefs who were approaching retirement. The haste with which Robert Brookings had reformed the school had produced problems which were becoming apparent only in the 1930s. Brookings had obliged the school to enter into a "crippling set of contracts" with the hospitals as an inducement to gain clinical teaching material. The alienation of the local profession from the imported faculty had reduced the local philanthropic support which the school could rely on for the long term.[51]

In order to salvage the situation, Gregg became intricately involved in a series of negotiations, discussions, and plans. He secured from the Rockefeller Foundation a "transfusion fund" of $400,000 and attempted to convince local donors to use their leverage to change the hospital situation. Gregg spent a great deal of time and effort in trying to disentangle Brookings' handiwork. His task was made somewhat easier when the federal government began supporting the construction of hospitals under the Lanham Act in areas congested by war production. Timely as it was, the federal grant underlined how the war was changing the context of medical education.[52]

In December 1940 Gregg proposed that the Rockefeller Foundation deal with the problems of the looming war by turning away from the policies it had been pursuing since the reorganization. In a memorandum to Fosdick which the president circulated among all the officers, Gregg suggested that the Foundation use 1941 to terminate with generous grants all the obligations it had accumulated so that when the war ended it would have a reserve of funds and time with which to aid in reconstruction. "The Scylla and Charybdis of foundations," he argued, "is on the one hand doing small things in a big way and on the other doing big things in a small way." The policy of the Foundation since 1928 had been "to do everything in a small way—everything in small amounts and for short periods." Gregg acknowledged that Fosdick had mitigated some of the problems, but the officers were still mired in "the thick of thin things." Gregg projected that if the Foundation did not clear its deck, two-thirds of the officers' time would be consumed in reviews and renewals of older projects. He predicted that after the war "our knowledge, our methods, and our money will be desperately important," and he wanted the Foundation to be in "the state of maximum elasticity and freedom of manoeuvre." [53]

Gregg pointed out that the policies of the reorganization had been premised on the prospective stability of college and university finances but that the "contracting universe of 1930–40" had annihilated that assumption. The inconstancy of Rockefeller Foundation support had a damaging effect on exactly what the Foundation was trying to aid: research and the recruitment and training of those who would undertake it. What Gregg decried as the "shibboleth of 'squarely within the program'" had the cumulative effect of diverting the officers from the important role of husbanding the research institutions by overloading them with the busy-work of renewal, extensions, and reviews. The policy of short-term grants had turned the Foundation's officers from "incubators" into "brooders," periodically doling out a meager subsistence to university researchers. Gregg warned that the Foundation was ignoring its "unique role" as "one of the few foundations large enough to do big things thoroughly" and was instead becoming "merely the largest single distributor of chicken feed" in the world. [54]

Weaver's response to Gregg's proposals brought into the open the differences between the two paradigms of foundation management which they represented. "There is at least one instance in which chicken feed is not despised," Weaver asserted, "and that is by a starving chicken. And once in a while even a chicken lays a golden egg." Weaver accused Gregg of "being caught up in the inertia of language," where the easy course was to "treat 'small' as meaning 'trivial' and 'big' as meaning 'important.'" Significant scientific advances, he pointed out, were synthesized out of smaller gains. Weaver felt that the "RF should solemnly dedicate itself to the discovery and support of important things," whether small or large. [55] Indeed, Weaver saw the Foundation itself as the synthesizer of new knowledge: "When we buy a large project of the pasted-up variety, we buy some excellent and some mediocre component parts. We would do better to buy only the excellent, and do our own pasting-up."[56] As Robert Kohler has pointed out, Weaver was the prototype of a role which became increasingly common during and after World War II: the manager of science.[57] Weaver saw his function and the foundation's role as an integrative force above and apart from the universities.

Gregg, in contrast, held to Flexner's view that the role of foundation philanthropy was to be the guardian of the university's integrity. Flexner had been a manager of the organization of knowledge, never a manager of organized knowledge like Weaver. Gregg laid great importance on what he termed the "ecology of the university," and he felt that that delicate ecology was being upset by the myriad demands placed upon it by the foundations and the growing number of specialized research agencies. "We are really in many cases," he regretfully noted, "a University playing hide and seek in other universities' buildings." The problem, he felt, was that no one was paying attention to the increasingly decrepit condition of the buildings.[58]

Weaver confessed that he was hesitant to pursue the debate of large versus small grants since he felt that "I have all the cards stacked against me."[59] But just the opposite was the case. Despite the personal affinity between Fosdick and Gregg, it was Weaver who captured the spirit and meaning of the 1928 reorganization which Fosdick had forged and was determined to defend. This is evident in each one's criticisms of the other's program.

Gregg regretted that the small-grant policy gave intellectually lazy officers an excuse to avoid sustained and engaged thinking which was necessary to the evaluation of larger projects.[60] Weaver felt the same charge could be laid at the door of the large-grant policy but only in reference to the trustees. He alluded to the "patience, time, and attention to technical detail" required "to prove to a Board of Trustees the importance of some 'small' thing." From his standpoint, a focus on large grants was "a formula which at one slick stroke appears to solve the problem of their [the trustees'] personal responsibility, appeals to their vanities, and requires a minimum of their time."[61] These two charges were not mutually exclusive but implied differing conceptions of the polity of a foundation. In Gregg's formulation, the initiative in policymaking lay with the officers, even if the trustees had ultimate responsibility. Weaver's model was one of more frank partnership: the trustees and the officers would be equally conversant with the "technical detail" involved.

But that partnership was more than administrative. Looming behind the Gregg-Flexner program were a number of tensions which were difficult to contain. A program of institutional leadership, which the large-grant policy suggested, quickly raised questions of elitism, definitive social management, and the role of patronage in determining institutional directions. Gregg was willing to address these problems candidly. He explicitly recognized that in organizing educational units, the foundation and the universities were dealing in a species of property which was increasingly valuable in technological society.[62] He urged frank recognition that the purpose of the university was to train an elite. "It is so strongly in our social traditions to be alert to the encroachments of the few upon the mass," he warned, "that we ignore the depredations of the mass upon the elite."[63]

The program supported by Fosdick and Weaver tried to avoid these troublesome questions by orienting itself toward unimpeachable goals which gave both the officers and the trustees a defined field of action and yet did not threaten the organizational legitimacy of the foundation. It was not surprising therefore that nothing came of Gregg's proposal. Although Fosdick found his idea "thoughtful and thought-provoking,"[64] the president was unwilling to resume what had proved a risky course twenty years earlier. Perhaps overestimating Fosdick's flexibility, Gregg privately reiterated his misgivings about the Foundation's course. In a letter which he asked Fosdick not to circulate without his permission, Gregg suggested that the Foundation was trying to "escape the responsibilities of our own maturity" by "giving Rockefeller dimes to worthy little investigative impeccabilities." Gregg wanted the Foundation to exercise institutional leadership by setting an example to the proliferating smaller foundations; he feared that "a pleasure in perfected trifles . . . will otherwise overtake us." Weaver's policy of keeping "theoretically aloof from pure physics, chemistry and mathematics though progress there would provide tomorrow's progress in biology," Gregg characterized as "just stupidity."[65] Unfortunately for Gregg, World War II accelerated just those trends in the organization of knowledge which distressed him.

The war seemed to vindicate the idea of organized research. "Many men have been impressed by the rewarding result to medicine of integrated scientific effort," one medical academic wrote. "There is a general feeling that methods of cooperation which have produced astonishing results in time of war should not be discarded in the years of peace." It was felt that "the exigency of the war has spurred forward looking men toward greater diligence," and that therefore "the record shows an imposing array of new and promising ideas."[66]

During the war the Organization for Scientific Research and Development under Vannevar Bush funded research in tropical medicine, antibiotics, aviation medicine, and many other areas which were vital to the war effort. As the war drew to a close, Bush planned to institutionalize his effort into a national science foundation, but he was taken by surprise when Roosevelt ordered the OSRD to begin planning for demobilization. The various medical projects still in operation were dealt out to the medical branches of the army and navy and the Public Health Service. The grants for penicillin research were given to the Public Health Service, which assigned them to be administered from the National Institute of Health. Previously, NIH had been mainly an intramural organization, performing its own work on a limited number of topics deemed to fall within the definition of public health restricted to infectious diseases. When the price of penicillin dropped dramatically, the project budget had a significant surplus, and the NIH inaugurated a grants program for medical research projects to take up the slack.[67]

That adventitious program was the beginning of the federal patronage of medical research under NIH. The widespread public perception that American technological and scientific expertise had won the war created the impression of an immanent scientific utopia. Adroit management of congressional testimony by such individuals as Mary Lasker made opposition to federal research aid almost impossible. The ability to present representative victims of disease put potential opponents in the untenable position of willfully withholding cures which awaited only concentrated, well-funded effort.[68]

Gregg realized that the shower of federal funds on the Depression-parched budgets of the nation's medical schools would only increase the problems of maintaining the institutional coherence of academic medicine. He warned that "unless the nature and value of research is more widely and more intelligently understood it will not flourish in our democracy."[69] He wanted the Rockefeller Foundation to be an example of such intelligence.

Accordingly, in March 1946 Gregg proposed that he present to the trustees "a frank account of the status of the medical schools of this country."[70] He wrote:

> The serious fact is that medical education in the United States is deteriorating and is likely to continue to fail the obligations as well as the opportunities placed before it by post war conditions unless substantial steps are taken to correct these serious changes. I believe we should point this out to the Trustees.[71]

Gregg maintained that medical education was entering a generational transition at the worst possible time. The decade of 1944–1955 was due to see a large number of retirements from those faculties reorganized with GEB funds between 1913 and 1927. The position of junior men which he had always recognized as strained was now critical. Students trained on accelerated schedules during the war were going to return and demand postgraduate courses, the most expensive type of training. Owing to high wartime taxes, private giving to medical education had dried up. The planned creation of new medical schools in the western states would put yet another demand on the limited supply of teachers. "In a short time," Gregg warned, "we shall not have the well trained young men available to receive and apply effectively grants for research work. It is no good buying expensive groceries if you ignore the cook's salary." The pending increases in federal funding did not give Gregg any solace: "I question pointedly if the Government will in its enthusiasm for research realize that money is needed in the first place and essentially for living costs and stable futures for those who can do the expected research."[72]

Gregg proposed to do what Flexner had urged him to do fifteen years earlier when he had assumed the directorship of the Medical Science Division. Gregg wanted to select a set of six or seven private medical schools "with an eye to their present excellence, and to the quality of their recent professional appointments, to their regional influence especially on State medical schools and to the likelihood of their not being aided by other private donors," and make large grants for endowment, conditional on other funds' being raised. Such a program would stimulate state medical schools and guarantee that future Rockefeller Foundation research grants could be put to capable use. Most important, Gregg stressed, such a move "would serve as a most valuable example to other foundations and to government in correcting the serious losses of the war and it would point to the deepest need of research—the maintenance of stable conditions for finding, training and supporting research men."[73]

Medical education was being threatened by what Gregg's assistant Robert S. Morison called "the magic wand theory of medical advance."[74] That theory had been dramatically reinforced by the research during the war, but the Rockefeller Foundation itself bore some responsibility:

> The growth of other organizations with objectives patterned on the Foundation's past procedures of temporary support for special projects only makes the question more acute. How is a university to maintain itself in sufficient health to perform the gymnasium implied by the acceptance of funds for new projects?[75]

This program did not necessarily mean more funds for Flexner's network. Morison criticized the appeal of University of Rochester president Alan Valentine to John D. Rockefeller III as "an unusually explicit expression of this infantile longing to return to the nourishing mothers who served so well in the past." Indeed it was thought that the large outside aid to such schools as Vanderbilt, Chicago, and Rochester had "hindered rather than helped these schools in building sound relations with their own communities."[76] But some sort of strategic leadership was needed if the institutional integrity of medical education was to be preserved.

In the late 1940s the Rockefeller Foundation was undergoing an administrative transition that made it even less likely that Gregg's proposals would be adopted. Fosdick was scheduled to retire in 1948, and the regime which succeeded him showed how successful he had been in molding the Foundation to his worldview. When he left the presidency, the board of trustees was dominated by the ideological heirs to the Wilsonian progressivism which he had championed: the internationalist wing of the Republican party. Men like John Foster Dulles, Walter Stewart, and Walter Gifford were more concerned with the external reach of American institutions than with their internal functioning.

The selection of Chester I. Barnard as Fosdick's successor emphasized the latter's enduring influence. The two men had followed similar careers, combining business (Barnard had risen to be president of New Jersey Bell Telephone) with public service (Barnard's work as director of the United

Service Organization in World War II was almost a direct continuation of Fosdick's as creator of the United War Fund in World War I). Barnard had been a trustee of the Rockefeller Foundation since 1940 and a member of its executive committee, so he was familiar with the course Fosdick had set. [77]

Barnard was America's foremost theorist of the managerial role, and his perspective was a codification of the ideas and attitudes adumbrated by Fosdick. Prompted by L. J. Henderson, the Harvard physiologist turned social theorist, Barnard put forth his views in somewhat inaccessible but nonetheless influential works, the most prominent being *The Functions of the Executive*. Henderson and Barnard were among the relatively few Americans who, before the intellectual migration of European scholars fleeing the Nazis, took seriously such European social theorists as Pareto and Michels. A rapport with questions of the organization of social leadership might seem to have predisposed Barnard to the Flexnerian paradigm of philanthropic management, but the opposite was the case. During the Atlantic crossing the European theories lost some of their hard edges and took on the flavor of American optimism. Barnard's work was characterized by an open-ended analysis which focused on the interrelation of formal and informal organizations, the dependency of authority on a democracy of behavior, and leadership as a two-way communication system. This vision could not accommodate Flexner's notions of institutional forms reflecting a moral order and the necessity of didactic intellectual leadership. Barnard's themes of "organization" and "management" became ways of talking about "institutions" and "elites" in ways which were less threatening to American democratic ideology. [78]

But the differences was not merely semantic; in philanthropic practice Barnard's views meant continuation of Fosdick's policy of concentrating on smaller programs which were both administratively and politically more manageable than the vexed questions of institutional leadership. It was not surprising, therefore, that Barnard vetoed Gregg's suggestion of some judiciously applied endowment grants to the leading medical schools. Management was exalted to the leadership. Barnard was perfectly content with the notion that the Rockefeller Foundation was an agency which farmed out its own research: in a Barnardian paraphrase of Gregg, an informal university operating within the formal universities. [79]

Even though his way was blocked at the Foundation, Gregg tried to exercise leadership in other areas. The National Fund for Medical Education was an instance. The growing federal commitment to medical research and education was viewed apprehensively by both the AMA, which feared federal regulation of medical education, and by some business leaders who wanted to restrict the growth of federal expenditures. Preliminary meetings were held in 1948 to found an organization to privately aid medical education. Representatives of the AMA, the American Association of Medical Colleges, and the foundations joined with delegates from the National Association of Manufacturers and the Chamber of Commerce to see what could be done to privately aid medical education. At the group's second conference Earl Buting of the National Association of Manufacturers ominously warned that federal aid of medical education "would be the opening wedge to a complete plan of socialized medicine"; he hoped his organization could provide $16,000,000 annually for the nation's medical schools.[80]

While some of the educators involved in the effort professed an extreme reluctance to have the federal government support medical education, others privately confessed to foundation officers that they were going along with the campaign in the expectation that it would fail to meet its goals and that then they could accept and even lobby for federal funds without reproach from private donors.[81]

Gregg shared that attitude. He commented archly at one meeting of the National Fund that "if private initiative is reserved to the making of money and never applied to the giving of it, it will be a setback for those who are championing the idea of private initiative."[82] Privately, he expressed his opinion that

> the issue of Government support to medical education and research was hardly any longer to be considered a possibility since it was an obvious reality, but nonetheless private support to education could do better than expend its energies trying its best to exclude Government; private initiative had certain freedom for experiment and considerable protection from waves of popular opinion.[83]

Gregg was also eager that the organized medical profession put up or shut up. He admonished a meeting of the American Association of Medical Colleges and the AMA that it was important to "realize that notoriously large doctor bills may very seriously limit the public's enthusiasm for supporting medical education."[84]

Once the National Fund for Medical Education had begun, Gregg urged it to "make a request for a very large sum of money from so wealthy and reactionary a profession as the AMA leadership now 'represents.'"[85] When the AMA in December 1950 voted only half a million dollars to the Fund, the normally circumspect Gregg could not refrain from comment. He wrote to the secretary of the AMA's Council on Medical Education and Hospitals that "the medical profession might sensibly be expected to contribute to the Fund, since most doctors have not paid back to their schools any appreciable fraction of the cost of the education received in those schools." But when the AMA's contribution was divided by its membership, it came to between $2.75 and $3.00 a member. Gregg drily expressed "the hope that the $500,000 grant will soon be repeated for the sake of the status of the AMA in the opinion of other possible donors to the National Fund for Medical Education."[86]

Gregg worried that it was "very near to an impossibility . . . to make a relatively small sum of money available to every school in the United States and at the same time make it highly selected and significant in its effect."[87] It was politically difficult for the National Fund to widely solicit funds and then selectively distribute them. As a possible solution to this dilemma Gregg devised a formula whereby the Fund would increase its contribution to a school in relation to the percentage of the school's student body from out of state. In that way, schools of national importance could be aided without a public declaration of their elite status.[88] But still, Gregg felt that the sums contributed were pathetic in relation to the institutional needs.

Gregg considered the rapid growth of nationwide charities concerned with single diseases to be another problem which made foundation leadership necessary. He was privately critical of the National Foundation for Infantile Paralysis, perhaps the quintessential example of such charities.[89] It had not only a focus on children but a national patron in the form of Franklin Roosevelt. Its "march of dimes" made it a charity that rich and poor alike could participate in. Gregg felt that the research grants made by such groups did not begin to meet the hidden costs incurred in taking the grants on. Too much stress was put, he felt, on specialist training to cope with the diseases. Gregg worried that "organizations like the NFIP can very easily skim cream that has taken years to accumulate and are paying very little attention to what it is that has produced the cream of ability that they now are using to do research work on short term grants.[90] He felt that research was too often discussed as "an abstraction" when the "reality" was "the living teachers and investigators" and what was really important was "the kind of life they lead and can plan to lead."[91]

By 1950, the amount of money the federal government was putting into medical research was far greater than the Rockefeller Foundation's contribution. Gregg argued again that the "enormous changes in tax supported maintenance of research and training justify a thorough review of the policy of the Medical Sciences." The federal government, he noted, was in effect imitating the policy the Foundation had pursued since 1928. If the Foundation was to "avoid quantitative comparisons with a now far more powerful competitor," it would have to do precisely what the government was not doing: supply long-term funds and even endowments. Only in this way could the Foundation even out a situation which was becoming dangerously unbalanced. Like Flexner, Gregg saw endowment as "the one type of valuable aid which the Government cannot give." "Furthermore, endowment gives an institution independence of government: Indeed, it could be claimed that adequate endowment of a private institution not only makes it independent of government—it makes government dependent on the private institution's dependable resources." Anticipating opposition, Gregg noted that the "argument that endowment means but little nowadays brings to mind the source of the Foundation's current income."[92]

But Gregg was again swimming up the political stream. The growth of federal funding for medical research and education was viewed by many in the foundation world as a model of the philanthropic role which was politically useful, particularly in the early 1950s. With the rise of McCarthyism, the foundations again came under attack, this time from the right. While congressional investigations exonerated the foundations of the specific charges of aiding un-American activities, their tenuous legitimacy was again underlined. The philanthropoids' defense stressed that the foundations were society's "venture capital," experimental laboratories developing mechanisms which the government could later adapt or ignore as the people in their wisdom saw fit.[93] This role was much less likely to invite political attack than the Flexnerian position that the foundations were in fact the leading forces of social change. In such an atmosphere, support for frankly elitist institutions was unlikely to win acceptance.

Thus, Gregg was stymied. In 1951, he left the directorship of the Medical Science Division to become vice-president of the Rockefeller Foundation, a new post designed so that his talents as a phrasesmith and public representative could be put to best advantage. Until his retirement from the Foundation in 1956, he continued periodically to urge the reconsideration of its policies toward endowment and institutional support, but none of his colleagues saw his point. Indeed, reorganizations of the Foundation's medical activities during Gregg's service as vice-president moved it even further away from his ideals. In 1955 the medical field was split between one area concerned with medical education and one concerned with medical research. That bifurcation which Gregg had deplored between the Medical Science and Natural Sciences had now been driven to the heart of medical education. Gregg was not consulted about these changes, but privately to his friends he expressed his "extreme . . . personal unhappiness, with the direction that the Rockefeller Foundation had been going ever since the appointment of Max Mason as President."[94] Despite being universally well liked at the Rockefeller Foundation, Gregg had always been an almost tragically lonely figure.[95] His disappointment with the course of Foundation policies could only have increased his sense of isolation.

Gregg's frustration in carrying out a program informed by Flexner's principles showed just how limited was what might be called the Flexnerian moment in the history of the American managerial elite. Flexner's program, which had focused on the integrity of institutional structures as the key to social progress, had given way to Fosdick's philosophy (more completely articulated by Barnard) which saw management as the crucial variable. While this shift in emphasis politically protected the executive function itself, from an institutional point of view it was debilitating. Gregg often bemoaned what he called the "neurotic unwillingness" of the Rockefeller Foundation to take seriously the consequences of its own permanence and influence.[96] He felt that the neglect of its own cumulative effect on American institutional life was all the more dangerous because of the elaborate reasoning and rationalizations attached to that neglect.

Flexner made much the same point in an illuminating exchange of letters with Warren Weaver in 1955. The program which the Rockefeller Foundation pursued under Bernard and his successor, Dean Rusk, ideally suited a manager of Weaver's temperament. He busied himself with a variety of activities and in 1955 was rewarded by being promoted to a new post which, to Gregg's final frustration, included authority over medical education. As he took up his new duties, Weaver solicited Flexner's "ideas as to what constitute the major present-day problems of medical education in the United States, and the steps which you think can and should be taken in order to overcome the difficulties." Weaver noted that the decision making in the Rockefeller Foundation was "a good deal less individualistic than it used to be nearly a half century ago," but he wanted his colleagues to have the benefit of Flexner's advice. [97]

Flexner responded that the major difficulty was Weaver himself and the style of philanthropic management he represented. Flexner noted that Weaver was "Vice-President for the Natural and Medical Sciences of the Rockefeller Foundation in charge of all natural sciences, medicine, and public health over the entire world," and that Weaver had "no schooling or experience qualifying you to discharge any such terrific responsibility." [98] Weaver's approach to the possibilities of Rockefeller Foundation action Flexner criticized (employing one of Gates's terms) as "scopey." He saw no indication that Weaver was "thinking and working under any limitations as to subject, place, or personnel." [99] "A man," Flexner asserted, "be he an Einstein, a Galileo, or a Harvey, must limit his field if he is to be an effective agent." [100] The particular program which Flexner recommended to Weaver was that which he himself had pursued: select several medical schools, "find out what they think their needs are, trust them, and help them liberally." [101] "Trust" had never been one of Flexner's practices, but he was not niggardly. Total cost was to Flexner an extraneous consideration; if the program was successful, "emulation will do the rest." [102]

Not easily put off, Weaver continued the correspondence, peppering Flexner with questions about the possible use of closed-circuit color television to aid in medical education, a proposal for a two percent surcharge on each doctor bill to help fund the nation's medical schools, and what relative mixture of national and international medical programs would be best. [103] Flexner was impatient with these vaporings, admonishing Weaver:

> I wonder whether you have ever heard an axiom which Goethe laid down in an essay he wrote in *Natur und Kunst* in 1802. He said, "In der Beschränkung zeigt sich erst der Meister" which I translate, "The master shows himself first by defining the limitations under which he works." Now I find in your letter no indication that you are thinking and working under any limitations as to subject, place, or personnel. [104]

In his defense, Weaver asserted that

> a philanthropic organization with large resources, is bound to look at the world of opportunity and say, "What ought we do?" . . . It does not do to say that no one is wise enough to make such decisions. These decisions *must be made.*[105]

Weaver protested that he was "not in the least assuming that I have the training, the experience, the wisdom, or the judgment to make such decisions," but that he was "a very small part of the Rockefeller Foundation," and that he could rely on collective judgments and wisdom. Weaver felt keenly the responsibility to evaluate all problems which had a bearing on "the welfare of mankind."[106]

Flexner scorned the idea that "your huge and undistinguished staff is any substitute for direct personal acquaintance on your part."[107] But the differences between the two men were not based on experience alone:

> Our ways of "facing" the problem differ, however, fundamentally. You seem to me to assume that you and your associates can analyze the world situation and select what is most important. I hold that the human mind does not work that way. The human mind, at its best, has *insight* and *"hunches."*[108]

Flexner maintained that a "foundation executive is like a shrewd statesman or politician—he instinctively perceives a situation favorable to action."[109] The point was not to devise rational procedures but to have "strength of judgment." Flexner worried that Weaver's studied proceduralism was preoccupation with context—a fatal timidity. Drawing another lesson from history, Flexner pointed out:

> When President Lincoln embarked on the Civil War, he knew very little about the financial or political problems which he and the country would have ultimately to face. He did his duty at the moment, as he saw it.[110]

Leadership could not always be rational.

After a summer's worth of Flexner's aphorisms and object lessons, Weaver called a halt to the correspondence. "I think it has become clear that you and I have sincere and energetically held differences of opinion concerning the basic philosophy of a foundation," he wrote to Flexner in understatement.[111] In a backhanded compliment, Weaver suggested to his colleagues at the Foundation that despite the "incredible immodesty and despite the ridiculous unfairness of some of his judgments about the activities of foundations today, nevertheless Dr. Flexner is worth listening to very carefully." On the whole, however, Weaver was unconvinced.

While he held Flexner up as someone worthy of veneration, he saw Flexner's views as hopelessly antique, his proposals as "obstructionist."[112]

The exchange between the two generations captured the changes in foundation management. If Flexner, in his stress on "hunches," impulse, and emulation represented the original charisma of philanthropic reform, Weaver, in his studied proceduralism and his reliance on collective rules, was an example of its routinization. To his loss, Gregg had been trapped between two eras of foundation policymaking.

Conclusion

Soon after Abraham Flexner's ninetieth birthday in November 1956, Lawrence Spivak asked the elderly educator to enliven America's Sunday morning with a television appearance on *Meet the Press*. Flexner, who had not trusted a journalist since E. L. Godkin, Gilded Age editor of the *Nation*, declined, pleading exhaustion from his recent celebration and noting, with a modesty which questioned Spivak's judgment, that "I have, I think, ceased to be news."[1]

Thirty years later, Flexner has become, if not news, at least a consistent topic of interest. He has become a lightning rod for many who study both the past and present structure of medical education. On the one hand, he is held responsible for the many ills of today's medical system (or non-system): high cost (produced by the reduction in the number of schools and practitioners), technical dehumanization (a result of his emphasis on science), and the creation of a professional structure overwhelmingly white, male, and unresponsive to popular concerns.[2] More sympathetic treatments view him as a well-intentioned reformer who simply could not have anticipated the myriad consequences of the reforms he promoted.[3] Still others suggest that Flexner was in fact the unhonored prophet of comprehensive, preventive medical care for all.[4]

Flexner has become what was once said of British prime minister Stanley Baldwin: a peg to hang myths on. Flexner himself contributed to this process by his willful distortions of the past in his autobiography and elsewhere. But, remarkable as it was, Flexner's record cannot bear the weight some would thrust upon it. Several scholars have already begun to unburden him. They have established that the reform of medical education did not spring full blown from Flexner's skull and that it had begun long before he let fly with his famous report.[5] Indeed, as Flexner himself said, the most important consequence of the Carnegie Foundation's Bulletin No. 4 was that Gates read it and Flexner was thereby brought to the General Education Board to organize his network of schools.[6]

The most salient aspects of Flexner's career were his entrepreneurial management of the organization of knowledge and the ideology which underlay it. The continuing interest in Flexner testifies to the importance of the central question he faced in that management: how can a democratic society organize and support systems for the training of elites of esoteric expertise? Before Flexner, the centrifugal tendencies of American democracy seemed to suggest that any success in that endeavor would be relatively modest and local. Flexner created a formula for a national hierarchy of institutions which would channel individual ambition by assigning positions according to universal, rational criteria. Flexner saw his meritocratic bureaucracy as consistent with democracy, but not itself democratic. Indeed, Flexner's system was premised on the continuation of leadership like his own which was not answerable to democratic values.

Flexner's success in establishing his policies was a tribute to both his political skill and his ideological timeliness. In the early twentieth century, Americans were uncharacteristically amenable to the idea of bureaucratic management, particularly if it could be portrayed as a technically expert antidote for corruption. Flexner promoted the full-time plan in just that fashion and put himself in a strategic position of leadership. But Flexner's managerial regime proved in time to be a transitional rather than a permanent system of philanthropic leadership for institutionalized knowledge. The separation which he envisioned between the values of democracy and the ideals of education was a chimera. Democratic questions were even more complicated in the institutional context of American university education. Flexner's leadership became unacceptable to bureaucratic managers within both the medical schools and the Rockefeller philanthropic boards.

Flexner's overthrow was part of the changing pattern of American bureaucratic policymaking. The paradigm of management which succeeded Flexner's was more congenial to a democratic political culture. That style, represented in the Rockefeller Foundation by Raymond Fosdick, Warren Weaver, and Chester Barnard, overlooked the questions of institutionalized values and organizational hierarchies and emphasized instead the functional goals of a self-determined program. This new policy not only made the foundation less explicitly elitist, it also redistributed power internally: it gave the trustees the initiative in determining broad lines of inquiry and the officers a mandate to engage in the management of knowledge.

The rise in federal funding for medical research and education after World War II brought the problem full circle. A century earlier, in 1855, institutions of medical education were organizational waifs, ignored and unsupported by the universities, private donors, the organized medical profession, and the government. By 1955, all those groups had become intricately involved in medical education. But while the level of financial support had unquestionably increased, whether there was a corresponding increase in the level of leadership remains a question. The irony was—and is—that the bureaucratic management of medical education is viewed as just as illegitimate when carried out by the (presumably) democratic government as it was when carried out by the foundations. But a yearning for leadership remains nonetheless. The late twentieth century echoes the nineteenth with laments over the lack of leadership and frustration with the intractability of the American system of medical education.[7]

Such dissatisfaction has prompted some to scan the horizon for a new Flexner who will slash medical education's Gordian knot of intertwined democratic and bureaucratic forces.[8] But if Abraham Flexner came again to the foundation boardrooms of New York, the government offices of Washington, or the precincts of the National Institutes of Health in Bethesda, it is probable that his welcome would be brief. Leadership like his would be even more quickly overthrown today that it was in his own time. But if Flexner did not have a viable answer to the problem of melding bureaucratic management with a democractic political culture, he was at least forthright in seeing it as a question.

Notes   Selected Bibliography   Index

Notes

Preface

1. Robert H. Wiebe, *The Search for Order, 1877–1920* (New York: Hill and Wang, 1967).

2. See Barry D. Karl and Stanley N. Katz, "The American Private Philanthropic Foundation and the Public Sphere, 1890–1930," *Minerva* 19 (1981): 236–270; Karl and Katz, "Philanthropy, Patronage, and Politics," *Daedalus* 116 (1987): 1–40: Barry D. Karl, "Philanthropy, Policy Planning and the Bureaucratization of the Democratic Ideal," *Daedalus* 105 (1976): 129–149.

3. Daniel M. Fox, "Abraham Flexner's Unpublished Report: Foundations and Medical Education, 1909–1928," *Bulletin of the History of Medicine* 54 (1980): 475–496, is a good brief discussion of Flexner's philanthropic career. A valuable discussion of how foundation staff could transmute a philanthropist's designs is to be found in Ellen Condliffe Lagemann, *Private Power for the Public Good: A History of the Carnegie Foundation for the Advancement of Teaching* (Middletown, Conn.: Wesleyan University Press, 1983).

4. See Kenneth E. Boulding, *The Organizational Revolution: A Study in the Ethics of Economic Organization* (New York: Harper, 1953); Louis Galambos, "The Emerging Organizational Synthesis in Modern American History," *Business History Review* 44 (1970): 279–290; Robert D. Cuff, "American Historians and the 'Organizational Factor,'" *Canadian Review of American Studies* 4 (1973): 19–31.

5. See Richard L. McCormick, *From Realignment to Reform: Political Change in New York State, 1839–1910* (Ithaca: Cornell University Press, 1981).

6. This description of the nineteenth-century state is from Morton Keller, *Affairs of State: Public Life in Late Nineteenth Century America* (Cambridge: Belknap, 1977).

7. Kenneth M. Ludmerer, *Learning to Heal: The Development of American Medical Education* (New York: Basic Books, 1985), pp. 5–7.

8. John Field, "Medical Education in the United States: Late Nineteenth and Twentieth Centuries," in C. D. O'Malley, ed., *The History of Medical Education* (Berkeley: University of California Press, 1970); Saul Jarcho, "Medical Education in the United States, 1910–1956," *Journal of the Mount Sinai Hospital* 26 (1959):

339–385. A more matter-of-fact discussion of Flexner's role is to be found in Paul Starr, *The Social Transformation of American Medicine* (New York: Basic Books, 1982); pp. 118–126.

9. E. Richard Brown, *Rockefeller Medicine Men: Medicine and Capitalism in America* (Berkeley: University of California Press, 1979); Stephen Kunitz, "Professionalism and Social Control in the Progressive Era: The Case of the Flexner Report," *Social Problems Journal* 22 (1974–75): 16–27; Gerald E. Markowitz and David K. Rosner, "Doctors in Crisis: A Study of the Use of Medical Education Reform to Establish Modern Professional Elitism in Medicine," *American Quarterly* 24 (1973): 83–107; Howard S. Berliner, "Philanthropic Foundations and Scientific Medicine," Sc.D. diss., Johns Hopkins School of Public Health, 1977. I am grateful to Mr. Berliner for providing me with a copy of his dissertation.

10. See Robert F. Arnove, ed., *Philanthropy and Cultural Imperialism: The Foundations at Home and Abroad* (Bloomington: Indiana University Press, 1982).

11. Charles E. Rosenberg, "Toward an Ecology of Knowledge: On Discipline, Context and History," in Alexandra Oleson and John Voss, eds., *The Organization of Knowledge in Modern America, 1860–1920* (Baltimore: Johns Hopkins University Press, 1979).

12. See, for example, Morris J. Vogel and Charles E. Rosenberg, eds., *The Therapeutic Revolution: Essays in the Social History of American Medicine* (Philadelphia: University of Pennsylvania Press, 1979).

13. Barry D. Karl, "The Power of Intellect and the Politics of Ideas," *Daedalus* 97 (1971): 1002–1035.

14. See my review of Arnove, *Philanthropy and Cultural Imperialism*, in *Bulletin of Atomic Scientists* (January 1984).

Introduction

1. John Morgan, *A Discourse on the Foundation of Medical Schools in America* (Baltimore: Johns Hopkins University Press, 1937), p. 32n.

2. See Joseph Kett, *The Formation of the American Medical Profession* (New Haven: Yale University Press, 1968); A McGehee Harvey and James Brodley III, *Two Centuries of American Medicine, 1776–1976* (Philadelphia: W. B. Saunders, 1976); Daniel Calhoun, *Professional Lives in America: Structure and Aspirations, 1750–1850* (Cambridge: Harvard University Press, 1965); George H. Daniels, *Science in American Society: A Social History* (New York: Knopf, 1971); Rosemary Stevens, *American Medicine and the Public Interest* (New Haven: Yale University Press, 1972).

3. Richard H. Shryock, *Medicine and Society in America, 1600–1860* (Ithaca: Cornell University Press, 1972), pp. 1–43.

4. Morgan, *Discourse*, p. 35.

5. Kett, *Formation of the American Medical Profession*, pp. 8–28; Calhoun, *Professional Lives in America*, pp. 15–31.

6. Kett, *Formation of the American Medical Profession*, pp. 13–30; Howard S. Miller, *Dollars for Research: Science and Its Patrons in Nineteenth-Century Amer-*

ica (Seattle: University of Washington Press, 1970); Merle Curti, Judith Green, and Roderick Nash, "Anatomy of Giving: Millionaires in the Late Nineteenth Century," *American Quarterly* 15 (1963): 416–435.

7. Kett, *Formation of the American Medical Profession*, p. 43.

8. Smithsonian Institution, *Miscellaneous Collections* 17 (1880): 141–144.

9. Daniel Drake, *Practical Essays on Medical Education and the Medical Profession in the United States* (Cincinnati: Rolf & Young, 1832; rpt. Baltimore: Johns Hopkins University Press, 1952), p. 98.

10. Kett, *Formation of the American Medical Profession*, p. 45.

11. See Ronald L. Numbers, ed., *The Education of American Physicians* (Berkeley: University of California Press, 1980).

12. Morris J. Vogel, *The Invention of the Modern Hospital: Boston, 1870–1930* (Chicago: University of Chicago Press, 1980); Charles E. Rosenberg, "Inward Vision and Outward Glance: The Shaping of the American Hospital, 1880–1914," *Bulletin of the History of Medicine* 53 (1979): 346–391. David Rosner, *A Once Charitable Enterprise: Hospitals and Health Care in Brooklyn and New York, 1885–1915.* (Princeton: Princeton University Press, 1982).

13. Quoted in Martin Kaufman, *American Medical Education: The Formative Years, 1765–1910* (Westport, Conn.: Greenwood Press, 1976), p. 144.

14. Quoted in Daniels, *Science in American Society*, p. 171.

15. Drake, *Practical Essays*, p. 91.

16. James G. Burrow, *AMA: Voice of American Medicine* (Baltimore: Johns Hopkins University Press, 1963), pp. 1–19.

17. Quoted in Kaufman, *American Medical Education*, p. 88.

18. Quoted in Daniels, *Science in American Society*, p. 162.

19. William Pepper, *Higher Medical Education: The True Interest of the Public and of the Profession* (Philadelphia: J. B. Lippincott, 1894), pp. 5, 6, 25.

20. Ibid., p. 21.

21. Ibid., p. 22.

22. Ibid., p. 33.

23. Hugh Hawkins, *Between Harvard and America: The Educational Leadership of Charles W. Eliot* (New York: Oxford University Press, 1972), pp. 59–61, 216, 280; Ludmerer, *Learning to Heal*, pp. 50–54; Ludmerer, "Reform at Harvard Medical School, 1869–1909," *Bulletin of the History of Medicine* 55 (1982): 343–370.

24. Wilson Allen Gay, *William James: A Biography* (New York: Viking, 1967), pp. 157–58. I am grateful to Richard von Mayerhauser for this citation.

25. Charles W. Eliot, "The New Education," *Atlantic Monthly* 23 (1869): 215.

26. Thomas F. Harrington, *The Harvard Medical School: A History, Narrative, and Documentary*, 3 vols. (New York: Lewis, 1905), 3:1407–1408; John H. Warner, "Physiology," in Numbers, *Education of American Physicians.*

27. Daniel Michael Bluestone, "From Pasture to Pasteur: An Architectural and Environmental History of the 1906 Harvard Medical School," B.A. thesis, Harvard College, 1975.

28. This controversy is usefully discussed with reference to British medicine in Judy Sadler, "Ideologies of 'Art' and 'Science' in Medicine," in Wolfgang Krohn et

al., eds., *The Dynamics of Science and Technology* (Dordrecht, Holland: D. Reidel, 1978), pp. 177–215.

29. Harrington, *Harvard Medical School*, pp. 1035, 1038, 1936; see also Henry J. Bigelow, *Medical Education in America* (Cambridge: Welch, Bigelow, 1871).

30. Hawkins, *Betweeen Harvard and America*, p. 61.

31. Harrington, *Harvard Medical School*, p. 1023.

32. Ibid., p. 1021.

33. Ibid., p. 1043.

34. Henry K. Beecher and Mark D. Altschule, *Medicine at Harvard: The First Three Hundred Years* (Hanover, N.H.: University Press of New England, 1977), p. 95.

35. Starr J. Murphy to John D. Rockefeller, December 19, 1901, Charles W. Eliot Papers, Nathan Pusey Library, Harvard University (Hereafter CEWP), box 104, folder 47.

36. Franklin Parker, *George Peabody* (Nashville: Vanderbilt University Press, 1971), p. 302; Alan M. Chesney, *The Johns Hopkins Hospital and the Johns Hopkins University School of Medicine*, 3 vols. (Baltimore: Johns Hopkins University Press, 1958), 1 : 16.

37. Hugh Hawkins, *Pioneer: A History of the Johns Hopkins University, 1874–1889* (Ithaca: Cornell University Press, 1960), pp. 3–20.

38. Ibid., pp. 19–20; Gert H. Brieger, "The California Origins of the Johns Hopkins Medical School," *Bulletin of the History of Medicine* 51 (1977): 339–352.

39. Hawkins, *Pioneer*, pp. 38–62; Laurence R. Veysey, *The Emergence of the American University* (Chicago: University of Chicago Press, 1965), pp. 16, 17, 164–165.

40. Simon Flexner and James Thomas Flexner, *William H. Welch and the Heroic Age of American Medicine* (New York: Viking Press, 1941); Donald Fleming, *William H. Welch and the Rise of Modern Medicine* (Boston: Little, Brown, 1954); Richard H. Shryock, *The Unique Influence of Johns Hopkins University on American Medicine* (Copenhagen: Ejnar Munksgaard, 1953).

41. Harvey Cushing, *The Life of Sir William Osler*, 2 vols. (Oxford: Clarendon Press, 1925).

42. See Gerald L. Gieson, "Divided We Stand: Physiologists and Clinicians in the American Context," in Vogel and Rosenberg, *Therapeutic Revolution*.

43. Chesney, pp. 88–89.

44. Ibid., pp. 193–197.

45. Ibid., pp. 197–218.

46. Martin B. Anderson, *The Right Use of Wealth* (New York, 1878), p. 24.

47. "Medical Colleges and Their Endowments," *JAMA* 2 (April 5, 1884): 377.

48. "Endowments," *JAMA* 1 (July 21, 1883): 58.

49. "Medical Colleges and Their Endowments," p. 377.

50. Henry B. Ward, Address of the President, *Proceedings of the Eighteenth Annual Meeting of the Association of American Medical Colleges* (Chicago: AAMC, 1908), p. 34.

51. Frank Billings, "State Medicine," *JAMA* 5 (September 19, 1885): 309–315.

52. Harrington, *Harvard Medical School*, p. 1105.

53. Charles W. Eliot, "The Exemption from Taxation of Church Property and the Property of Educational and Charitable Institutions," in *Exemption from Taxation* (Boston: privately printed, 1910), p. 42.

54. Charles W. Eliot, *The Working of the American Democracy: An Address Delivered before the Fraternity Phi Beta Kappa of Harvard University* (Cambridge: John Wilson and Son, 1888), p. 12.

55. Eliot, "Exemption from Taxation," p. 37.

56. Ibid., p. 24.

57. Ibid., pp. 37, 35–36.

1. Experiments in Philanthropic Reform

1. See Charles Rosenberg, *No Other Gods* (Baltimore: Johns Hopkins University Press, 1976).

2. The best biography of Carnegie is James Frazier Wall, *Andrew Carnegie* (New York: Oxford University Press, 1970).

3. Andrew Carnegie, "A Confession of Religious Faith," *Miscellaneous Writings of Andrew Carnegie*, ed. Burton J. Hendrick (New York: Doubleday, 1933), p. 295.

4. Ibid., p. 297.

5. John White, "Andrew Carnegie and Herbert Spencer: A Special Relationship," *Journal of American Studies* 13 (1979): 68.

6. Andrew Carnegie, "Wealth," *North American Review* 148 (1889): 653, 656, 662.

7. Ibid., p. 662.

8. Andrew Carnegie, "The Best Fields for Philanthropy," *North American Review* 149 (1889): 685, 691–692.

9. Allan Nevins, *Study in Power: John D. Rockefeller, Industrialist and Philanthropist,* 2 vols. (New York: Scribners, 1953), remains the best biography of the founding Rockefeller.

10. Frederick T. Gates, *Chapters in My Life* (New York: Free Press, 1977), is Gates's autobiography.

11. Richard Storr, *Harper's University: The Beginnings* (Chicago: University of Chicago Press, 1966), pp. 9–11; Gates, *Chapters in My Life*, pp. 91–98.

12. Frederick Gates to Dr. Stephens, January 20, 1891, Frederick Taylor Gates Papers, Rockefeller Archive Center, Pocantico Hills, N.Y. (hereafter FTGP), box 4.

13. Quoted in Storr, *Harper's University*, p. 31.

14. Ibid., pp. 18–34.

15. Frederick T. Gates to Dr. Morehouse, February 3, 1891, FTGP, box 4.

16. Gates to Dr. Stephens, January 10, [1891], FTGP, box 4.

17. Storr, *Harper's University*, pp. 45–51.

18. Gates to Harry Pratt Judson, April 6, 1908, FTGP, box 4.

19. Gates, *Chapters in My Life*, p. 159.

20. E. Fletcher Ingals to William Rainey Harper, March 18, 26, April 8, May 11, 1892, University of Chicago Presidents' Papers, 1889–1925, Department of Special

Collections, Regenstein Library, University of Chicago (hereafter UCP), box 57, folder 10; Harper to F. M. Sperry, August 8, 1902, UCP, box 58, folder 11.

21. George C. Hopkins to Harper, March 3, 1893, UCP, box 58, folder 9.

22. Ingals to Harper, January 10 and September 30, 1893, UCP, box 57, folder 10.

23. Ingals to Harper, January 22, 1894, UCP, box 57, folder 10.

24. Ingals to Harper, March 7, 1894, UCP, box 57, folder 10.

25. Berliner, "Philanthropic Foundations and Scientific Medicine."

26. Ingals to Harper, January 17, 1896, and January 24, 1898, UCP, box 57, folders 10 and 11.

27. Quoted in Storr, *Harper's University*, p. 134.

28. Ingals to Harper, January 27, 1898, UCP, box 57, folder 11.

29. Ingals to Harper, January 17, 1899, UCP, box 57, folder 12.

30. Ingals to Harper, April 27, 1899, UCP, box 57, folder 12.

31. Gates to Harper, June 19, 1898, quoted in Storr, *Harper's University*, p. 143.

32. Gates to Thomas W. Goodspeed, December 28, 1915, FTGP, box 2.

33. The edition Gates read was probably William Osler, *Principles and Practice of Medicine*, 2d ed. (New York: D. Appleton, 1896).

34. Gates, *Chapters in My Life*, p. 182.

35. Storr, *Harper's University*, pp. 143–144.

36. Gates to Harper, January 8, 1898, quoted in Storr, *Harper's University*, p. 144.

37. Gates to Goodspeed, January 12, 1898, quoted in Storr, *Harper's University*, p. 144.

38. "Mr. Gates on Full-Time," typescript, n.d., Simon Flexner Papers, microfilmed at Rockefeller Archive Center, Pocantico Hills, N.Y. (hereafter SFP).

39. Gates to Thomas Goodspeed, January 19, 1898, quoted in Storr, *Harper's University*, p. 145.

40. Seth Low to T. Mitchell Prudden, August 8, 1900, Columbia University Archives, Low Library, Columbia University (hereafter CUA).

41. Prudden to Low, September 19, 1900, CUA.

42. Low to John D. Rockefeller, Jr., November 7, 1900, CUA.

43. Minutes of the Scientific Directors, Rockefeller Institute for Medical Research, January 11 and March 8, 1902, Record Group 110.2, box 1, Rockefeller University Collection, Rockefeller Archive Center, Pocantico Hills, N.Y. (hereafter cited thus: RU-RG 110.2-box 1).

44. Florence R. Sabin, *Franklin Paine Mall: The Story of a Mind* (Baltimore: Johns Hopkins University Press, 1934), pp. 75, 82.

45. Lewellys F. Barker to W. R. Harper, August 19, 1901, UCP, box 14, folder 29; [Barker], "Notes for President Harper," n.d., UCP, box 58, folder 11.

46. Lewellys F. Barker, "Medicine and the Universities," *Record* 7 (July 1902): 88.

47. Ibid., p. 89.

48. "Mr. Gates on Full-Time."

49. Rockefeller junior to Harper, October 10, 1903, UCP, box 56, folder 11.

50. Rockefeller junior to Martin A. Ryerson, July 10, 1902, UCP, box 56, folder 16.

51. "Statement made October 5th, 1903 by the President to the Trustees . . . ," UCP, box 58, folder 11.

52. Rockefeller junior and Gates to Ryerson, September 26, 1902, UCP, box 58, folder 11.

53. Rockefeller junior and Gates to Ryerson, October 22, 1903, UCP, box 56, folder 11.

54. Storr, *Harper's University*, p. 290.

55. Harper to Rockefeller senior, February 22, 1905, UCP, box 56, folder 17.

56. Nicholas Murray Butler to Starr J. Murphy, October 3, 1902, CUA.

57. Murphy to Butler, October 30, 1902; Butler to Murphy, March 10, 1903, CUA.

58. Bluestone, "From Pasture to Pasteur," pp. 72–83.

59. Murphy to F. B. Mallory, September 23, 1901, CWEP, box 104, folder 47.

60. Mallory to Murphy, September 27, 1901, CWEP, box 104, folder 47.

61. Minutes of the Scientific Directors, May 10, 1901, RU-RG 110.2-box 1.

62. A. Flexner to S. Flexner, "Friday," [1898], SFP.

63. Minutes of the Scientific Directors, April 12, 1902, RU-RG 110.2-box 1.

64. Telegram, Rockefeller senior to Rockefeller junior, June 14, 1902, in Minutes of the Scientific Directors, June 14, 1902, RU-RG 110.2-box 1; see also Minutes of May 5, 1903, ibid.

65. Gates to Rockefeller senior, June 3, 1905, FTGP, box 4, folder 79.

66. Ibid.; "Memo by Mr. Gates," October 7, 1908, FTGP, box 2, folder 26.

67. Frederick T. Gates, "Thoughts on Medical Missions and the Teachings of Jesus," Rockefeller Family Archives, 30 Rockefeller Plaza, N.Y.

68. Frederick T. Gates, "Philanthropy and Civilization," [1923?], Frederick T. Gates Collection, Countway Library of Medicine, Harvard University Medical School, Boston.

69. Frederick T. Gates, "Corporation Privileges," n.d., FTGP, box 1, folder 11.

70. Frederick T. Gates, "The Purpose of the Rockefeller Foundation with Suggestions as to the Policy of Administration," [1905 or 1906], FTGP, box 2, folder 26.

71. Frederick T. Gates, "Competition vs. Cooperation," n.d., FTGP, box 1, folder 13.

72. Minutes of the Scientific Directors, June 13, 1907, RU-RG 110.2-box 1.

73. A handwritten copy of Welch's statement is in the William H. Welch Papers, Alan M. Chesney Medical Archives, Johns Hopkins Medical School, Baltimore (hereafter WHWP), box 20.

74. Ibid.

75. Ibid.

76. Ibid.

77. Starr J. Murphy to Gates, July 14, 1908, Rockefeller Family Archives.

78. See Russell C. Maulitz, "Physician versus Bacteriologist: The Ideology of Science in Clinical Medicine," in Vogel and Rosenberg, *Therapeutic Revolution*.

79. William H. Welch, "Medicine and the University," *JAMA* 50 (1908): 1.

80. William H. Welch to F. P. Mall, n.d., WHWP, box 20.

81. This distinction is discussed in Charles E. Rosenberg, "Toward an Ecology of Knowledge: On Discipline, Context and History," in Oleson and Voss, *Organization of Knowledge in Modern America*. A provocative discussion of the concept of professionalism is Magali Sarfatti Larson, *The Role of Professionalism: A Sociological Analysis* (Berkeley: University of California Press, 1977).

82. Maulitz, "'Physician versus Bacteriologist.'"

83. See A. McGehee Harvey, "Rufus Cole and the Hospital of the Rockefeller Institute," and Saul Benison, "The Development of Clinical Research at the Rockefeller Institute before 1929," both in *Trends in Biomedical Research, 1901–1976, Proceedings of the Second Rockefeller Archive Center Conference*, December 10, 1976.

84. A. McGehee Harvey, "Samuel J. Meltzer: Pioneer Catalyst in the Evolution of Clinical Science in America," *Perspectives in Biology and Medicine* 21 (1978): 431–440.

85. Samuel J. Meltzer, "The Science of Clinical Medicine: What it Ought to Be and the Men to Uphold It," reprinted in J. McKeen Cattell, ed., *Medical Research and Education* (New York: Science Press, 1913), pp. 438, 428–429 431.

86. Ibid., pp. 432, 439, 430.

87. Burrow, *AMA*, pp. 34–35.

88. *Second Annual Conference of the Council on Medical Education of the American Medical Association* (Chicago: American Medical Association, 1908), p. 66.

89. Ingals to Harper, January 29, 1900, UCP, box 57, folder 13.

90. See Lagemann, *Private Power for the Public Good.*

91. Henry S. Pritchett, autobiographical fragment, Carnegie Corporation files, New York (hereafter CCF).

92. Lagemann, *Private Power for the Public Good*, pp. 19–24.

93. Henry S. Pritchett, "How Science Helps Industry in Germany," *Review of Reviews* 33 (1906): 167.

94. Lagemann, *Private Power for the Public Good*, pp. 11–65.

95. Ibid., passim; see also Howard J. Savage, *Fruit of an Impulse: Forty-Five Years of the Carnegie Foundation, 1905–1950* (New York: Harcourt, Brace, 1953).

96. CFAT, *Annual Report*, 1908, p. 150.

97. CFAT, *Annual Report*, 1907, p. 43.

98. Ibid.

99. Ibid., p. 66.

100. CFAT, *Annual Report*, 1908, p. 149.

101. Henry S. Pritchett, "Democracy and Education," reprint from *Lancet-Clinic*, March 20, 1915, CCF.

102. CFAT, *Annual Report*, 1908, p. 157.

103. Ibid., pp. 165–166.

104. Abraham Flexner, *An Autobiography* (New York: Simon and Schuster, 1960), is an unreliable source on Flexner's life but a revealing example of his temperament.

105. Ibid., pp. 51–55.

106. Ibid., pp. 63–64.

107. A. Flexner to S. Flexner, June 12, 1906, SFP.

108. Abraham Flexner, *The American College: A Criticism* (New York: Century, 1908), p. 178.

109. Flexner, *Autobiography*, p. 71.

110. Flexner to Henry S. Pritchett, November 4, 1909, Abraham Flexner Papers, Library of Congress (hereafter AFP), box 17.

111. Flexner, *Autobiography*, p. 79.

112. Abraham Flexner, *Medical Education in the United States and Canada*, CFAT Bulletin no. 4 (New York: Carnegie Foundation for the Advancement of Teaching, 1910), p. ix.

113. Ibid., p. 13.

114. Donna Bingham Munger, "Robert Brookings and the Flexner Report: A Case Study of the Reorganization of Medical Education," *Journal of the History of Medicine and Allied Sciences* 23 (1968): 356–371; Kenneth M. Ludmerer, "The Reform of Medical Education at Washington University," *Journal of the History of Medicine and Allied Sciences* 35 (1980): 149–173.

115. Autobiographical fragment in Pritchett to Floyd C. Shoemaker, May 1, 1933, CCF.

116. Pritchett to Flexner, October 20, 1909, AFP, box 17.

117. Flexner, *Autobiography*, p. 81.

118. Abraham Flexner, "A Report on the Medical Department of Washington University," n.d., AFP, box 17.

119. Ibid.

120. Ludmerer, *Learning to Heal*, pp. 167–169.

121. Munger, "Robert Brookings and the Flexner Report," p. 365.

122. Anson Phelps Stokes to Flexner, June 24, 1910, AFP, box 10.

123. W. T. Therkeld to Flexner, February 21, 1910, AFP, box 19.

124. Charles W. Dabney to Flexner, May 5, 1910, AFP, box 18.

125. A. W. Harris to Pritchett, March 14, 1910, AFP, box 20.

126. *New York Times*, June 12, 1910.

127. Frederick W. Hamilton to Flexner, February 19, 1910, AFP, box 21.

128. Pritchett to Hamilton, February 25, 1910, AFP, box 21.

129. *Acts* 17 : 30.

130. Hamilton to Pritchett, March 12, 1910, AFP, box 21.

131. Flexner to Hamilton, March 15, 1910, AFP, box 21.

132. Flexner, *Medical Education in the United States and Canada*, pp. 19, 143, 153.

133. Ibid., p. xiii, xi.

134. See Robert P. Hudson, "Abraham Flexner in Perspective: American Medical Education, 1865–1910," *Bulletin of the History of Medicine* 46 (1972): 545–561.

135. H. P. Judson to H. S. Pritchett, January 10, 1916, UCP, box 57.

136. See Rosemary Stevens, *Medical Practice in Modern England: The Impact of Specialization and State Medicine* (New Haven: Yale University Press, 1966).

137. Flexner, *Medical Education in the United States and Canada*, pp. 105, 102.

138. Ibid., p. 154.

139. Ibid., pp. 101, 72.

140. Michael Schudson, "The Flexner Report and the Reed Report: Notes on the History of Professional Education in the United States," *Social Science Quarterly* 55 (1974) : 347–361.

141. Flexner, *Medical Education in the United States and Canada*, p. 144.

142. Abraham Flexner, "Aristocratic and Democratic Education," *Atlantic Monthly* 108 (1911) : 391.

143. Ibid., p. 390.

144. Ibid., p. 392.

145. Ibid.

146. Ibid., pp. 394, 395.

147. Ibid.

148. Flexner, *Medical Education in the United States and Canada*, p. 155.

2. The Transformation of Philanthropic Reform

1. A. Flexner to S. Flexner, November 1, 1912, SFP:

2. General Education Board, *Annual Report for the Year 1928–1929* (New York: General Education Board, 1929), p. 49.

3. A. Flexner to S. Flexner, May 18, 1912. SFP.

4. Ludmerer, *Learning to Heal*, pp. 207–213; H. David Banta, "Abraham Flexner: A Reappraisal," *Social Science and Medicine* 5 (1971) : 545.

5. Flexner, typescript, "The History of Full-Time Clinical Teaching," AFP, box 11; Flexner, *Autobiography*, p. 112.

6. Flexner, *Autobiography*, pp. 109–110.

7. Frederick T. Gates to William H. Welch, January 10, 1911, WHWP, box 20.

8. Gates to Welch, January 6, 1911, WHWP, box 20.

9. Chesney, *Johns Hopkins Hospital and the Johns Hopkins University School of Medicine*, Vols. 2 and 3; Cushing, *Life of Sir William Osler;* W. G. MacCallum, *William Stewart Halsted* (Baltimore: Johns Hopkins University Press, 1930); Fleming, *William H. Welch and the Rise of Modern Medicine*, p. 171 and passim; Flexner and Flexner, *William H. Welch and the Heroic Age of American Medicine*.

10. Fleming, *William H. Welch and the Rise of Modern Medicine*, pp. 168, 171.

11. Flexner, *Autobiography*, p. 110.

12. The report is entitled simply "The Johns Hopkins School." One copy, with Welch's marginalia, is in the General Education Board Collection, Rockefeller Archive Center, Pocantico Hills, N.Y., series 1, subseries 4, box 588, folder 6262 (hereafter cited thus: GEB 1-4-588-6262); another copy is in AFP, box 19.

13. Ibid., p. 36.

14. Ibid., pp. 23, 21, 17, 21.

15. Mall to his sister, December 12, 1886, quoted in Sabin, *Franklin Paine Mall*, p. 75.

16. Flexner, *Autobiography*, p. 113.

17. "The Johns Hopkins School," pp. 25–26.

18. Flexner, *Autobiography*, p. 8.

19. "The Johns Hopkins School," pp. 4, 21, 4.

20. A provocative presentation is in Burton J. Bledstein, *The Culture of Professionalism* (New York: W. W. North, 1976).

21. A. Flexner to S. Flexner, November 26, 1881, see also Abraham to Simon, n.d. [1893], SFP.

22. Anne Crawford Flexner was the author of several plays produced in New York and Europe, including the popular *Marriage Game*. See Abraham to A. C. Flexner, February 26, 1924, box 7, AFP.

23. Flexner to Morris Cohen, June 27, 1921, SFP-APS.

24. "The Johns Hopkins School," p. 14.

25. Flexner, *Autobioraphy*, pp. 112–113.

26. Howard Kelly to William Osler, May 1, 1911, Full-time volume, Harvey Cushing Papers, History of Medicine Library, Yale University (hereafter HCP-FT).

27. Ibid.

28. Kelly to Osler, May 9, 1911, HCP-FT.

29. Kelly to Osler, May 29, 1911, HCP-FT.

30. Ibid.

31. Lewellys F. Barker to Flexner, March 7, 1911, AFP, box 19.

32. A. Flexner to S. Flexner, August 23, 1911, SFP.

33. Lewellys F. Barker, "Some Tendencies in Medical Education in the United States," reprinted in Cattell, *Medical Research and Education*, pp. 275–277.

34. Osler to Barker, March 24, 1914, quoted in Lewellys F. Barker, *Time and the Physician* (G. P. Putnam's Sons, 1942), p. 202.

35. *Whole-Time Clinical Professors: A Letter to President Remsen from William Osler* (n.p., n.d.), pp. 4, 10, 8, 9.

36. A Flexner to S. Flexner, June 9, 1911, SFP.

37. A. Flexner to J. Whitridge Williams, GEB 1-4-588-6262.

38. Flexner, *Autobiography*, p. 115.

39. Howard Kelly to Wiliam Osler, October 21, 1913, HCP-FT.

40. Abraham Flexner, *Medical Education in Europe*, CFAT Bulletin no. 6 (New York: Carnegie Foundation for the Advancement of Teaching, 1912); Abraham Flexner, *Prostitution in Europe* (New York: Century, 1912).

41. A. Flexner to S. Flexner, September 20, 1911, SFP.

42. A. Flexner to S. Flexner, November 1, 1912, SFP.

43. A. Flexner to S. Flexner, October 28, 1912, SFP.

44. Welch to Barker, January 13, 1914, Lewellys F. Barker Papers, Alan M. Chesney Medical Archives, Johns Hopkins Medical School (hereafter LFBP).

45. A. Flexner to S. Flexner, June 15, 1911, SFP; Welch to A. Flexner, October 19, 1913, GEB 1-4-588-6262.

46. A copy of the contract is in GEB 1-4-588-6263.

47. A copy of the petition is in the Dean's Office Files of the Harvard Medical School, Countway Library of Medicine, Boston (hereafter HMS-DOF), file RF-GEB, 1913–1922.

48. Ibid.

49. Ibid.

50. Beecher and Altschule, *Medicine at Harvard*, makes this distinction on pp. 175–188.

51. Harvard petition.

52. Henry Christian to Charles W. Eliot, November 1, 1913, HMS-DOF, file RF-GEB, 1913–1922.

53. Ibid.

54. *New York Times*, October 23, 1913.

55. Christian to A. Lawrence Lowell, January 9, 1914, copy in HCP-FT.

56. Harvey Cushing to Lowell, March 30, 1911, HCP-FT.

57. Cushing note, n.d. [1914], HCP-FT.

58. Lowell to Cushing, April 4, 1914, HCP-FT.

59. Cushing note, February 2, 1914, HCP-FT.

60. Lowell to Cushing, March 6, 1915, HCP-FT.

61. Walter Cannon to Cushing, March 3, 1915, HCP-FT.

62. Alexander Cochrane to Lowell, April 15, 1915, HCP-FT.

63. Jean Alonzo Curran, *Founders of the Harvard School of Public Health with Biographical Notes, 1909–1946* (New York: Josiah Macy, Jr., Foundation, 1970), pp. 1–11.

64. Barbara Rosenkrantz, "Cart before Horse: Theory, Practice, and Professional Image in American Public Health, 1870–1920," *Journal of the History of Medicine and Allied Sciences* 229 (1974): 55–73.

65. Curran, *Founders of the Harvard School of Public Health*, pp. 12–15; Thomas B. Turner, *Heritage of Excellence: The Johns Hopkins Medical Institution, 1914–1947* (Baltimore: Johns Hopkins University Press, 1974), pp. 44–52.

66. Jerome Greene to Charles W. Eliot, November 11, 1915, CWEP, box 416, folder RF.

67. Eliot to Greene, November 12, 1915, CWEP, box 416, folder RF.

68. Eliot to Flexner, February 10, 1916, CWEP, box 403-1, folder GEB, 1908–1917.

69. Flexner to Eliot, February 11, 1916, CWEP, Box 403-1, folder GEB, 1908–1917.

70. Greene to Eliot, June 13, 1916, CWEP, box 416, folder RF.

71. William S. Thayer to Eliot, October 3, 1916, CWEP, box 408, folder: Harvard Medical School Committee on Application to the GEB, 1916–1917.

72. "Provisional memorandum about aid for the Harvard Medical School from the General Education Board," CWEP, box 408, folder: HMS committee.

73. Eliot to Wallace Buttrick, December 15, 1916, CWEP, box 408, folder: HMS committee.

74. "Provisional memorandum . . ."

75. Ibid.

76. Buttrick to Eliot, December 26, 1916, CWEP, box 403-1, folder: GEB, 1908–1917.

77. Eliot to Buttrick, December 28, 1916, CWEP, box 403-1, folder: GEB, 1908–1917.

78. Memorandum, January 30, 1917, CWEP, box 408, folder: HMS committee.
79. Walter Cannon, "Notes on the GEB Memorandum," CWEP, box 408, folder: HMS committee.
80. William S. Thayer, "Comments on Dr. Buttrick's Memorandum," n.d., CWEP, box 408, folder HMS committee.
81. Eliot to Buttrick, April 24, 1917, CWEP, box 403-1, folder: GEB, 1908–1917.
82. See Eliot to Buttrick, May 17, 1917, CWEP, box 403-1, folder: GEB, 1908–1917.
83. F. G. Shattuck to Henry S. Pritchett, May 18, 1917, CCF.
84. Pritchett to Shattuck, May 22, 1917, CCF.
85. Shattuck to Pritchett, June 5, 1917, CCF.
86. Shattuck to Pritchett, June 12, 1917, CCF.

3. Building a System of National Management

1. C. W. Eliot to J. D. Greene, February 17, 1914, Rockefeller Foundation Archives, Record Group 3, series 900, box 21, folder 159. (Hereafter cited thus: RF 3-900-21-159); Graham Adams, *The Age of Industrial Violence, 1910–1915* (New York: Columbia University Press, 1966), pp. 146–147.
2. Arthur Dean Bevan, chairman of the AMA Council on Medical Education, was a typical exponent of this view. See his "Headship and Organization of Clinical Departments of First-Class Medical Schools," *Science*, n.s. 41 (March 12, 1915): 388–390; and "Medical Education and the Hospital," *JAMA* 60 (March 20, 1913): 974–979.
3. See, for example, *Washington Times*, November 11, 1913.
4. Henry S. Pritchett, "A Statement on the Medical Schools," made at the May 20, 1918, meeting of the board of the Carnegie Corporation, CCF; "Report on Applications for Aid to Medical Education," November 28, 1919, ibid.; Pritchett to Flexner, May 30, 1919, ibid.
5. Flexner, *Medical Education in Europe*, p. 112.
6. Flexner, *Autobiography*, pp. 136–148.
7. Flexner, *Medical Education in the United States and Canada*, p. 216.
8. A. Flexner to S. Flexner, April 15, 1909, SFP; A. Flexner to Henry S. Pritchett, April 17, 1909, February 7 and 8, 1910, AFP, box 17.
9. See Franklin H. Martin to Pritchett, April 12, 1915, and November 16, 1915, CCF.
10. Arthur Dean Bevan to Pritchett, January 14, 1914, CCF.
11. E. Fletcher Ingals to H. P. Judson, August 3, 1916, UCP, box 20, folder 1.
12. See Frederick T. Gates to Judson, June 19, 1916, UCP, box 34, folder 3; Flexner to Judson, February 4, 1916, UCP, box 33, folder 19.
13. Abraham Flexner, "A Plan for the Development of Medical Education in Chicago," AFP, box 14.
14. Ibid.
15. Ibid.

16. Ibid.

17. Flexner to Judson, July 11, 1916, UCP, box 33, folder 19.

18. Flexner to Julius Rosenwald, November 4, 1916, box 8, Julius Rosenwald Papers, Department of Special Collections, Regenstein Library, University of Chicago, folder 24; Flexner to Judson, November 10, 1916, UCP, box 33, folder 19.

19. Judson to Flexner, November 21, 1916, UCP, box 33, folder 19.

20. Flexner to Judson, May 10, 1917, UCP, box 33, folder 19; C. W. Vermeulern, *For the Greatest Good to the Greatest Number: A History of the Medical Center of the University of Chicago, 1927–1977* (Chicago: Vice-President for Public Affairs, University of Chicago, 1977), pp. 6–8.

21. Flexner to Judson, November 23, 1916, UCP, box 33, folder 19.

22. Albert R. Lamb, *The Presbyterian Hospital and the Columbia-Presbyterian Medical Center, 1868–1943* (New York: Columbia University Press, 1955), pp. 35–71.

23. Ibid., p. 74.

24. Nicholas Murray Butler to Edward S. Harkness, November 30, 1910, CUA.

25. Lamb, *Presbyterian Hospital and Columbia-Presbyterian Medical Center*, p. 75.

26. Ibid., pp. 78–79.

27. Harkness to Butler, March 24, 1914, CUA.

28. Walter Lambert to Butler, July 27, 1915, CUA.

29. Harkness to Butler, September 29, 1915, CUA.

30. Lambert to Butler, September 24, 1915, CUA.

31. Butler to Lambert, September 27, 1915, CUA.

32. Butler to Pritchett, October 5, 11, 14 and November 10, 1915, CUA.

33. Butler to Henry S. Pritchett, November 10, 1915, CUA.

34. Butler to Pritchett, November 24, 1915, CUA.

35. Quoted in Lambert to Butler, July 20, 1916, CUA.

36. Lambert to Robert W. de Forest, June 2, 1916, CUA.

37. Rockefeller junior to Flexner, January 30, 1917, GEB 1-5-700-7208.

38. Butler to Wallace Buttrick, February 3, 1917, GEB 1-5-700-7208.

39. Flexner to Anson Phelps Stokes, June 10, 1931, AFP.

40. Abraham Flexner, "Memorandum on Columbia University and Medical Education," copy in CCF.

41. Flexner to W. Sloane, December 10, 1917, GEB 1-5-700-7209.

42. Pritchett to Butler, n.d., CUA.

43. Butler to Pritchett, December 26, 1917, CUA.

44. Lambert to Butler, May 4, 1918, CUA.

45. See A. Flexner to S. Flexner, July 18, 1918, SFP; "Enclosure A" in Butler to Pritchett, December 12, 1918, CCF; Flexner to Buttrick, November 8, 1918, and Buttrick to Flexner, November 11, 1918, GEB 1-5-700-7209.

46. Butler to Pritchett, February 28, 1919, CCF.

47. Butler to Pritchett, December 17, 1918, January 9 and 14, 1919, CUA.

48. Pritchett to Buttrick, February 24, 1919, CCF.

49. Pritchett to Flexner, May 7, 1918, AFP, box 17.

50. Pritchett to Flexner, May 19, 1919, AFP, box 17.

51. Pritchett to Flexner, April 4, 1918, AFP, box 17.

52. Pritchett to Buttrick, November 11 and 25, 1919, GEB 1-4-589-1005.

53. A. Flexner to S. Flexner, July 18, 1918, SFP.

54. William Darrach, "Memorandum on the School of Medicine," December 13, 1919, CCF.

55. See note 2, above.

56. Barker, "Some Tendencies in Medical Eduaction."

57. Reprinted as Theodore C. Janeway, "Outside Professional Engagements by Members of Professional Faculties," *Educational Review* 56 (March 1918): 207–219.

58. Ibid., pp. 208, 212, 213.

59. J. Morris Slemons to Flexner, April 10, 1918, GEB 1-4-590-6288.

60. George Blumer to Flexner, April 15, 1918, GEB 1-4-590-6288.

61. Ibid.

62. Abraham Flexner, "Medical Education in the United States: A Program," GEB 1-5-702-7225.

63. "Memorandum Regarding Mr. Rockefeller's Gift to Be Devoted to the Improvement of Medical Education in the United States," GEB 1-5-702-7225.

64. Ibid.

65. Ibid.

66. Flexner to Arthur Dean Bevan, March 7, 1914, copied in Bevan to Pritchett, March 10, 1914, CCF.

67. Abraham Flexner, "Memorandum for Dr. Vincent re Medical Education," December 30, 1919, GEB 1-5-702-7225.

68. Vincent to Flexner, November 30, 1919, GEB 1-5-702-7225.

69. Flexner, "Memorandum for Dr. Vincent re Medical Education."

70. Ibid.

71. Ibid.

72. It is worth noting that the General Education Board had in the past supported public activities in agriculture, and the Rockefeller Sanitary Commission provided funds by which state boards of health hired physicians. Gates was a member of the board of both bodies when these steps were taken. See Ettling, *The Germ of Laziness: Rockefeller Philanthropy and Public Health in the New South* (Cambridge: Harvard University Press, 1981). It is possible, indeed likely, that his position on this question had hardened over the years as a result of political opposition to Rockefeller philanthropic activities. There is also a strain in the philanthropic tradition which saw the American South as almost a colonial dependency. Thus just as philanthropic boards cooperated with governments in overseas colonial development, so they could aid the southern states, although such cooperation would not be appropriate in a prosperous "developed" state which should be required to tax itself for its own gain. I am grateful to an anonymous colleague for pointing out Gates's earlier acquiescence in public-private cooperation.

73. Abraham Flexner, "Medical Department, University of Iowa," December 12, 1920, GEB 1-5-704-7224.

74. Ibid.

75. W. R. Boyd to Flexner, November 28, 1921, GEB 1-5-704-7224.
76. Flexner to W. Dean, May 15, 1922; W. R. Boyd to Flexner, September 29, 1922, GEB 1-5-704-7244.
77. Flexner to W. Jessup, May 26, 1922, GEB 1-5-704-7244.
78. A. Flexner to S. Flexner, August 13, 1922, SFP.
79. S. Flexner to William H. Welch, October 13, 1922, SFP.
80. Frederick T. Gates, typescript headed "This is the Gedney Paper," FTGP, box 3.
81. Ibid.
82. Ibid.
83. Flexner to Henry S. Pritchett, November 1, 1922, GEB 1-5-704-7244.
84. Ibid.
85. Ibid.
86. Pritchett to Flexner, October 31, 1922, GEB 1-5-704-7244.
87. Pritchett to J. R. Angell, November 3, 1922, CCF.
88. W. R. Boyd to Flexner, November 16, 1922, GEB 1-5-704-7244.
89. Flexner to W. R. Boyd, November 17, 1922, GEB 1-5-704-7244.
90. Flexner to W. W. Bierly, April 19, 1923; Winford Smith to Flexner, May 15, 1923, GEB 1-5-704-7244.
91. Flexner to Gates, November 25, 1922, GEB 1-5-704-7244.
92. Gates to Flexner, December 2, 1922, GEB 1-5-704-7244.
93. See Gates's memo "Gifts to the States and a Medical Policy," FTGP, box 6.
94. Abraham Flexner to Anne Crawford Flexner, March 8, 1916, AFP, box 1.

4. The Perils of Management

1. A. Flexner to Charles W. Eliot, May 2, 1921, CWEP, box 404-1.
2. Flexner to Rockefeller junior, April 22, 1921, Rockefeller Family Archives, box 20.
3. Alan Gregg, Oral History Memoir, Department of Special Collections, Butler Library, Columbia University.
4. Flexner to Edwin R. Embree, May 6, 1921, GEB 1-4-711.
5. Flexner to Embree, n.d., "Dear Pupil," GEB 1-4-711.
6. Ibid.
7. Flexner to Embree, May 6 and 10, 1921, GEB 1-4-711.
8. Flexner to Embree, May 24, 1921, GEB 1-4-711.
9. Charles W. Eliot to Wallace Buttrick, March 5, 1920, CWEP, box 404-1.
10. Buttrick to Eliot, December 12, 1921, CWEP, box 404-1.
11. Embree to Flexner, May 29, 1921, GEB 1-4-711.
12. George E. Vincent to Richard M. Pearce, September 26, 1923, RF 3-906-1-3; Vincent diary entry, April 19–20, 1922, ibid.
13. Donald Fisher, "The Rockefeller Foundation and the Development of Scientific Medicine in Great Britain, "*Minerva* 16 (1978): 20–41.
14. Gregg, Oral History Memoir, p. 140.
15. Commonwealth Fund, "Report of the General Director," March 4, 1919, Commonwealth Fund files, New York, N.Y. See also A. McGehee Harvey and Susan

L. Abrams, *For the Welfare of Mankind: The Commonwealth Fund and American Medicine* (Baltimore: Johns Hopkins University Press, 1986).

16. "Suggestions and Recommendations as to Possible Activities for the Commonwealth Fund," December 13, 1919, Commonwealth Fund files.

17. Frederick P. Keppel to Pritchett, July 11, 1929, CCF.

18. Henry S. Pritchett, "The Relation of Medical Education to Medical Progress," enclosed in Pritchett to Wallace Buttrick, March 15, 1921, GEB 1-2-26-2783.

19. Ibid.

20. Ibid.

21. Robert M. Lester, *A Thirty Year Catalog of Grants* (New York: Carnegie Corporation of New York, 1942), p. 233.

22. Pritchett, "The Relation of Medical Education to Medical Progress."

23. Ibid.

24. Ibid.

25. F. P. Keppel, Interview Memorandum, February 16, 1927, CCF.

26. Flexner, *Autobiography*, p. 200.

27. Turner, *Heritage of Excellence*, p. 176.

28. J. S. Ames to Flexner, April 30, 1935, AFP, box 15; Flexner to Ames, May 1, 1935, ibid.; Flexner to M. C. Winternitz, October 26, 1923, Yale Medical School Archives. Department of Special Collections, Yale University Library, box 3.

29. Lewis Mayers and Leonard V. Harrison, *The Distribution of Physicians in the United States* (New York: General Education Board, 1924).

30. Harvey Cushing, "The Clinical Teacher and the Medical Curriculum," *JAMA* 82 (March 15, 1924): 841.

31. Harvey Cushing to Flexner, April 6, 1921, HCP-FT.

32. Flexner to Cushing, April 18, 1921, HCP-FT.

33. Abraham Flexner, *Medical Education: A Comparative Study* (New York: Macmillan, 1924), pp. 3–4.

34. Ibid., p. 4.

35. Ibid., p. 5.

36. A. Flexner, "Foundations: Ours and Others," 1925, RF 3-900-22-165.

37. A. Flexner, "A Modern University," *Atlantic Monthly* 136 (October 1925): 535.

38. Flexner, "Foundations: Ours and Others."

39. Abraham Flexner, "Is Social Work a Profession?" *Proceedings of the National Conference of Charities and Corrections* 42 (1915): 578.

40. Ibid., p. 579.

41. Ibid., p. 581.

42. Flexner, "Foundations: Ours and Others."

43. Flexner to Rufus Cole, March 2, 1923, Rufus Cole Papers, American Philosophical Society, Philadelphia.

44. Flexner to Richard M. Pearce, May 1, 1920, RF 3-906-2-11.

45. Flexner, "A Modern University," p. 534.

46. Flexner, "Foundations: Ours and Others."

47. Flexner, "A Modern University," p. 533.

48. William James, "The Social Value of the College-Bred," *McClure's Magazine* 30 (1908): 420.

49. Flexner, "A Modern University," pp. 540–541.

50. Thomas Milton Rivers, *Tom Rivers: Reflections on a Life in Medicine and Science: An Oral History Memoir*, prepared by Saul Benison (Cambridge: MIT Press, 1967), p. 64.

51. Wallace Buttrick to Flexner, March 9, 1920, GEB 1-4-488-6266.

52. Flexner to J. Whitridge Williams, April 21, 1921, GEB 1-4-589-6267.

53. Flexner to Winford Smith, March 17, 1921, GEB 1-45-589-6267.

54. G. Canby Robinson, *Adventures in Medical Education* (Cambridge: Harvard University Press, 1957), pp. 161–164.

55. William H. Welch to Flexner, April 29, 1921, GEB 1-4-589-6267.

56. J. Whitridge Williams to Flexner, April 9, 1921, GEB 1-4-589-6267.

57. Abraham Flexner, "Memorandum regarding Johns Hopkins Medical School and Hospital: May 3, 1921," GEB 1-4-589-6267.

58. GEB, Minutes of Meeting, May 26, 1921, GEB, 1-4-589-6267.

59. Flexner to Frank Goodnow, February 2, 1922, CCF; Henry Harlan to H. S. Pritchett, February 2, 1922, ibid.

60. Frank Goodnow and Henry Harlan to H. S. Pritchett, February 2, 1922, CCF.

61. Pritchett to Goodnow, May 29, 1922, CCF.

62. Henry S. Pritchett, "Memorandum concerning the Application of the Johns Hopkins Medical School," n.d., CCF.

63. Walter Palmer to Flexner, May 25, 1921, GEB 1-4-589-6267; Alfred E. Cohn to Franklin C. McLean, March 1, 1922, Franklin McLean Papers, Department of Special Collections, Regenstein Library, University of Chicago (hereafer McLP), box 1; Turner, *Heritage of Excellence*, p. 109; Robinson, *Adventures in Medical Education*, pp. 164–166.

64. Flexner to William H. Welch, May 15, 1922, GEB 1-4-589-6268.

65. Abraham Flexner, "Confidential Comments on the Memorandum Prepared by Messrs. MacCallum, Howland, and Weed," February 26, 1923, GEB 1-4-590-6277.

66. General Education Board, *Annual Report*, 1922–23, pp. 21–22.

67. Flexner, *Medical Education*, p. 18.

68. Theodore Billroth, *The Medical Sciences in the German Universities* (New York: Macmillan, 1924), p. 85.

69. A. Flexner to S. Flexner, July 4, 1920, SFP.

70. Billroth, *Medical Sciences in the German Universities*, p. ix.

71. Quoted in Genevieve Miller, "Medical History," in Numbers, *Education of American Physicians*, p. 298.

72. Flexner, "Confidential Comments on the Memorandum Prepared by Messrs. MacCallum, Howland, and Weed."

73. Turner, *Heritage of Excellence*, p. 190.

74. Ibid., p. 191.

75. A. McGehee Harvey, *Science at the Bedside: Clinical Research in American Medicine, 1905–1945* (Baltimore: Johns Hopkins University Press, 1981), pp. 78–104.

76. Alfred E. Cohn, *Medicine, Science, and Art* (Chicago: University of Chicago Press, 1931), pp. 126–128.

77. Ibid., pp. 126–132.

78. Ibid., p. 136.

79. A. E. Cohn to Robert K. S. Lim, March 20, 1926, Rufus Cole Papers.

80. A. Flexner to S. Flexner, February 1, 1924, SFP.

81. Flexner to H. P. Judson, January 28, 1920, UCP, box 59, folder 61.

82. Judson to Francis W. Peabody, February 20, 1920, UCP, box 59, folder 61.

83. Peabody to Judson, March 25, 1920, UCP, box 59, folder 11.

84. Judson to Peabody, April 21, 1920, UCP, box 19, folder 13.

85. A. Flexner to S. Flexner, March 27, 1920, SFP.

86. Wiliam B. Wherry to Wilbur Post, April 3, 1923, UCP, box 20, folder 3.

87. "Memorandum of Interview with Dr. Rufus Cole," May 28, 1923, UCP, box 20, folder 3.

88. Ibid.

89. E. D. Burton to J. R. Angell, July 25, 1923, UCP, box 20, folder 3.

90. Flexner to Angell, July 31, 1923, SFP.

91. Angell to Burton, July 28, 1923, UCP, box 20, folder 3.

92. F. Blake to Burton, August 1, 1923, UCP, box 20, folder 3.

93. "Memorandum to Members of the Committee on the Medical School," August 13, 1923, UCP, box 20, folder 3.

94. Flexner to Burton, August 29, 1923, UCP, box 20, folder 3.

95. Harold H. Swift to Burton, August 29, 1923, UCP, box 20, folder 3.

96. "Memorandum of Interview with Dr. Seem regarding Franklin C. McLean," September 22, 1923, UCP, box 20, folder 3.

97. See Marshall R. Urist, "Phoenix of Physiology and Medicine: Franklin Chambers McLean," *Perspectives in Biology and Medicine* 49 (Autumn 1975): 23–58.

98. See Peter Buck, *American Science and Modern China* (New York: Cambrige University Press, 1980); Mary Brown Bullock, *An American Transplant: The Rockefeller Foundation and Peking Union Medical College* (Berkeley: University of California Press, 1981).

99. Urist, "Phoenix of Physiology and Medicine," p. 31.

100. A. E. Cohn to F. C. McLean, December 30, 1922, McLP, box 1.

101. McLean to Burton, December 16, 1924, UCP, box 20, folder 3.

102. Burton to Dean Lewis, July 3, 1924, UCP, box 20, folder 7.

103. Lewis to Burton, July 5, 1924, UCP, box 20, folder 7.

104. Lewis to Burton, n.d., UCP, box 20, folder 7.

105. H. H. Swift to Burton, September 25, 1924, UCP, box 20, folder 7.

106. Burton to Flexner, September 29, 1924, UCP, box 20, folder 4.

107. Flexner to Burton, October 2, 1924, UCP, box 20, folder 7.

108. D. Phemister to Burton, December 8, 1924, UCP, box 20, folder 7.

109. Burton to McLean, December 15, 1924, UCP, box 20, folder 7.

110. H. H. Swift to Burton and Wilbur Post, December 5, 1923, UCP, box 20, folder 4.

111. Ibid.

112. "Memorandum of Lunch Meeting," December 19, 1923, UCP, box 20, folder 4.

113. "Memorandum of telephone call," December 20, 1923, UCP, box 20, folder 4.

114. Burton to D. Wilder, December 24, 1923, UCP, box 20, folder 4.

115. Leslie B. Arey, *Northwestern University Medical School, 1859–1975; A Pioneer in Educational Reform* (Evanston, Ill.: Northwestern University, 1979), pp. 293–301.

116. H. H. Swift to Burton, February 7, 1923, UCP, box 59, folder 3.

117. F. McLean to Burton, December 16, 1924, UCP, box 20, folder 5.

118. H. H. Swift to Burton, February 16, 1925, UCP, box 20, folder 3.

119. Flexner to Burton, March 10, 1924, UCP, box 20, folder 5.

120. Ibid.

121. Burton to Flexner, March 15, 1924, UCP, box 20, folder 4.

122. Winford Smith to Burton, December 20, 1923, UCP, box 20, folder 4.

123. "Program for the Development of the Graduate School of Medicine . . . ," April 8, 1926, UCP, box 115, folder 8.

124. Max Mason to Flexner, October 30, 1926, University of Chicago Presidents' Papers, ca. 1925–1945, Department of Special Collections, Regenstein Library, University of Chicago (hereafter UCP-II), box 70, folder 3.

125. Flexner to Max Mason, November 3, 1925, UCP-II, box 70, folder 3, emphasis in the original.

126. "Memorandum of Conference," December 17, 1927, UCP-II, box 15, folder 20.

127. Ibid.

128. Rufus Cole, "Hospital and Laboratory," *Science* n.s. 66 (December 9, 1927): 545–552.

129. A. E. Cohn to McLean, November 5, 1927, McLP, box 1.

130. Copy of the proposal is in GEB 1-4-590-6277.

131. Flexner, "Confidential Comments on the Memorandum Prepared by Messrs. MacCallum, Howland, and Weed."

132. Ibid.

133. Flexner to J. Morris Selmons, April 11, 1918, GEB 1-4-590-6288.

134. Karl, "Philanthropy, Policy Planning, and the Bureaucratization of the Democratic Ideal," p. 150; Ettling, *Germ of Laziness*, pp. 207–209.

135. Flexner to Alan Gregg, June 17, 1922, GEB 1-300-19-1952.

136. Francis W. Peabody, *Doctor and Patient* (New York: Macmillan, 1930), p. 95.

5. The Reorganization of Philanthropic Management

1. Alfred D. Chandler, Jr., *Strategy and Structure: Chapters in the History of American Industrial Enterprise* (Cambridge: MIT Press, 1962); Ellis W. Hawley, *The Great War and the Search for Modern Order* (New York: St. Martin's Press, 1984); Barry D. Karl, *The Uneasy State* (Chicago: University of Chicago Press, 1984).

2. William Darrach to Wallace Buttrick, April 13, 1920, GEB 1-5-701-7212.

3. Abraham Flexner, "Reflections on Dr. Darrach's Budget," GEB 1-5-701-7212.

4. Flexner to Darrach, April 20, 1921, GEB 1-5-701-7213.

5. Nicholas Murray Butler to William Barclay Parsons, November 9, 1920, CUA.

6. Henry S. Pritchett to Flexner, December 23, 1920, GEB 1-5-701-7212.

7. Ibid.

8. Pritchett to Buttrick, February 7, 1921, GEB 1-5-701-7213.

9. Pritchett to Parsons, January 19, 1921, CCF.

10. "Memorandum re College of Physicians and Surgeons, Columbia University," May 9, 1921, CCF.

11. Rockefeller junior to Flexner, April 25, 1921, GEB 1-5-701-7213.

12. "Memorandum," December 28, 1923, GEB 1-5-701-7213.

13. Frederick T. van Beuren, Jr., "Full-Time: The Letter or the Spirit?" *JAMA* 84 (May 19, 1925): 1324.

14. A. Flexner to S. Flexner, January 15, 1925, SFP.

15. T. Debevoise to W. Rose, November 24, 1924, GEB 1-5-701-7214.

16. Debevoise to Rose, November 24, 1924, GEB 1-5-701-7214.

17. "Memorandum of Interview," January 3, 1925, GEB 1-5-701-7214.

18. A. Flexner to S. Flexner, April 15, 1925, SFP.

19. Flexner, "Memorandum on General Parsons' Proposed Letter," n.d., GEB 1-5-701-7214.

20. A. Flexner to S. Flexner, April 15, 1925, SFP.

21. A. Flexner to S. Flexner, April 22, 1925, SFP.

22. Ibid.

23. Pritchett to Flexner, June 3, 1925, GEB 1-5-701-7215.

24. Dean Sage to Flexner, February 3, 1925, GEB 1-5-701-7214.

25. A. Flexner to S. Flexner, June 13, 1925, SFP.

26. Debevoise to Rose, July 8, 1925, GEB 1-5-701-7215.

27. Flexner to Stephen Baker, October 1, 1925, GEB 1-5-701-7215.

28. Baker to Flexner, December 16, 1925; "Agreement between the General Education Board and the Trustees of Columbia University in the City of New York, December 28, 1925," GEB 1-5-701-7215.

29. Ray Lyman Wilbur, *Memoirs* (Stanford: Stanford University Press, 1960).

30. Quoted in Harry Atkins, *The Dean: Willard C. Rappleye and the Evolution of American Medical Education* (New York: Josiah Macy, Jr., Foundation, 1975), p 15.

31. Ibid., p. 16.

32. Ibid., p. 28.

33. Ibid., p. 45.

34. Flexner, *Medical Education*, p. 45.

35. S. Flexner to A. Flexner, May 2, 1914, SFP.

36. *Preliminary Report of the Commission on Medical Education* (New Haven, 1927), p. 9.

37. *Third Report of the Commission on Medical Education* (New Haven, 1928), p. 61.

38. Ibid., p. 27.

39. *Final Report of the Commission on Medical Education* (New York: Office of the Director, 1932), p. 13.

40. General Education Board, *Annual Report for the Year 1928–1929* (New York: General Education Board, 1929), p. 49.

41. D. L. Edsall to Flexner, May 22, 1926, HMS-DOF.

42. Edsall to R. M. Pearce, May 4, 1927, David L. Edsall Papers, Countway Library of Medicine, Harvard University Medical School (hereafter DLEP), box 5, folder 175.

43. "Memoranda concerning Projected Developments in the Harvard Medical School and Hospitals Associated Therewith," n.d., HMS-DOF.

44. Edsall to Flexner, July 1, 1926, HMS-DOF.

45. Ibid.

46. Edsall to Pearce, April 5, 1927, HMS-DOF.

47. Edsall to Pearce, May 4, 1927, DLEP, box 5, folder 175.

48. Hans Zinsser, "The Perils of Magnanimity: A Problem in American Education," *Atlantic Monthly* 159 (1927): 246–250.

49. Ibid., p. 248.

50. Ibid., p. 249.

51. Flexner to F. C. McLean, January 26, 1927, McLP, box 1.

52. A. Flexner to S. Flexner, May 6, 1926, SFP.

53. G. E. Vincent to Julius Rosenwald, June 16, 1924, Rosenwald Papers, box 22, folder 8.

54. A. P. Stokes to E. R. Embree, April 15, 1924, RF 3-1-906-2-11.

55. Debevoise to Frederic T. Gates, October 7, 1925, Rockefeller Family Archives.

56. A. Flexner to S. Flexner, August 27, 1924, SFP; Flexner to Lewis Weed, February 1, 1927, Dean's Office Files, Alan M. Chesney Medical Archives, Johns Hopkins Medical School.

57. Raymond B. Fosdick, *John D. Rockefeller, Jr.: A Portrait* (New York: Harper and Brothers, 1956), p. 421.

58. Raymond B. Fosdick, *Chronicles of a Generation: An Autobiography* (New York: Harper and Brothers, 1958), pp. 20, 42.

59. Ibid., pp. 61–213.

60. Rockefeller junior to H. P. Judson, January 30, 1920, UCP, box 35.

61. Robert E. Kohler, "A Policy for the Advancement of Science: The Rockefeller Foundation, 1924–1929," *Minerva* 16 (1978): 488. My understanding of the reorganization was greatly helped by reading Kohler.

62. Raymond B. Fosdick, "Memorandum on Reorganization," January 18, 1928, RF 3-900-17-124.

63. The Rockefeller Foundation: A Statement by the President . . .," February 24, 1926," RF 3-900-17-121.

64. R. M. Pearce to Raymond B. Fosdick, April 16, 1926, RF 3-900-17-121.

65. Fosdick to Rockefeller junior, October 6, 1927, RF 3-900-17-123.

66. Rockefeller junior to Fosdick, December 15, 1926, RF 3-900-17-120.

67. The Rockefeller Foundation: Agenda for the Special Conference Meeting, February 23–25, 1925," January 15, 1925, RF 3-900-17120.

68. Vincent to Fosdick, January 5, 1926, RF 3-900-17-121.
69. Flexner to Charles Howland, April 13, 1927, RF 3-900-17-123.
70. A. Flexner to S. Flexner, January 5, 1928, SFP.
71. Ibid.
72. Flexner to Howland, April 13, 1927, RF 3-900-17-123.
73. A. Flexner to S. Flexner, January 5, 1928, SFP.
74. Flexner, "Memorandum regarding the General Education Board," January 4, 1927, RF 3-318-1-3.
75. Ibid.
76. Ibid.
77. Ibid.
78. Pearce to Fosdick, April 16, 1926, RF 3-900-17-121.
79. George Vincent, "Memorandum on AF's Paper," January 3, 1927, RF 3-900-17-123.
80. "Memorandum of a meeting at the Harvard Club . . . May 5, 1927," RF 3-900-17-123; "Memorandum on the Reorganization of the Boards," May 13, 1927, RF 3-900-17-123.
81. "Memorandum of meeting held at the Whitehall Club, January 19, 1928," RF 3-900-17-124; Raymond B. Fosdick, "Memorandum on Reorganization," January 18, 1928, RF 3-900-17-124; Fosdick to S. Flexner, November 1, 1927, RF 3-900-17-123; Memorandum, October 17, 1927, RF 3-900-17-123; George Vincent, "Memorandum on Policies and Organization of the Rockefeller Boards," January 29, 1927, RF 3-900-17-123; Vincent, "Memorandum on AF's Paper," January 13, 1927, RF 3-900-17-123; Fosdick to Vincent, December 15, 1926, RF 3-918-1-1.
82. S. Flexner to A. E. Cohn, August 25, 1926, SFP.
83. See Vernon K. Dibble, *The Legacy of Albion Small* (Chicago: University of Chicago Press, 1975).
84. Fosdick to Rockefeller junior, February 15, 1927, RF 3-900-17-123.
85. Raymond B. Fosdick, *The Old Savage in the New Civilization* (Garden City, N.Y.: Doubleday, Doran, 1928), pp. 14–15.
86. Ibid., pp. 27, 135.
87. Frederick Soddy, *Science and Life* (New York, E. P. Dutton, 1920), p. 44.
88. Memorandum on Policies and Organization of the Rockefeller Boards," January 1927, RF 3-900-17-123.
89. Fosdick to Vincent, March 7, 1928, RF 3-900-17-124.
90. The letter can be found in RF 3-900-17-124.
91. Flexner, "Memo," March 29, 1928, AFP, box 3.
92. A. Flexner to Anne Crawford Flexner, April 4, 1928, AFP, box 3.
93. Vincent to Fosdick, May 28, 1928, Raymond B. Fosdick Papers, Mudd Library, Princeton University (hereafter RFBP), box 19, item 17321.
94. Flexner, *Autobiography*, pp. 223–224.
95. Flexner to Fosdick, April 19, 1928, RBFP, box 19, item 99.
96. Fosdick to Flexner, May 8, 1928, RBFP, box 19, item 17321.
97. Flexner, "To My Friends," May 28, 1928, Julius Rosenwald Papers, box 15, folder 2.

98. *New Republic* 55 (June 6, 1928): 56.
99. A. E. Cohn to F. McLean, May 28, 1928, McLP, box 1.
100. A. E. Cohn to Flexner, June 6, 1928, McLP, box 1.
101. A. Flexner to S. Flexner, July 24, 1928, SFP.
102. A. Flexner to S. Flexner, April 29, 1928, SFP.
103. A. Flexner to S. Flexner, July 24, 1928, SFP.
104. A. Flexner to S. Flexner, June 1, 1928, SFP.
105. A. Flexner to S. Flexner, July 13, 1928, SFP.
106. A. Flexner to S. Flexner, August 23, 1928, SFP.
107. A. Flexner to S. Flexner, December 29, 1928, SFP.
108. S. Flexner to A. Flexner, January 15, 1929, SFP.
109. A. Flexner to Bernard Flexner, February 12, 1929, SFP.
110. A. Flexner to S. Flexner, January 3, 1929, SFP.
111. A. Flexner to S. Flexner, June 1, 1928, SFP.

6. ''*Administrative Tabes*''

1. For a particularly admiring view, see Wilder Penfield, *The Difficult Art of Giving: The Epic of Alan Gregg* (Boston: Little, Brown, 1967).
2. Flexner to R. B. Fosdick, July 16, 1936, RBFP, box 26.
3. Alan Gregg to David L. Edsall, January 28, 1936, box 16. Alan Gregg Papers, National Library of Medicine (hereafter AGP).
4. Minute, January 3, 1929, RF 3-906-1-1.
5. ''Report of the Special Committee on the Division of Medical Education of the RF,'' December 9, 1928, RF 3-906-1-7.
6. Ibid.
7. Ibid.
8. Gregg to Edsall, January 28, 1936, AGP, box 16.
9. A. Flexner to S. Flexner, August 30, 1928, SFP.
10. Gregg, Oral History Memoir, pp. 1, 6, 11, 18, 28.
11. Penfield, *Difficult Art of Giving*, p. 209.
12. Ibid., p. 216.
13. Memorandum, March 8, 1933, RF 3-906-1-4.
14. W. S. Leathers to Gregg, June 24, 1931, RF 1.1-200-116-1427.
15. Frederick Woodward to Robert McDougal, January 14, 1929, UCP-II, box 70, folder 3.
16. McDougal to Woodward, January 22, 1929, UCP-II, box 70, folder 3.
17. Franklin McLean, ''Memorandum to Dr. Lillie,'' April 10, 1932, McLP, box 2; see also Morris J. Vogel, *The Invention of the Modern Hospital; Boston, 1870–1930* (Chicago: University of Chicago Press, 1980), pp. 97–119.
18. Flexner to F. C. McLean, May 13, 1930, UCP-II, box 70, folder 5.
19. Robert Maynard Hutchins to H. H. Swift and F. C. McLean, April 23, 1930, UCP-II, box 115, folder 12.
20. Thomas E. Donnelly to Hutchins and Swift, December 19, 1930, UCP-II, box 70, folder 3.

21. Untitled memo, UCP-II, box 70, folder 4.

22. Untitled memo, RF 1.1-216-6-69.

23. Ibid.

24. McLean to Hutchins, June 17, 1932, McLP, Vol. II.

25. Ibid.

26. Donnelly to Hutchins, September 24, 1934, UCP-II, box 70, folder 4.

27. Henry S. Houghton to Woodward, September 28, 1934, UCP-II, box 70, folder 4.

28. Robert Maynard Hutchins, "Memorandum for the Committee on Instruction and Research and the Special Committee on Medical Affairs," February 7, 1939, UCP-II, box 70, folder 4.

29. "Minutes of the Special Meeting on Trends in Medical Care and Education . . . June 5, 1945," RF 3-900-25-193.

30. Robert E. Kohler, "Warren Weaver and the Rockefeller Foundation Program in Molecular Biology: A Case Study in the Management of Science," in Nathan Reingold, ed., *The Sciences in the American Context: New Perspectives* (Washington: Smithsonian Institution Press, 1979): Warren Weaver, *Scene of Change* (New York: Scribners, 1970), p. 59.

31. Gregg to Fosdick, May 21, 1951, AGP, box 16.

32. Fosdick, *Chronicle of a Generation*, p. 250; Penfield, *Difficult Art of Giving*, p. 224.

33. Gregg, "The Strategy of Our Program in Psychiatry," November 1937, RF 3-906-2-17.

34. Warren Weaver, Oral History Memoir, Department of Special Collections, Butler Library Columbia University, p. 296.

35. Weaver, *Scene of Change*, p. 3.

36. Kohler, "Warren Weaver and the Rockefeller Foundation Program in Molecular Biology."

37. Alan Gregg, "Memorandum to Mr. Fosdick re the MS," November 11, 1934, AGP, box 9.

38. Alan Gregg, "Statement for RF Meeting," April 12, 1934, AGP, box 16.

39. Alan Gregg, "Memorandum to Mr. Fosdick re Fluid Research," November 13, 1934, AGP, box 16.

40. Extract from the Report of the Committee on Appraisal, December 11, 1934, RF 3-900-24-189.

41. Gregg to Edsall, January 28, 1936, AGP, box 16.

42. Ibid.

43. Ibid.

44. Fosdick to Gregg, January 29, 1935, AGP, box 16; Gregg to Edsall, January 28, 1936, ibid.

45. Alan Gregg, "Prophecy on RBF," February 7, 1936, AGP, box 16.

46. Raymond B. Fosdick, "Relations between the Medical Sciences and the Natural Sciences," December 10, 1937, AGP, box 16.

47. Ibid.

48. Gregg to Fosdick, October 23, 1937, AGP, box 16; "Dear Ray," n.d., ibid.

49. "Dear Ray," May 3, 1939, AGP, box 16.

50. Rockefeller Foundation, *Annual Report*, 1939, p. 197; ibid., 1941, p. 165.

51. Alan Gregg, diary, October 28, 1937, RF 1.1-218-1-5; Evarts A. Graham to Gregg, April 12, 1937, ibid.

52. Rockefeller Foundation resolution 38056, April 6, 1938, RF 1.1-228-1-5; Gregg, diary, July 31, 1940, RF 1.1-228-1-7; R. R. Bradley to Gregg, September 30, 1943, RF 1.1-228-1-9.

53. Gregg to Fosdick, November 12, 1940, RF 3-900-21-160.

54. Ibid.

55. Warren Weaver to Fosdick, [November 27, 1940], RF 3-900-21-160.

56. Ibid.

57. Kohler, "Warren Weaver and the Rockefeller Foundation Program on Molecular Biology," p. 265.

58. Alan Gregg, "Limitations and Size of Projects," March 5, 1937, AGP, box 9.

59. Weaver to Fosdick, [November 27, 1940], RF 3-900-21-160.

60. Gregg to Fosdick, July 16, 1943, AGP, box 16.

61. Weaver to Fosdick, November 27, 1940, RF 3-900-21-160.

62. Alan Gregg, memorandum on the University of Chicago, n.d., RF 1.1-216-6-69.

63. Alan Gregg, "North American Responsibilities for the University, 1934–1954," *Science* 89 (June 23, 1939): 573.

64. Handwritten note on Gregg to Fosdick, November 12, 1940, RF 3-900-21-160.

65. Gregg to Fosdick, July 16, 1943, AGP, box 16.

66. A. A. Weech, "Medical Science at War," *Journal of the Association of American Medical Colleges* 21 (1946): 104–13.

67. A. N. Richards to Vannevar Bush, May 18, 1945, National Archives, Record Group 227, OSRD-CMR General Correspondence; see also Irwin Stewart, *Organizing Scientific Research for War: The Administrative History of the Office of Scientific Research and Development* (Boston: Little, Brown, 1948); Vannevar Bush, *Endless Horizons* (Washington: Public Affairs Press, 1946).

68. Stephen P. Strickland, *Politics, Science, and Dread Disease: A Short History of United States Medical Research Policy* (Cambridge: Harvard University Press, 1972).

69. Alan Gregg, "The Essential Need of Fundamental Research for Social Progress," *Science* n.s. 101 (March 16, 1945): 258.

70. Gregg to Fosdick, March 11, 1946, RF 3-906-1-5.

71. Ibid.

72. Ibid.

73. Ibid.

74. Robert S. Morison to Fosdick, February 13, 1947, RF 3-906-1-5.

75. Ibid.

76. Morison to Fosdick, May 7, 1947, RF 3-906-1-5.

77. A brief biography of Barnard is in William B. Wolf, *The Basic Barnard: An Introduction to Chester I. Barnard and His Theories of Organization and Manage-*

ment (Ithaca: Cornell University, New York State School of Industrial and Labor Relations, 1974).

78. See Chester I. Barnard, *The Functions of the Executive* (Cambridge: Harvard University Press, 1938), and *Organization and Management: Selected Papers* (Cambridge: Harvard University Press, 1948).

79. Wolf, *Basic Barnard*, p. 34.

80. "Minutes of Conference on the Financing of Medical Education," July 22, 1948, RF 1.2-139-200a-1247.

81. Memorandum, "National Fund for Medical Education, Interview with Mr. James B. Conant," March 25, 1949, Commonwealth Fund files.

82. Gregg, diary, January 18, 1949, RF 1.2-139-200a-1248.

83. Ibid., August 30, 1948, RF 1.2-139-200a-1247.

84. "Memorandum on Meeting, July 22, 1948," RF 1.2-139-200a-1247.

85. Gregg, diary, November 29, 1950, RF 1.2-140-200a-1240.

86. Gregg to Donald Anderson, November 18, 1950, RF 1.2-140-200a-1250.

87. Gregg to Lester J. Evans, March 1, 1951, RF 1.2-200a-140-1251.

88. Gregg to Devereux C. Josephs, March 15, 1950, RF 1.2-140-200a-1251.

89. See David Sills, *The Volunteers: Means and Ends in a National Organization* (Glencoe, Ill.: Free Press, 1957).

90. Gregg to Philip M. Wagner, July 12, 1949, RF 2-200-National Foundation for Infantile Paralysis, box GC 160.

91. Ibid.

92. Alan Gregg, "A Program in the Medical Sciences," RF 3-906-1-9.

93. John Lankford, *Congress and the Foundations in the Twentieth Century* (River Falls: Wisconsin State University, 1964), p. 446; Richard Clovard, "Risk-Capital Philanthropy: The Ideological Defense of Innovation," in George K. Zollschan and Walter Hirsch, eds., *Explorations in Social Change* (Boston: Houghton-Mifflin, 1964).

94. A. Baird Hastings, Oral History Memoir, National Library of Medicine, p. 342.

95. Penfield, *Difficult Art of Giving*, p. 189.

96. Gregg to Julia M. H. Carson, January 23, 1948, RF 3-900-21-162.

97. Weaver to Flexner, May 18, 1955, AFP, box 15.

98. Flexner to Weaver, August 2, 1955, AFP, box 15.

99. Ibid.

100. Ibid.

101. Flexner to Weaver, May 23, 1955, AFP, box 15.

102. Ibid.

103. Ibid.

104. Flexner to Weaver, August 2, 1955, AFP, box 15.

105. Weaver to Flexner, August 12, 1955, AFP, box 15.

106. Ibid.

107. Flexner to Weaver, August 2, 1955, AFP, box 15.

108. Flexner to Weaver, August 23, 1956, AFP, box 15.

109. Ibid.
110. Ibid.
111. Weaver to Flexner, October 18, 1955, AFP, box 15.
112. Warren Weaver, "Notes on Medical Education," RF 3-921-1-2.

Conclusion

1. Flexner to Lawrence E. Spivak, November 14, 1956, AFP, box 14.
2. E. Brown, *Rockefeller Medicine Men*, Markowitz and Rosner, "Doctors in Crisis," Kunitz, "Professionalism and Social Control in the Progressive Era," H. D. Banta, "Medical Education: Abraham Flexner, a Larger Perspective on the Flexner Report," *International Journal of Health Services* 5 (1975): 593–592.
3. Fox, "Abraham Flexner's Unpublished Report," Carleton B. Chapman, "The Flexner Report by Abraham Flexner," *Daedalus* 103 (1974): 105–117.
4. Steven Jonas, *Medical Mystery: The Training of Doctors in the United States* (New York, 1978).
5. Ludmerer, *Learning to Heal;* Hudson, "Abraham Flexner in Perspective."
6. Flexner to Warren Weaver, May 23, 1955, AFP, box 15.
7. Richard L. Landau, "The Real Crisis in American Medicine—No Leadership," *Perspectives in Biology and Medicine* 15 (1972): 351–355.
8. Chapman, "Flexner Report by Abraham Flexner," p. 117.

Selected Bibliography

Primary Sources

ARCHIVES AND MANUSCRIPT COLLECTIONS

Baltimore, Md. Johns Hopkins Medical School. Alan Mason Chesney Medical Archives.
    Dean's Office Files
    Lewellys F. Barker Papers
    William H. Welch Papers
Bethesda, Md. National Library of Medicine.
    Alan Gregg Papers
Boston, Mass. Harvard University Medical School. Countway Library of Medicine.
    David L. Edsall Papers
    Frederick T. Gates Collection
    Harvard Medical School, Dean's Office Files
Cambridge, Mass. Harvard University. Pusey Library.
    Charles W. Eliot Papers
Chicago, Ill. University of Chicago. Regenstein Library. Department of Special Collections.
    Franklin C. McLean Papers
    Julius Rosenwald Papers
    Presidents' Papers
New Haven, Conn. Yale University. History of Medicine Library.
    Harvey Cushing Papers
New York, N.Y. Carnegie Corporation.
    Historical Files
New York, N.Y. Columbia University. Low Library.
    Columbia University Archives.
New York, N.Y. Commonwealth Fund.
    Historical Files

New York, N.Y. 30 Rockefeller Plaza.
    Rockefeller Family Archives
Philadelphia, Pa. American Philosophical Society.
    Rufus I. Cole Papers
    Simon Flexner Papers
Princeton, N.J. Princeton University. Mudd Library.
    Raymond B. Fosdick Papers
Pocantico Hills, North Tarrytown, N.Y. Rockefeller Archive Center.
    Frederick T. Gates Papers
    Simon Flexner Papers
    General Education Board Collection
    Rockefeller Foundation Archives
    Rockefeller University Collection
Washington, D.C. Library of Congress.
    Abraham Flexner Papers
    Andrew Carnegie Papers
    Henry S. Pritchett Papers

ORAL HISTORIES

Columbia University Oral History Collection. Butler Library.
    Alan Gregg
    Warren Weaver
National Library of Medicine Oral History Collection.
    A. Baird Hastings

REPORTS

Carnegie Corporation. *Annual Report.* 1914–1950.
Carnegie Foundation for the Advancement of Teaching. *Annual Report.* 1906–1911.
General Education Board. *General Education Board: An Account of Its Activities.* 1902–1914.
General Education Board. *Review and Final Report.* 1902–1964.
Rockefeller Foundation. *Annual Report.* 1913–1960.

BOOKS

A Manual of the Public Benefactions of Andrew Carnegie. Washington, D.C.: Carnegie Endowment for International Peace, 1919.
Anderson, Martin B. *The Right Use of Wealth.* New York, 1878.
Barker, Lewellys. *Time and the Physician.* New York: G.P. Putnam and Sons, 1942.
Barnard, Chester I. *The Functions of the Executive.* Cambridge: Harvard University Press, 1938.

Barnard, Chester I. *Organization and Management: Selected Papers.* Cambridge: Harvard University Press, 1948.

Bigelow, Henry T. *Medical Education in America.* Cambridge: Welch, Bigelow, 1871.

Billroth, Theodore. *The Medical Sciences in the German Universities.* New York. Macmillan, 1924.

Bush, Vannevar. *Endless Horizons.* Washington: Public Affairs Press, 1946.

Carnegie, Andrew. *Miscellaneous Writings.* Ed. Burton J. Hendricke. New York: Doubleday, 1933.

Cattell, J. McKeen, ed. *Medical Research and Education.* New York: Science Press, 1913.

Cohn, Alfred E. *Medicine, Science, and Art: Studies in Interrelations.* Chicago: University of Chicago Press, 1931.

Commission on Medical Education, AMA. *Final Report of the Commission on Medical Education.* New York: Office of the Director of Study, 1932.

Drake, Daniel. *Practical Essays on Medical Education and the Medical Profession in the United States.* Cincinnati: Rolf and Young, 1832. Rpt. Baltimore: Johns Hopkins University Press, 1952.

Eliot, Charles W. *The Working of the American Democracy: An Address Delivered before the Fraternity Phi Beta Kappa of Harvard University. July 28, 1888.* Cambridge; John Wilson and Son, 1888.

Exemption from Taxation: Addresses, Reports, Judicial Proceedings, Legislative Bills, Acts, and Other Documents Relating to the Exemption of Massachusetts Colleges and Universities for Taxation. Boston. Printed for the Colleges and Universities of the Commonwealth, 1910.

Flexner, Abraham. *Abraham Flexner: An Autobiography.* New York: Simon and Schuster, 1960.

Flexner, Abraham. *The American College: A Criticism.* New York: Century, 1908.

Flexner, Abraham. *Daniel Coit Gilman, Creator of the American Type of University.* New York: Harcourt, Brace, 1946.

Flexner, Abraham. *Do Americans Really Value Education?* Cambridge: Harvard University Press, 1927.

Flexner, Abraham. *Funds and Foundations: Their Policies, Past and Present.* New York: Harper and Brothers, 1952.

Flexner, Abraham. *Medical Education: A Comparative Study.* New York: Macmillan, 1925.

Flexner, Abraham. *Medical Education in Europe.* Bulletin no. 6. New York: Carnegie Foundation for the Advancement of Teaching, 1912.

Flexner, Abraham. *Medical Education in the United States and Canada.* Bulletin no. 4. New York: Carnegie Foundation for the Advancement of Teaching, 1910.

Flexner, Abraham. *Universities: American, English, German.* New York: Oxford University Press, 1930.

Fosdick, Raymond B. *Chronicle of a Generation: An Autobiography.* New York: Harper and Brothers, 1958.

Fosdick, Raymond B. *The Old Savage in the New Civilization.* Garden City, N.Y.: Doubleday, Doran, 1928.

Keppel, Frederick P. *The Foundation: Its Place in American Life*. New York: Macmillan, 1930.

Laski, Harold J. *Dangers of Obedience*. New York: Harper and Brothers, 1930.

Lester, Robert M. *A Thirty Year Catalog of Grants*. New York: Carnegie Corporation of New York, 1942.

Mayers, Lewis, and Harrison, Leonard V. *The Distribution of Physicians in the United States*. New York: General Education Board, 1924.

Morgan, John. *A Discourse on the Foundation of Medical Schools in America*. Baltimore: Johns Hopkins University Press, 1937.

Osler, William. *Principles and Practice of Medicine*. 2d ed. New York: D. Appleton, 1896.

Peabody, F. W. *Doctor and Patient*. New York: Macmillan, 1930.

Pepper, William, *Higher Medical Education: The True Interest of the Public and of the Profession*. Philadelphia: J. B. Lippincott, 1894.

Robinson, G. Canby. *Adventures in Medical Education: A Personal Narrative of the Great Advance of American Medicine*. Cambridge: Harvard University Press, 1957.

Rockefeller, John D. *Random Reminiscences of Men and Events*. New York: Doubleday, Page, 1909.

Soddy, Frederick, *Science and Life*. New York: E. P. Dutton, 1920.

Weaver, Warren. *Scene of Change*. New York: Scribners, 1970.

Zinsser, Hans. *As I Remember Him: The Biography of R.S.* Boston: Little, Brown, 1940.

ARTICLES

Barker, Lewellys F. "Medicine and the Universities." *University of Chicago Record* 7 (1902): 83–94.

Bevan, Arthur Dean. "Headship and Organization of Clinical Departments of First-Class Medical Schools." *Science* n.s. 41 (1915): 388–390.

Bevan, Arthur Dean. "Medical Education and the Hospital." *Journal of the American Medical Association* 60 (1913): 974–979.

Billings, Frank. "State Medicine." *Journal of the American Medical Association* 5 (September 19, 1885): 309–315.

Carnegie, Andrew. "The Best Fields for Philanthropy." *North American Review* 149 (December 1889): 682–698.

Carnegie, Andrew. "Wealth." *North American Review* 148 (June 1889): 653–664.

Cole, Rufus. "Hospital and Laboratory." *Science* n.s. 66 (December 9, 1927): 545–552.

Colwell, N. P. "Present Needs of Medical Education." *Journal of the American Medical Association* 82 (1924): 838–840.

Cushing, Harvey. "The Clinical Teacher and the Medical Curriculum." *Journal of the American Medical Association* 82 (1924): 839–841.

Eliot, Charles W. "The New Education: Its Organization." *Atlantic Monthly* 23 (1869): 203–220.

"Endowments." *Journal of the American Medical Association* 1 (July 21, 1883): 58.

Flexner, Abraham. "Aristocratic and Democratic Education." *Atlantic Monthly* 108 (1911): 386–395.

Flexner, Abraham. "Is Social Work a Profession?" *Proceedings of the National Conference of Charities and Corrections* 42 (1915): 576–590.

Flexner, Abraham. "A Modern University." *Atlantic Monthly* 136 (1925): 530–541.

Gregg, Alan. "A Critique of Medical Research." *Proceedings of the American Philosophical Society* 87 (1944): 313–320.

Gregg, Alan. "The Essential Need of Fundamental Research for Social Progress." *Science* n.s. 101 (March 16, 1945): 257–259.

Huxley, Thomas. "Address on University Education." *American Addresses, with a Lecture on the Study of Biology.* New York: D. Appleton, 1890.

Janeway, Theodore C. "Outside Professional Engagements by Members of Professional Faculties." *Educational Review* 56 (1918): 207–219.

Kirkland, James A. "Recent History of Vanderbilt University." *Methodist Review* (Nashville) 59 (April 1910): 343–358.

"Medical Colleges and Their Endowments." *Journal of the American Medical Association* 2 (April 5, 1884): 377.

Pritchett, Henry S. "How Science Helps Industry in Germany." *Review of Reviews* 33 (1906): 167–170.

Pusey, William Allen. "Medical Education and Medical Service." *Journal of the American Medical Association* 84 (1925): 281–285, 365–369, 431–437, 513–515, 592–595.

Stockard, Charles R. "The Laboratory Professor and the Medical Sciences in the United States." *Journal of the American Medical Association* 74 (1920): 229–234.

Vincent, George E. "The Doctor and the Changing Order." *Survey* 55 (January 1, 1926): 409–411.

Ward, Henry B. "Address of the President." *Proceedings of the Eighteenth Annual Meeting of the Association of American Medical Colleges* (Chicago: AAMC, 1908).

Welch, William H. "Medicine and the University." *Journal of the American Medical Association* 50 (1908): 1–3.

Witherspoon, J. A. "Medical Education Past and Present." *Journal of the American Medical Association* 80 (1923): 1191–1194.

Zinsser, Hans. "The Next Twenty Years." *Science* n.s. 74 (1931): 397–404.

Zinsser, Hans. "The Perils of Magnanimity: A Problem in American Education." *Atlantic Monthly* 159 (1927): 246–250.

Zinsser, Hans. "Relationship of the Fundamental Laboratory to Clinical Teaching." *Journal of the American Medical Association* 92 (1929): 1399–1402.

Secondary Sources

THESES AND DISSERTATIONS

Berliner, Howard S. "Philanthropic Foundations and Scientific Medicine." Sc.D. dissertation, Johns Hopkins School of Public Health, 1977.

Bluestone, Daniel Michael. "From Pasture to Pasteur: An Architectural and Environmental History of the 1906 Harvard Medical School." B.A. thesis, Harvard College, 1975.

Howe, Barbara. "The Emergence of the Philanthropic Foundation as an American Social Institution, 1900–1920." Ph.D. dissertation, Cornell University, 1976.

BOOKS

Adams, Graham. *The Age of Industrial Violence, 1910–1915; The Activities and Findings of the U.S. Commission on Industrial Relations.* New York: Columbia University Press, 1966.

American Foundation. *Medical Research: A Mid-Century Survey.* 2 vols. Boston: Little, Brown, 1955.

Anderson, Odin W. *The Uneasy Equilibrium: Private and Public Financing of Health Services in the United States, 1875–1965.* New Haven: College and University Press, 1968.

Arey, Leslie B. *Northwestern University Medical School, 1859–1979; A Pioneer in Educational Reform.* Evanston, Ill.: Northwestern University, 1979.

Atkins, Harry. *The Dean: Willard C. Rappleye and the Evolution of American Medical Education.* New York: Josiah Macy, Jr., Foundation, 1975.

Beecher, Henry K., and Altschule, Mark D. *Medicine at Harvard: The First Three Hundred Years.* Hanover, N.H.: University Press of New England, 1977.

Bledstein, Burton J. *The Culture of Professionalism: The Development of Higher Education in America.* New York: W. W. North, 1976.

Bonner, Thomas Neville. *American Doctors and German Universities: A Chapter in International Intellectual Relations, 1870–1914.* Lincoln: University of Nebraska Press, 1963.

Bonner, Thomas Neville. *Medicine in Chicago, 1850–1950.* Madison, Wis.: American History Research Center, 1957.

Bordley, James, III, and Harvey, A. McGehee. *Two Centuries of American Medicine, 1776–1976.* Philadelphia: W. B. Saunders, 1976.

Boulding, Kenneth E. *The Economy of Love and Fear.* Belmont, Calif. Wadsworth, 1973.

Boulding, Kenneth E. *The Organizational Revolution: A Study in the Ethics of Economic Organization.* New York: Harper, 1953.

Bremner, Robert H. *American Philanthropy.* Chicago: University of Chicago Press, 1960.

Brown, E. Richard. *Rockefeller Medicine Men: Medicine and Capitalism in America.* Berkeley: University of California Press, 1979.

Buck, Peter. *American Science and Modern China.* New York: Cambridge University Press, 1980.

Bullock, Mary Brown. *American Transplant: The Rockefeller Foundation and Peking Union Medical College.* Berkeley: University of California Press, 1981.

Burrow, James G. *AMA: Voice of American Medicine*. Baltimore: Johns Hopkins University Press, 1963.

Calhoun, Daniel. *Professional Lives in America: Structure and Aspirations, 1750–1850*. Cambridge: Harvard University Press, 1965.

Chandler, Alfred D., Jr. *Strategy and Structure*. Cambridge: Massachusetts Institute of Technology Press, 1962.

Chesney, Alan M. *The Johns Hopkins Hospital and the Johns Hopkins University School of Medicine*. 3 vols. Baltimore: Johns Hopkins University Press, 1958 and 1963.

Commonwealth Fund. *Historical Sketch, 1918–1962*. New York, 1962.

Corner, George W. *A History of the Rockefeller Institute, 1901–1953: Origins and Growth*. New York: Rockefeller Institute Press, 1967.

Corner, George W. *Two Centuries of Medicine: A History of the School of Medicine of the University of Pennsylvania*. Philadelphia: J. B. Lippincott, 1965.

Crowe, Samuel J. *Halsted of Johns Hopkins*. Springfield, Ill.: Charles C. Thomas, 1957.

Curran, Jean Alonzo. *Founders of the Harvard School of Public Health with Biographical Notes, 1909–1940*. New York: Josiah Macy, Jr., Foundation, 1970.

Curti, Merle, and Nash, Roderick. *Philanthropy in the Shaping of American Higher Education*. New Brunswick, N.J.: Rutgers University Press, 1965.

Cushing, Harvey. *The Life of Sir William Osler*. 2 vols. Oxford: Clarendon Press, 1925.

Daniels, George H. *Science in American Society: A Social History*. New York: Alfred A. Knopf, 1971.

Deitrick, J. E., and Berson, R. D. *Medical Schools in the United States at Midcentury*. New York: McGraw-Hill, 1953.

Dupree, A. Hunter. *Science in the Federal Government*. Cambridge: Belknap Press of Harvard University Press, 1957.

Elliot, Edward Charles, and Chambers, M. M. *Charters of Philanthropies: A Study of the Charters of Twenty-nine American Philanthropic Foundations*. New York: Carnegie Foundation for the Advancement of Teaching, 1939.

Ettling, John. *The Germ of Laziness: Rockefeller Philanthropy and Public Health in the New South*. Cambridge: Harvard University Press, 1981.

Evans, Lester J. *The Crisis in Medical Education*. Ann Arbor: University of Michigan Press, 1964.

Feinstein, Alvan. *Clinical Judgment*. Baltimore: Williams and Wilkins, 1967.

Fleming, Donald. *William H. Welch and the Rise of Modern Medicine*. Boston: Little, Brown, 1954.

Flexner, Abraham. *Henry S. Pritchett: A Biography*. New York: Columbia University Press, 1943.

Flexner, Simon. *The Evolution and Organization of the University Clinic*. London: Oxford University Press at the Clarendon Press, 1966.

Flexner, Simon, and Flexner, James Thomas. *William H. Welch and the Heroic Age of American Medicine*. New York: Viking Press, 1941.

Fosdick, Raymond B. *Adventure in Giving: The Story of the General Education Board*. New York: Harper and Brothers, 1962.

Fosdick, Raymond B. *John D. Rockefeller, Jr.: A Portrait*. New York: Harper and Brothers, 1956.

Fosdick, Raymond B. *The Story of the Rockefeller Foundation*. New York: Harper and Brothers, 1952.

Fremont-Smith, Marion F. *Foundations and Government: State and Federal Law and Supervision*. New York: Russell Sage Foundation, 1965.

Fulton, John R. *Harvey Cushing: A Biography*. Springfield, Ill.: Charles C. Thomas, 1946.

Gay, Wilson Allen. *William James: A Biography*. New York: Viking, 1967.

Goodspeed, Thomas Wakefield. *William Rainey Harper, First President of the University of Chicago*. Chicago: University of Chicago Press, 1928.

Hagedorn, Herman. *Brookings: A Biography*. New York: Macmillan, 1936.

Harvey, A. McGehee. *Aventures in Medical Research: A Century of Discovery at Johns Hopkins*. Baltimore: Johns Hopkins University Press, 1976.

Harvey, A. McGehee. *The Interurban Clinical Club, 1905–1976: A Record of Achievement in Clinical Science*. Interurban Clinical Club, 1976.

Harvey, A. McGehee. *Science at the Bedside: Clinical Research in American Medicine, 1905–1945*. Baltimore: Johns Hopkins University Press, 1981.

Harvey, A. McGehee, and Abrams, Susan L. *For the Welfare of Mankind: The Commonwealth Fund and American Medicine*. Baltimore: Johns Hopkins University Press, 1986.

Harvey, A. McGehee, and McKusick, Victor A. *Osler's Textbook Revisited*. New York: Appleton-Century-Crofts, 1967.

Hawkins, Hugh. *Between Harvard and America: The Educational Leadership of Charles W. Eliot*. New York: Oxford University Press, 1972.

Hawkins, Hugh. *Pioneer: A History of the Johns Hopkins University, 1874–1889*. Ithaca, New York: Cornell University Press, 1960.

Hirsch, Edwin F. *Frank Billings*. Chicago: University of Chicago Press, 1966.

Hollis, Ernest V. *Philanthropic Foundations and Higher Education*. New York: Columbia University Press, 1938.

Kaufman, Martin. *American Medical Education: The Formative Years, 1765–1910*. Westport, Conn.: Greenwood Press, 1976.

Keele, K. D. *The Evolution of Clinical Methods in Medicine*. London: Pitman Medical Publishers, 1963.

Kendall, Patricia L. *The Relationship between Medical Educators and Medical Practitioners: Sources of Strain and Occasions for Cooperation*. Evanston, Ill.: Association of American Medical Colleges, 1965.

Kett, Joseph. *The Formation of the American Medical Profession*. New Haven: Yale University Press, 1968.

Kidd, Charles Vincent. *American Universities and Federal Research*. Cambridge: Belknap Press of Harvard University Press, 1959.

Kiser, Clyde V. *The Milbank Memorial Fund: Its Leaders and Its Work, 1905–1974*. New York: Milbank Memorial Fund, 1975.

Krause Elliott A. *Power and Illness: The Political Sociology of Health and Medical Care.* New York: Elsevier, 1977.

Lagemann, Ellen Condliffe. *Private Power for the Public Good: A History of the Carnegie Foundation for the Advancement of Teaching.* Middletown, Conn.: Wesleyan University Press, 1983.

Lamb, Arthur R. *The Presbyterian Hospital and the Columbia-Presbyterian Medical Center, 1868–1943: A History of a Great Medical Adventure.* New York: Columbia University Press, 1955.

Lankford, John. *Congress and the Foundations in the Twentieth Century.* River Falls: Wisconsin State University, 1964.

Larson, Magali Sarfatti. *The Role of Professionalism: A Sociological Analysis.* Berkeley: University of California Press, 1977.

Lemaine, Gerald; Macleod, Roy; Mulkay, Michael; and Wingart, Peter, eds. *Perspectives on the Emergence of Scientific Disciplines.* Chicago: Aldine, 1976.

Ludmerer, Kenneth M., *Learning to Heal: The Development of American Medical Education.* New York: Basic Books, 1985.

MacCallum, W. G. *William Stewart Halsted.* Baltimore: Johns Hopkins University Press, 1930.

McCloskey, Robert Green. *American Conservatism in the Age of Enterprise: A Study of William Graham Sumner, Stephen J. Field, and Andrew Carnegie.* Cambridge: Harvard University Press, 1951.

Miller, Howard S. *Dollars for Research: Science and Its Patrons in Nineteenth-Century America.* Seattle: University of Washington Press, 1970.

Mims, Edwin. *Chancellor Kirkland of Vanderbilt.* Nashville: Vanderbilt University Press, 1940.

Nevins, Allan. *Study in Power: John D. Rockefeller, Industrialist and Philanthropist.* 2 vols. New York: Scribners, 1953.

Numbers, Ronald L. *Almost Persuaded: American Physicians and Compulsory Health Insurance, 1912–1920.* Baltimore: Johns Hopkins University Press, 1977.

Numbers, Ronald L., ed. *The Education of American Physicians.* Berkeley: University of California Press, 1980.

Oleson, Alexandra, and Voss, John, eds. *The Organization of Knowledge in Modern America, 1860–1920.* Baltimore: Johns Hopkins University Press, 1979.

Owen, David. *English Philanthropy, 1660–1960.* Cambridge: Belknap Press of Harvard University Press, 1964.

Parker, Franklin. *George Peabody: A Biography.* Nashville: Vanderbilt University Press, 1971.

Penfield, Wilder. *The Difficult Art of Giving: The Epic of Alan Gregg.* Boston: Little, Brown, 1967.

Reingold, Nathan, ed. *The Sciences in the American Context: New Perspectives.* Washington: Smithsonian Institution Press, 1979.

Ringer, Fritz. *The Decline of the German Mandarin: The German Academic Community, 1880–1933.* Cambridge: Harvard University Press, 1969.

Rockefeller Archive Center. *Trends in Biomedical Research, 1901–1976: Proceed-*

Selected Bibliography

ings of the Second Rockefeller Archive Center Conference. December 10, 1976.
[North Tarrytown, N.Y.]: The Center, c. 1977.

Rosenberg, Charles. *No Other Gods: On Science and American Social Thought.*
Baltimore: Johns Hopkins University Press, 1976.

Rosner, David. *A Once Charitable Enterprise: Hospitals and Health Care in Brooklyn and New York, 1885–1915.* Princeton, N.J.: Princeton University Press, 1982.

Rothstein, William G. *American Physicians in the Nineteenth Century.* Baltimore:
Johns Hopkins University Press, 1972.

Rudolph, Frederick. *The American College and University: A History.* New York:
Vintage Books, 1962.

Sabin, Florence Rhea. *Franklin Paine Mall: The Story of a Mind.* Baltimore: Johns
Hopkins Press, 1934.

Savage, Howard T. *Fruit of an Impulse: Forty-five Years of the Carnegie Foundation, 1905–1950.* New York: Harcourt, Brace, 1953.

Shryock, Richard H. *The Development of Modern Medicine: An Interpretation of
the Social Factors Involved.* Madison: University of Wisconsin Press, 1979.

Shryock, Richard H. *Medicine and Society in America: 1600–1860.* Ithaca: Cornell
University Press, 1972.

Sills, David. *The Volunteers: Means and Ends in a National Organization.* Glencoe,
Ill.: Free Press, 1957.

Starr, Paul. *The Social Transformation of American Medicine.* New York: Basic
Books, 1982.

Stevens, Rosemary. *American Medicine and the Public Interest.* New Haven: Yale
University Press, 1972.

Stevens, Rosemary. *Medical Practice in Modern England: The Impact of Specialization and State Medicine.* New Haven: Yale University Press, 1966.

Stewart, Irwin. *Organizing Scientific Research for War: The Administrative History
of the Office of Scientific Research and Development.* Boston: Little, Brown, 1948.

Storr, Richard T. *Harper's University: The Beginnings.* Chicago: University of Chicago Press, 1966.

Strickland, Stephen P. *Politics, Science, and Dread Disease: A Short History of
United States Medical Research Policy.* Cambridge: Harvard University Press,
1972.

Strickland, Stephen P. *Sponsored Research in American Universities and Colleges.*
Washington: American Council on Education, 1967.

Strickland, Stephen P., and Strickland, Tamara T. *The Markle Scholars.* New York:
Markle Foundation, 1976.

Turner, Thomas B. *Heritage of Excellence: The Johns Hopkins Medical Institution,
1914—1947.* Baltimore: Johns Hopkins University Press, 1974.

Vermeulern, C. W. *For the Greatest Good to the Greatest Number: A History of the
Medical Center of the University of Chicago, 1927–1977.* Chicago: Vice-President
for Public Affairs, University of Chicago, 1977.

Veysey, Laurence R. *The Emergence of the American University.* Chicago: University of Chicago Press, 1980.

Vogel, Morris J., and Rosenberg, Charles E., eds. *The Therapeutic Revolution: Es-*

says in the Social History of American Medicine. Philadelphia: University of Pennsylvania Press, 1979.

Wall, Joseph Frazier. *Andrew Carnegie.* New York: Oxford University Press, 1970.

Weiskotten, H. G.; Schwitalla, A. M.; Cutter, W. D.; and Anderson, H. H. *Medical Education in the United States, 1934–1939.* Chicago: AMA Council on Medical Education and Hospitals, 1940.

Whitaker, Ben. *The Philanthropoids: Foundations and Society.* New York: William Morrow, 1979.

Whitehead, John S. *The Separation of College and State: Columbia, Dartmouth, Harvard, and Yale, 1776–1876.* New Haven: Yale University Press, 1973.

Wiebe, Robert H. *The Search for Order, 1877–1920.* New York: Hill and Wang, 1967.

Wolf, William B. *The Basic Barnard: An Introduction to Chester I. Barnard and His Theories of Organization and Management.* Ithaca: New York School of Industrial and Labor Relations, Cornell University, 1974.

Wooster, James Willett. *Edward Stephen Harkness, 1874–1940.* New York, 1949.

ARTICLES

Ayers, Leonard P. "The Seven Great Foundations: IV. The General Education Board." *Journal Of Education* 72 (October 6, 1910): 316–317.

Ayers, Leonard P. "The Seven Great Foundations: V. The Carnegie Foundation for the Advancement of Teaching." *Journal of Education* 72 (October 13, 1910): 340–341.

Banta, H. David. "Abraham Flexner: A Reappraisal." *Social Science and Medicine* 5 (1971): 655–661.

Beach, Mark. "Professional versus Professorial Control of Higher Education." *Educational Record* 49 (1968): 267–268.

Benison, Saul. "Poliomyelitis and the Rockefeller Institute: Social Effects and Institutional Response." *Journal of the History of Medicine and Allied Sciences* 29 (1974): 74–92.

Berliner, Howard S. "New Light on the Flexner Report: Notes on the AMA-Carnegie Foundation Background." *Bulletin of the History of Medicine* 51 (1977): 603–609.

Brieger, Gert H. "The California Origins of the Johns Hopkins Medical School." *Bulletin of the History of Medicine* 51 (1977): 339–352.

Brieger, Gert H. "The Original Plans for the Johns Hopkins and Their Historical Significance." *Bulletin of the History of Medicine* 39 (1965): 518–528.

Burnham, John C. "Psychiatry, Psychology, and the Progressive Movement." *American Quarterly* 12 (1960): 457–465.

Chapman, Carleton B. "The Flexner Report by Abraham Flexner." *Daedalus* 103 (Winter 1974): 105–117.

Clovard, Richard. "Foundations and Professions: The Organizational Defense of Autonomy." *Administrative Science Quarterly* 6 (September 1961): 167–184.

Clovard, Richard. "Risk-Capital Philanthropy: The Ideological Defense of Innovation." In George K. Zollschan and Walter Hirsch, eds., *Explorations in Social Change*, pp. 728–748. Boston: Houghton Mifflin, 1964.

Coben, Stanley. "Foundation Officials and Fellowships: Innovation in the Patronage of Science." *Minerva* 14 (Summer 1966).

Curti, Merle E. "American Philanthropy and the National Character." *American Quarterly* 10 (Winter 1958): 420–437.

Curti, Merle E. "History of American Philanthropy as a Field of Research." *American Historical Review* 62 (January 1957): 353–363.

Curti, Merle E. "Tradition and Innovation in American Philanthropy." *Proceedings of the American Philosophical Society* 105 (1961): 146–156.

Curti, Merle; Green, Judith; and Nash, Roderick. "Anatomy of Giving: Millionaires in the Late Nineteenth Century." *American Quarterly* 15 (Fall 1963): 416–435.

Fisher, Donald. "The Rockefeller Foundation and the Development of Scientific Medicine in Great Britain." *Minerva* 16 (Spring 1978): 20–41.

Fleming, Donald. "The Full-Time Controversy." *Journal of Medical Education* 30 (1955): 398–406.

Fox, Daniel M. "Abraham Flexner's Unpublished Report: Foundations and Medical Education, 1909–1928." *Bulletin of the History of Medicine* 54 (1980): 475–496.

Gelfand, Toby. "The Origins of a Modern Concept of Medical Specialization: John Morgan's Discourse of 1765." *Bulletin of the History of Medicine* 50 (1976): 511–535.

Harvey, A. McGehee. "Samuel J. Meltzer: Pioneer Catalyst in the Evolution of Clinical Science in America." *Perspectives in Biology and Medicine* 21 (1978): 431–440.

Hudson, Robert P. "Abraham Flexner in Perspective: American Medical Education, 1865–1910." *Bulletin of the History of Medicine* 46 (1972): 545–561.

Karl, Barry D. "Philanthropy, Policy Planning, and the Bureaucratization of the Democractic Ideal." *Daedalus* 105 (Fall 1976): 129–149.

Karl, Barry D. "The Power of Intellect and the Politics of Ideas." *Daedalus* 97 (Summer 1968): 1002—1035.

Kohler, Robert E. "The Management of Science: The Experience of Warren Weaver and the Rockefeller Foundation Programs in Molecular Biology." *Minerva* 14 (1976): 279–306.

Kunitz, Stephen. "Professionalism and Social Control in the Progressive Era: The Case of the Flexner Report." *Social Problems Journal* 22 (October 1974): 16–27.

Landau, Richard L. "The Real Crisis in American Medicine—No Leadership." *Perspectives in Biology and Medicine* 15 (1972): 351–355.

Ludmerer, Kenneth M. "Reform at Harvard Medical School, 1869–1909." *Bulletin of the History of Medicine* 55 (1982): 343–370.

Ludmerer, Kenneth M. "The Reform of Medical Education at Washington University." *Journal of the History of Medicine and Allied Sciences* 35 (1980): 149–173.

Markowitz, Gerald E., and Rosner, David Karl. "Doctors in Crisis: A Study of the Use of Medical Education Reform to Establish Modern Professional Elitism in Medicine." *American Quarterly* 4 (March 1973): 83–107.

Means, James Howard. "Experiences and Opinions of a Full-Time Medical Teacher." *Perspectives in Biology and Medicine* 2 (1959): 127–162.

Morison, Robert S. "Foundations and Universities." *Daedalus* 93 (Fall 1964): 1109–1142.

Munger, Donna Bingham. "Robert Brookings and the Flexner Report." *Journal of the History of Medicine and Allied Sciences* 23 (October 1968): 356–371.

Purcell, Edward A. "Service Intellectuals and the Politics of Science." *History of Education Quarterly* 5 (September 1975): 97–110.

Rosenkrantz, Barbara. "Cart before Horse: Theory, Practice, and Professional Image in American Public Health, 1870–1920." *Journal of the History of Medicine and Allied Sciences* 229 (1974): 55–73.

Sadler, Judy. "Ideologies of 'Art' and 'Science' in Medicine: The Transition from Medical Care to Application of Technique in the British Medical Profession." In Wolfgang Krohn et al., eds., *The Dynamics of Science and Technology*, pp. 177–215. Dordrecht, Holland: D. Reidel, 1978.

Schudson, Michael. "The Flexner Report and the Reed Report: Notes on the History of Professional Education in the United States." *Social Science Quarterly* 55 (1974): 347–361.

Stevens, David Harrison. "Life and Work of Trevor Arnett." *Phylon* 16 (1955): 127–140.

Strickland, Stephen P. "Integration of Medical Research and Health Policies." *Science* n.s. 173 (1971): 1093–1103.

Urist, Marshall R. "Phoenix of Physiology and Medicine: Franklin Chambers McLean." *Perspectives in Biology and Medicine* 49 (Autumn 1975): 23–58.

Wyllie, Irvin Gordon. "The Search for an American Law of Charity, 1776–1844." *Mississippi Valley Historical Review* 46 (September 1959): 203–221.

Index